RACISM ON TRIAL

RACISM ON TRIAL

THE CHICANO FIGHT FOR JUSTICE

Ian F. Haney López

The BELKNAP PRESS of HARVARD UNIVERSITY PRESS
Cambridge, Massachusetts & London, England   2003

Library of Congress Cataloging-in-Publication Data

Haney-López, Ian.
Racism on trial : the Chicano fight for justice / Ian F. Haney López
  p. cm.
Includes bibliographical references and index.
ISBN 0-674-01068-X (alk. paper)
  1. Mexican Americans—Civil rights—California—East Los Angeles—History—
20th century. 2. Mexican Americans—Race identity—California—East Los Angeles.
3. Mexican Americans—Legal status, laws, etc.—California—East Los Angeles—History—20th century. 4. Political activists—Legal status, laws, etc.—California—East
Los Angeles—History—20th century. 5. East Los Angeles (Calif.)—Trials, litigation,
etc. 6. Civil rights movements—California—East Los Angeles—History—20th century. 7. East Los Angeles (Calif.)—Race relations. 8. Racism—California—East Los
Angeles—History—20th century. 9. United States—Race relations—Case studies.
10. Racism—United States—Case studies. I. Title.

F869.E18 H36 2003
305.868'72079493—dc21   2002038267

For my wife,

Deborah Drickersen Córtez

Racial beliefs and practices harm large segments of our population. Yet few of us see society's current state as unnatural or unjust; most deny that race or other structural forces limit the life chances of individuals and groups. We do not believe that our attitudes or actions are based on racial considerations. Instead, race has become common sense: accepted but barely noticed, there though not important, an established fact that we lack the responsibility, let alone the power, to change. The color line has come to seem a fiction, so little do we apprehend its daily mayhem.

In contrast, activists in the civil rights and racial pride movements of the late 1960s forcefully challenged the common sense of race by demanding new rights and by building new identities. In 1968 the residents of East Los Angeles, then and now the heart of the largest Mexican community in this country, took to the streets to fight for better schools and to protest police brutality in their community.[1] To understand and define their place in the United States, the Mexican insurgents articulated a new racial identity for themselves. Before 1968, leaders of the Mexican community had claimed to be white. After that year, and still to this day, many Mexicans insisted instead that they were Chicanos, proud members of a brown race. This book uses two criminal prosecutions of Chicano activists to explore efforts by the Mexican community to grapple with racism and, more importantly, with the nature of their racial identity.

Latino identity may hold the key to the future of race relations in this country. The 2000 census ranks Latinos as the largest minority group in the United States, comprising 12.5 percent of the population.[2] Latinos are also one of the fastest growing groups, having increased in size by more than 50 percent during the 1990s. They already outnumber African Americans, and within a few years will outnumber all other minority groups combined.[3] While California accounts for almost a third of the total Latino population, Latinos are dispersed throughout the United States. They represent a quarter of the West's population and one tenth of the people in the South and the Northeast. Nine states claim a Latino population greater than 500,000 and twenty-two more have Latino populations over 100,000.

But if Latinos are the largest minority group, what race are they? Consider the situation of Mexicans in the United States. Long the predominant Latino group, people of Mexican descent account for roughly 60 percent of all Latinos. Puerto Ricans and Cubans, the next two largest Latino groups, constitute respectively only 9.6 percent and 3.5 percent of that population. In 1930 the census counted Mexicans as a part of a "Mexican race"; from 1940 through 1970 the census enumerated them as white; and since 1980 the census has included that group as part of a broader Hispanic category that supposedly is independent of race.[4]

These conflicting understandings of Mexican identity currently co-exist in the United States. Many non-Mexicans consider Mexicans to be racial inferiors, although many also consider them to be an ethnic group rather than a race. Meanwhile, Mexicans are almost evenly divided in whether they think that they're white, and some insist that Mexicans are a cultural but not a racial group.[5] The question of Mexican identity mirrors a larger conundrum that applies to all Latinos. Non-Latinos do not know how to consider this group, while 42 percent of Latinos identify themselves as "some other race" and 48 percent claim that they are white.[6]

Contradictory notions of Mexican or Latino identity do not

stem primarily from mistakes about how to apply terms like race, nationality, ethnicity, culture, and so on. Confusion inheres in those labels themselves and not simply in how they are applied, for these terms denote overlapping ways of conceptualizing group differences.[7] Discomfort about whether a group is "truly" a race rather than an ethnicity, a culture, and so forth should exist for all groups. Mexicans should be considered no less, though no more, a race than whites, blacks, Asians, Native Americans, and Pacific Islanders—the categories currently used by the census—for all are races only to the extent that they have been socially constructed as such.[8]

Uncertainty regarding Mexican identity principally stems from the fact that Mexicans in the United States have straddled the border between white and non-white identity for the last 150 years. It is not that Mexicans are a race but not an ethnicity, or a nationality but not a culture. Rather, such labels have served as ammunition in the longstanding fight over the social status of Mexicans. The question of Mexican identity elicits strongly contradictory intuitions because no consensus exists, among non-Mexicans or within the Mexican community, on where to place Mexicans in the prevailing racial order.

Meanwhile, racial dynamics continue to change. Historically, Anglo society constructed Mexicans and other Latino groups as non-white. But now various Latino and Asian communities, for instance the Cubans and the Japanese, increasingly hold nearly white status. And growing numbers of minority individuals—those with fair features, wealth, political connections, or high athletic, artistic, or professional accomplishments—can achieve virtually a white identity. This is not to say that these groups and individuals are fully white, for that racial designation, like all others, operates on a sliding scale. Some people remain more white than others. Nevertheless, the boundaries of whiteness are expanding to incorporate communities and individuals who would have been constructed as non-white just a few decades ago. In turn, this expansion fuels the growing sense among many, particularly among those who regard themselves as white, that race is now an artifact of the past. The fair treatment and high status of some minorities ostensibly proves that our society has reached the end of race and racism.

But race and racism continue to distort almost every social encounter and warp almost every facet of our social structure. While whites have preserved their superior status, in part by extending privileges to some, many in our society remain victimized by the brutal politics of race. Our society still constructs whole populations as non-white: large numbers of us remain beyond the care of the rest, impoverished and incarcerated, disdained and despised, feared and forsaken. Is this our future? How will those historically considered to be non-white respond to current racial barriers? Should they agitate for a white identity, or organize around a non-white self-conception? What will be the reaction of those secure in their white status, and of those whose claim to white identity is more tenuous? I contend that these questions come down to this: As a society, will we confront and remake the racial common sense that perpetuates inequality? The answer will set the trajectory of race relations in the twenty-first century.

In this book I examine a critical moment of racial transformation within the Mexican community in East Los Angeles during the late 1960s. I do so partly because the story of Mexican militancy is not well known, but more importantly because it tells us something about the nature and future of race in the United States. The legal history of the Chicano movement in Los Angeles illuminates a sustained struggle by a key constituency to negotiate the tension between white and non-white status. The activists' efforts emphasize the potentially emancipatory consequences of directly engaging with racial ideas and practices. This book is about the racial world we continually recreate in our daily lives, and about how we might improve that world. It is written especially for those who understand, like many of the Chicano insurgents, that justice is the most important word in race relations.[9]

CONTENTS

Justice is the most important word in race relations.

—*Rubén Salazar*

During a single week in March 1968, ten thousand East Los Angeles students charged into the streets to protest abysmal conditions in the local high schools. For years, parents and community leaders had fruitlessly complained to local school officials about dilapidated buildings, gross overcrowding, hostile teachers, and prison-like environments that consistently produced nothing but high drop-out rates. That spring, fed up with their mistreatment and inspired by the protest politics sweeping the country, students took matters into their own hands. Their walkout drew the largest Mexican community in the United States onto the turbulent field of popular protest. Shouting "Education for All" and "Chicano Power," the young demonstrators not only vented years of community frustration with indifferent officials and inferior schools, they voiced a new identity for Mexicans in the United States. After that violent spring, they were Chicanos.

Since the 1930s, members of the Mexican community had insisted, in the face of a strong presumption by Anglo society to the contrary, that Mexicans were white. Indeed, community leaders promoted the term "Mexican American" to convey an assimilationist ideology stressing white identity. Now, for the first time, Mexicans asserted a different racial conception: Chicanos defined themselves as proud members of a brown race, thereby rejecting not only the previous generation's assimilationist orientation but their racial pretensions as well. In East Los Angeles, this sea-change in racial identity took months, not years.

To be sure, the Chicano rejection of whiteness occurred within the larger context of longstanding Anglo-Mexican tensions in the Southwest. In addition, even before the late 1960s, many members of the Mexican community had understood themselves in other terms. More recent immigrants, people in the working class, and those with darker features often identified themselves not in terms of race but rather through their cultural and familial ties to Mexico. More directly anticipating the Chicano movement, many Mexican youths in the 1940s and 1950s rejected their parents' racial aspirations, developing a hip, alienated Pachuco culture that fashioned itself as neither Mexican nor American. Nevertheless, prior to the Chicano movement, no segment of the Mexican community had self-consciously embraced and affirmatively proclaimed a brown identity. The Chicano movement heralded the emergence of a new, quintessentially racial politics that sought to turn non-white status into a badge of pride. This book traces the advent of that new racial politics and explores its significance today.

I have three principal goals in this book: to describe the evolution of a non-white racial identity among Mexicans in East Los Angeles during the Chicano movement years; to illustrate how racial thinking leads to and stems from legal violence; and to offer a general theory of race as common sense that helps us to fathom not only the rise of the Chicano movement but also current racial dynamics.

I use "Mexicans" here in a particular fashion. By this term I mean people in the United States descended from the inhabitants of the southwestern region acquired from Mexico in the mid-nineteenth century, as well as permanent immigrants from Mexico and their descendants. I do not mean nationals of Mexico but United States residents. I adopt this definition in order to have a term that carries no racial connotation. In contrast, I reserve for more particular usage the labels "Mexican Americans" and "Chicanos." "Mexican Americans" refers to Mexican community members who insisted that Mexicans are white, and "Chicanos" refers to those who argued instead that Mexicans constitute a non-white race.[1] Few scholars make this distinction, and many community members today accept Chicano and Mexican American as synonyms.[2] Nevertheless, I emphasize these labels' original racial connotations both to sharpen my discussion of the Chicano movement and to emphasize that, like all racial ideas, Mexican racial identity is a cultural product that cannot be taken for granted.

Two criminal prosecutions arising directly from the 1968 student demonstrations provide the primary vehicle for examining the Chicano movement in East Los Angeles. The first case began in late May 1968, when the Los Angeles Grand Jury indicted thirteen community leaders and college students for allegedly encouraging the high school protesters. These defendants were charged with a variety of misdemeanors, ranging from disturbing the peace to trespassing on school grounds—offenses that would usually result in fines or, at worst, a few days of incarceration. But they were also accused of conspiracy, a felony charge routinely used by law enforcement at that time against groups engaged in civil disobedience or protest actions. Because of the conspiracy charge, the defendants faced potential sentences of up to forty-five years in prison. These defendants became popularly known as the East L.A. Thirteen. Their court case, even more than the initial demonstrations at the high schools, politically mobilized the Mexican community.

In response to the community's agitation, the State of California hosted an educational conference in the spring of 1969 at the Biltmore Hotel in downtown Los Angeles to address the "needs" of Mexican students. When Governor Ronald Reagan rose to give the keynote address, East Los Angeles residents in the audience stood to boo him. Simultaneously, fires ignited with road flares erupted on several floors of the hotel. As a result of these events, the Los Angeles Grand Jury indicted six persons on felony charges of burglary, arson, and conspiracy; the defendants, who became known as the Biltmore Six, faced possible life sentences.

Together these two cases provide an important window onto the Chicano movement, partly because the defendants included leaders from such prominent Chicano organizations as the United Mexican American Students (UMAS) and the Brown Berets and partly because the cases frame the rise and collapse of the Chicano movement in Los Angeles. More importantly for our purposes, though, these cases provide a unique view of one of the Chicano movement's definitive features—they reveal the insurgents' struggle to understand not only the constant discrimination they faced but also the nature of their own identity.

In Part One of this book, I describe the legal and racial battles that took place in the *East L.A. Thirteen* and *Biltmore Six* cases. Both groups of defendants chose for their lawyer Oscar Acosta, a volcanic figure who shared the militants' antipathy for the police and the courts. He billed himself as the only genuine Chicano lawyer on the grounds that he truly hated the law. For Acosta and most of the defendants, the cases represented an opportunity to publicize the Chicano cause. The defense principally argued that discrimination against Mexicans tainted the selection of those who sat on the indicting grand juries and that the Los Angeles Superior Court judges who chose the grand jurors were responsible. To provide a basis for this defense, Acosta called to the witness stand as many judges as he could subpoena, and one by one, hour by hour he interrogated them about their alleged discriminatory conduct. Over the course of both cases, Acosta cornered more than a hundred judges in the witness box, "snap[ping] for their throats," he would say, "with a smile, a slight twist of the eyes."[3]

To prevail on the discrimination claim, not only did Acosta have to demonstrate bias but, first and foremost, he had to prove that Mexicans constituted an identifiable and distinct minority group in Los Angeles. This seemed straightforward: Mexicans comprised one in every eight Los Angeles county residents, with a vast population concentrated into the relatively tiny area of East Los Angeles, by choice but also by a history of de jure and de facto segregation in housing, the labor market, and schools. Nevertheless, Acosta and the defendants struggled to show in court that Mexicans existed as a distinct group that could be discriminated against. To some extent, this difficulty stemmed from the Mexican community's past successes in arguing that Mexicans were white. I use Part One to explore how the defendants understood themselves in terms of both race and racism. In addition, I trace the rise of East Los Angeles and examine historically the racial construction of Mexicans.

In Part Two I analyze the allegations raised in the Chicano cases that the Los Angeles Superior Court judges discriminated against Mexicans. Chicanos often claimed that racism generally, and legal racism in particular, proved that they were not white. This claim is something of a surprise, because overt racism against Mexicans was waning by the time of the Chicano movement. Yet discrimination against that group continued, and the Chicano cases exemplify this paradox. Judge after judge seemed to testify honestly that he (the overwhelming majority of judges were men) did not intend to discriminate against Mexicans or any other group. Yet between 1959 and 1969, when Mexicans made up one of every eight Los Angeles residents, they accounted for only one of every fifty-eight Los Angeles grand jurors. Only four Mexicans served on a Los Angeles grand jury during this period, out of a total of 233 grand jury members.[4]

To explain this paradox of declining overt prejudice and persistent discrimination, I offer an analysis of the Chicano cases that draws on the now widely accepted view that race is a social construction. In this view, race is not a fundamental biological division but rather reflects a given society's understanding of various superficial differences among people, both physical and cultural.[5] But simply stating that race is socially constructed does not answer the key questions raised by the Chicano movement cases. If race is a matter of social beliefs, how do ideas about race operate—how do they arise, spread, and gain acceptance? What is the relationship between race as a set of ideas and racism as a set of practices? How have racial ideas created the structures of inequality that mar our social world?

I introduce the notion of race as "common sense" to answer these questions.[6] I suggest that what we think we know often takes the form of common sense—a complex set of background ideas that people draw upon but rarely question in their daily affairs. These background ideas do much of our thinking for us, for they provide ways to comprehend and act in the world that we constantly draw upon, thus sparing ourselves the need to repeatedly reconsider the already familiar. Our breakfast routines, the route we drive to work or walk home from school, our style of dress—these are stock ideas and practices that we have absorbed and heavily rely upon but to which we give little thought. They are codes of thinking and acting that facilitate the minutiae of our lives. That minutiae takes on great significance, for it helps to constitute our identities and our world views. We are not fully rational beings carefully considering anew each decision, the contours of who we are, or the nature of the world around us. Instead, our beliefs, our selves, and our sense of reality reflect what we understand to be common sense.

I argue that racial ideas operate within this sphere of common sense—that we regularly rely on, yet infrequently examine, assumptions about race. Most people think little about race, save perhaps to deny its continued importance. Yet most people uncritically accept racial distinctions as a natural and necessary component of society. We depend upon racial ideas in conceiving of ourselves, in conducting our relationships with others, and in comprehending the social world. We "know" what race we are with great certainty, and yet we give this question little or no thought. Race informs how we view, and treat, the "white," "black," "brown" and "yellow" people we interact with, even if we do not consciously think about them in racial terms. We readily accede to structures of social inequality, without fathoming that racial ideas help to render such inequality "normal."

Race as common sense is more than just ideas. The common sense of race also informs repertoires of behavior. We follow the scripts laid out for us by common sense not only in our thinking but in our decision-making and in our actions. When we uncritically rely on racial ideas, we often, in turn, practice racism. We treat people according to their place in the racial hierarchies created by society and, by doing so, perpetuate those hierarchies. The segregation in our cities and workplaces—or, more concretely, the dilapidated conditions in the schools that supposedly served East Los Angeles—resulted from actions based on widely accepted racial ideas.

I do not mean to suggest that all action takes place on the common sense level, for intentional racism still plays a large part in constructing the society we now live in. Nevertheless, racial common sense has long played a prominent role in both fostering discriminatory behavior and in rendering such behavior normal and legitimate. Today, after several decades of declining overt prejudice, it is likely that most racism is unconsidered and reflexive, the product of thoughtless reliance on background ideas of race. Racism is now most often common sense.

Racism as common sense, I contend, explains the discrimination at issue in the Chicano cases. Called upon to pick grand jurors from a cross-section of Los Angeles county, the judges instead consistently nominated their friends and neighbors. Under questioning by Acosta, the judges denied that they ever intended to discriminate against Mexicans or anyone else; they insisted that they desired only to pick qualified persons for the grand jury. But as became clear in their testimony, patterns of social, educational, residential, and workplace segregation ensured that the judges had few Mexican acquaintances, save perhaps their gardeners, and that they regarded Mexicans as unqualified to serve on the grand jury. The judges assumed that persons like themselves—white, older, affluent, and male, or married to someone like that—deserved that honor. For the judges, it was simply indisputable that people like themselves were dependable, competent, and qualified, meriting not only a seat on the grand jury but the esteem accorded friends. Likewise, it was common knowledge to the judges that Mexicans were, well, inferior. Intentional discrimination was unnecessary. To systematically exclude Mexicans from the Los Angeles grand jury, the judges only had to rely on what seemed to them common sense.

The judges' blind acceptance of ideas regarding the superiority of whites and the inferiority of Mexicans tainted not only grand jury selection but a range of judicial functions. Common sense racism also explains police practices in East Los Angeles, practices that involved pervasive hostility and brutality toward Mexicans. To be sure, conscious bigotry permeated the Los Angeles police and sheriff's departments; yet common sense ideas of race contributed significantly to the distortion of law enforcement in East L.A. The police disdained the residents there as racial inferiors and approached them armed with preconceptions regarding their deficient character, innate criminal tendencies, propensity for senseless violence, and unbridled taste for alcohol. Judicial bias and police malpractice together imposed a reign of legal violence on East Los Angeles that can be largely explained by the operation of race as common sense. The result was a constant, unremarkable, unconsidered racism that exacted its toll in human lives.

Many Chicanos insisted that legal violence against the Mexican community proved that Mexicans were non-white. Although this violence took various forms, the Chicano activists almost always pointed to direct physical violence, the sort that bashed heads, broke bones, and wrecked lives. Scholars commonly define law abstractly, as a body of court decisions and legislative statutes. In these terms, legal violence might be taken to refer to rhetorical or symbolic offenses, the kind suffered in a courtroom or through group disregard expressed in formal laws. I do not mean to diminish the importance of such violence or to imply some sharp distinction between physical and psychic harm.[7] But it was not primarily the formal or symbolic systems of law that convinced Chicanos they were brown. Rather, the massive police presence, the constant police brutality, the hostile judges, and the crowded jails convinced Mexicans that they were not white. "Law" for Chicanos, and in turn in this book, means the police and the courts, and legal violence refers principally to the physical force these institutions wield. Law carried out on the street—as opposed to law on the books—convinced many Mexicans that they were Chicanos.

Although the Chicano insurgents cited racism and legal violence to prove that they were brown, neither sufficiently explains this new racial identity's emergence. After all, racism against the Mexican community stretched back well more than a hundred years and had been much more virulent before 1968. Similarly, law enforcement had aggressively and brutally mistreated the Mexican community for decades. Indeed, one scholar argues that legal repression spurred Mexican political mobilization in East Los Angeles in the 1930s and 1940s.[8] That may be, but in the decades before 1968 the Mexican community reacted to such racism and repression by declaring a white identity, not by insisting, as the Chicanos did, on a brown one.

In Part Three, I examine the development and contours of the new Chicano racial ideology of the late 1960s.[9] The Chicano movement arose in a period of broad social mobilization spearheaded by the black struggle for civil rights. The black movement inspired many groups, including the Chicanos, and also provided important lessons about protest tactics and organizing strategies. Yet for Mexicans the black struggle's greatest impact may have come not through lessons learned directly but through the civil rights movement's indirect influence on racial common sense. Since the mid-1950s, the spectacle of black protesters encountering violent repression had transfixed the nation. This imagery

linking together protest, legal violence, and race became embedded in common sense. The scenes from Selma and Birmingham,
and later Watts and Detroit, powerfully communicated that
whites would respond with violent resistance to minorities who
protested social inequality. This message's racial component—
that the conflict pitted blacks against whites—was obvious. In
turn, the very quality of being obvious made this component that
much more a matter of common sense: when minorities protested, legal violence followed. This tripartite linkage among
protest, repression, and race strongly contributed to the rise of a
brown identity among Mexicans in East Los Angeles.

When news of the arrests of the East L.A. Thirteen spread, the
Mexican community almost immediately conceptualized the
mass indictments and potentially lengthy sentences in rhetoric
that tracked the common sense connections established during
the black struggle. Before the arrests, there had been relatively
little talk of a brown racial identity; in their wake, a new language quickly emerged that painted the activists as racial militants persecuted by the police for demanding justice. No doubt
the Black Power movement directly influenced this rhetoric. But
the Chicano analysis drew more heavily on the new common
sense that linked protest, repression, and race. I contend that the
Chicano activists turned to race—and not to other potential
bases of group solidarity such as class, nationality, or culture—
because the social context made it "obvious" to them that Mexicans were yet another racial minority protesting social injustice
and in turn encountering legal violence.

Activist newspapers from East Los Angeles such as *La Raza*
and *La Causa* recorded the militants' changing politics and
worldviews and demonstrate that racial common sense strongly
influenced the development of Chicano racial identity. The most
sophisticated of such papers, *La Raza* covered the Chicano
movement's start in East Los Angeles. As the organ for the
Brown Berets, *La Causa* chronicled the evolving ideas of a radical Chicano group. Both newspapers show that, while the mili-

tants hotly debated questions such as the social position of Mexicans and racism's role in the community's life, they rarely directly
engaged questions about Mexican racial identity. Instead, they
drew upon the protest-repression-race connection, and, more
importantly, they accepted popular conceptions of race almost
wholesale. Thus, the militants believed that they were brown as a
matter of descent and biology, not by virtue of having made a
political choice—they understood themselves to be recognizing
facts of nature, not inventing them. The Chicano movement remade Mexican racial identity but did so while accepting and in
turn proclaiming that race determined individual identity, gender
relations, and group destiny. Common sense impelled not only
the shift to Chicano identity, but also the form it took.

I close with an epilogue that draws central lessons from the
Chicano movement and traces into the present several strands of
the East L.A. Chicano story. Defense lawyer Oscar Acosta disappeared in the mid-1970s, judges in Los Angeles continue to discriminate against Latinos in grand jury selection, the legal system
increasingly protects rather than prohibits racial discrimination,
and the Chicano movement's principal legacy seems to be racial
pride rather than structural change. Meanwhile, the level of legal
violence in our society grows, as does its role in constructing racial identities. We now live in the midst of a "war on crime" and
a "war on terrorism." These crusades are fought largely on racial
terrain; they reflect our society's decision to deploy extraordinary
force against persons who, while described almost exclusively as
"criminals" or "terrorists," in fact are predominantly minorities.
The legal violence deployed in the name of these wars further en-
trenches racial ideas, both among the targets of state force and
for society as a whole. More than ever, we know ourselves by
how the police and the courts treat us. If we receive respect, courtesy, fair treatment, and due process, we are white; if we are harassed, beaten, arrested, or detained by executive fiat, we are
black, brown, yellow, or red. Neither the differing treatment nor
the assumptions regarding racial identity stem primarily from in-

tentional racism, I contend, but rather are largely matters of common sense.

We as a country find ourselves today where the East Los Angeles protesters were on the eve of the high school walkouts. We must remedy deep inequalities structured along racial lines, and we must devise conceptions of race and racism that allow us to do so. We should learn from the judges and the police in East Los Angeles, and also from the Chicano militants who fought them, what happens when ideas about race and status are allowed to remain in the background, unexamined and unquestioned by people divided by race.

LITIGATING MEXICAN IDENTITY

1

THE CHICANO MOVEMENT CASES

               In 1968 more Mexicans made their home in Los Angeles than lived in the states of Colorado, New Mexico, and Arizona combined.[1] The heart of this vast population was East Los Angeles.

    Then, as today, leaving the corporate high-rises and squat government buildings of downtown Los Angeles to travel just a mile or two east, crossing over the wide concrete aqueduct that carries the Los Angeles River in a shallow trickle, is to journey into the Mexican world of East L.A. It is a world of three-story commercial buildings strung out along four-lane thoroughfares, the bright signs worn with age, the roads gritty, spotted, choked with parked cars; of dun-colored tract homes and California bungalows on small lots, some pretty and well-tended, others in disrepair; of crowded apartment buildings scattered about, few with any charm. It is a community of small Mexican restaurants painted in reds and greens, of corner grocery stores where radios blare *rancheras* and Spanish-language commercials hawk cheap furniture and used cars, a place where people and their complicated lives spill into the streets.

    In 1968 the population of East Los Angeles was relatively poor. Among its 105,033 residents, median family income was less than three-quarters that in Los Angeles City.[2] It was also comparatively young and uneducated: nearly 44 percent of the

population was under twenty years of age, compared with 33
percent in the city, and just over a quarter had completed high
school, while in Los Angeles as a whole 62 percent had high
school degrees.[3] But more striking, almost all East Los Angeles
residents were Mexican: 87 percent of the population bore Spanish surnames, of whom an estimated 95 percent traced their origins to Mexico; in the city, the Spanish-surnamed population
came to only 18 percent.[4] (Today, 97 percent of East Los Angeles's 124,000 residents are Latino, making it, according to
the 2000 census, the densest concentration of Latinos in the
country.)[5]

The Mexican community in East Los Angeles was not
blighted and hopeless, however.[6] Rather, in 1968 the community
was relatively settled and stable, even more stable, by some measures, than Los Angeles as a whole. Owner-occupied homes accounted for slightly more of the residences in East Los Angeles
than in the city; and one-quarter more people than in Los Angeles as a whole were living in the same home in 1970 that they
had occupied in 1965.[7] Nor was the East L.A. community primarily made up of immigrants. Rather, as in the Southwest generally, in 1968 about 85 percent of the Mexican population held
U.S. citizenship by birth, and more than half had been in the
United States at least three generations.[8] East Los Angeles at that
time is perhaps best described as a working-class community
afflicted by the usual hardships of poverty, poor infrastructure,
and scarce jobs. Yet, it was also a minority community, and this
fact played a powerful role in the unique problems confronting
its Mexican residents.

EDUCATIONAL CRISIS

The local school system, in particular the four East Los Angeles
high schools—Garfield, Roosevelt, Lincoln, and Wilson—constituted a long-standing concern in the community. These schools,
with a student body over three-quarters Mexican, provided the
barest education.[9] During the 1950s and into the 1960s, only

half of the Mexican students who entered the Los Angeles public school system completed high school.[10] Partly, this attrition stemmed from the Eastside schools' deteriorated physical conditions: they were large dilapidated concrete buildings surrounded by stretches of crumbling pavement and high chainlink fences. The result could also be traced to scant resources and severe overcrowding. Thousands of students jammed hallways and classrooms designed for hundreds; they ate in shifts in the cafeteria and scrambled to find restrooms not closed for lack of maintenance; they shared tattered and outdated books and science equipment, when available at all.

But a large part of the problem in the East Los Angeles schools was race. Racial politics exacerbated the school board's indifference to the plight of East Los Angeles's children; meanwhile, inside the classroom, faculties were overwhelmingly white. Only 3 percent of the teachers and 1.3 percent of the administrators at the East L.A. schools bore Spanish surnames. Bigoted views of Mexican students distorted how teachers and administrators conceived of their roles as educators.[11] As one junior high teacher explained, "We will keep trying . . . but there is nothing you can do with those kids, they can't discuss, they can't talk, all you can do is give them seat work to keep them busy and keep them under control."[12] Another "solution" was to declare them mentally impaired: although Mexicans comprised 14 percent of California's elementary and secondary students in 1968, they accounted for 40 percent of the students shunted into separate educational programs for the "mentally handicapped."[13]

In response to the local schools' wretched conditions, East Los Angeles's residents organized in the 1950s to seek reform.[14] College-educated professionals from the small Mexican middle class led this effort.[15] They held public hearings and met with state legislators, school board members, and administrators. Despite their campaign, little changed in the East Los Angeles schools. Community organizing continued to focus on the school system into the 1960s, when new groups emerged to demand educa-

tional reform in East L.A., groups that resorted to a more militant politics of confrontation.

A NEW GENERATION

The mid-1960s witnessed a growing radicalization among Mexican youth. Inspired by black and white radicals who rejected dia-
logue with community power brokers and government officials,
militant young Mexicans increasingly thought that social change
depended upon confronting the institutions that they considered
directly responsible for inequitable community conditions—the
establishment," in the parlance of the day.

During the 1960s, various Mexican groups coalesced
throughout the Southwest, including a farm worker's union in
California's Central Valley, a land-grant movement in New Mexico, and a youth organization in Colorado. Among the groups
that formed in Los Angeles during this time, several stand out. In
1967 Mexican college students convened a regional conference
to discuss their role in the struggle for social change. Calling
themselves United Mexican American Students (UMAS), they
voted to establish Mexican student organizations on college
campuses throughout Los Angeles to address issues confronting
themselves and their community.[16] In February 1968 UMAS
sponsored a conference at the University of California at Los Angeles that stressed pride in Mexican heritage, culture, and language, as well as the need for Mexicans to "strive for power as a
group, in the manner of militant Negro Black Power groups."[17]

High school students also organized. In 1966 they formed a
group called Young Citizens for Community Action (YCCA),
which concentrated at first on educational issues. Later, especially as the group's focus switched more to police brutality,
YCCA became radicalized, abandoning a program that emphasized access to elected officials in favor of one that stressed mass
mobilization and demonstrations. To mark this increased militancy, the group changed its name to the Brown Berets and
adopted the following pledge: "I wear the Brown Beret because it

signifies my dignity and pride in the color of my skin and race."[18] The politics of insurgency in East Los Angeles included a dramatic new willingness to claim a non-white identity as the basis for solidarity and mobilization.

At least initially, these new groups focused on education. The launching of activist-oriented community newspapers around this time strengthened the campaign for educational reform. *La Raza*, the movement's leading paper, ran numerous articles on the atrocious conditions in local schools.[19] In December 1967, *La Raza* forcefully challenged parents to ask themselves tough questions concerning the educational realities at the Eastside schools: "Why is there a 40 to 50% chance my child will not graduate from high school? Why is there a chance my child will be among the lowest in the nation in reading ability? Why is there a chance my child will never know the language, culture and history of his own people? Why is there a chance my child's abilities and talents will never be discovered and developed in our schools?"[20] *La Raza* aimed its message not solely at the parents in East L.A. but also at the Los Angeles school board: "It is now apparent that our voices are not being heard," the paper editorialized. "So, to hell with it. Merry Christmas brother. 1968 will be different. Next year the community is going to be heard one way or another."[21]

BLOWOUT!

La Raza's end-of-year message proved prescient. In the fall of 1967 high school students in East Los Angeles began developing plans to walk out of their schools. Sal Castro, a civics teacher at Lincoln High School and himself a product of the East Los Angeles barrio, joined in the nascent mobilization. Castro gave the students the following advice: "Before you even think about blowing-out, why don't you write your grievances, all these things that are wrong in the school, not only the things that are wrong in your school, but the things that you remember were wrong in the elementary schools because, you see, you don't want to change things just in the high schools; you also want to think about your little brothers and sisters and also your kids when you get married. There has to be a change, a complete change."[22]

By early spring of 1968, a consensus had developed among students that they would stage mass walkouts. With the assistance of Castro, the student activists enlisted the help of the UMAS chapters in Los Angeles, as well as the support of various college professors, professionals, and clergy already active in community politics.[23] The Brown Berets, many of them high school students or recent graduates, also joined in planning the walkouts. The student militants formed strike committees at Garfield, Roosevelt, and Lincoln high schools. They also formed a central committee to draft demands and coordinate any actual strikes.

The committee formulated thirty-six demands, including such things as reduced class size, more teachers and counselors, expanded library facilities, and an end to the requirement that students contribute janitorial services. By and large, however, the demands focused on community control of the schools: the students called for bilingual education, more Mexican teachers, the implementation of a citizen review board, and the establishment of a Parents' Council.[24] The students planned to present the demands to the school board, coupled with a threat to walk out if the demands were not met.[25]

On Friday, March 1, 1968, however, the principal of Wilson High canceled the senior class play, sparking student anger. Influenced by the talk of strikes circulating generally, students at Wilson staged an unplanned walkout during the lunch period.[26] The central strike committee quickly convened to consider whether to call for a general strike at Garfield, Roosevelt, and Lincoln. Before they reached a decision, the students at Garfield took matters into their own hands. On Tuesday, March 5, nearly 2,000 students stormed out of Garfield High School. Brandishing placards and yelling at the top of their lungs, the student demonstrators chanted "Education, Not Eradication," "Walk Out Today, Or Drop Out Tomorrow," "We are not 'Dirty Mexicans,'" and "Teachers, Sí, Bigots, No." As both a proclamation and a demand, they also shouted "Chicano Power."[27]

In part due to the advice of Sal Castro, who cautioned the students to show solidarity or risk division and failure, the coordinating committee immediately called for walkouts at Lincoln and Roosevelt.[28] Fearing police violence, Castro and the central committee encouraged members of UMAS and the Brown Berets to attend in order to maintain order and protect the high school students. It is clear, though, that UMAS and the Brown Berets did more than simply protect the students; they also played an important role in encouraging them to walk out. The Brown Berets, in particular, arrived at various schools with picket signs and probably called in the false fire alarms and bomb threats that forced school officials to move students out of the classrooms.

On Wednesday, March 6, 2,700 students walked out of Garfield; at Roosevelt, despite locked gates and the arrival of the police, 500 determined students also marched out.[29] Friday, March 8, marked the last day of school protests that spring. Students from the various schools walked out simultaneously and met at Hazard Park for a 9:00 A.M. rally. At Lincoln High School, Sal Castro insisted on accompanying his students. According to Castro, the high school principal came to his classroom at 8:45 A.M. and warned him against joining the protest. "The Principal came into the classroom and said . . . 'You are not going.' And I said, 'I am going.' I said, 'My responsibility as a teacher is with the kids. If I am here in an empty classroom, I mean, who am I teaching, an empty wall?'"[30] Castro also recalled heavy rain that morning, and the students' determination to walk out anyway. "At 8:55, not only was it raining, but it began raining harder in the Lincoln area. It was really coming down. I looked out the window and I said, 'My gosh.' You know, I thought about peace marches and other demonstrations, and when there is bad weather like that, they just call them off, they

say, 'Forget it, we'll try again tomorrow.' These kids—these kids
knew what they wanted. In the driving rain, kids without rain-
coats, without umbrellas, some kids in T-shirts, were walking
out. Wave upon wave upon wave, they came . . . I was out there
in the rain, my face wet. The kids didn't know it, but I was cry-
ing."[31]

As Castro emphasized, "The kids had such a fervent desire to
let the whole community know their real problems."[32] And the
community seemed to be listening. At the Hazard Park rally, the
students were joined not only by Julian Nava, the only Mexican
on the County Board of Education, but also by their U.S. Congressman, Ed Roybal, the first Mexican elected to federal office
from California. During one week in March 1968, perhaps ten
thousand students walked out of area high schools in a political
storm that rolled through East Los Angeles, sweeping its Mexican residents into the politics of protest.

AFTER THE WALKOUTS

As the walkouts continued during the first week of March, the
police and sheriff's departments increased their presence in the
community, patrolling the schools and arresting protesters.[33]
Meanwhile, the thunder set off by the mass demonstrations rum-
bled out far beyond East Los Angeles. Reporters from the *Los
Angeles Times* and other papers throughout the Southwest con-
verged on East L.A., and headlines about the walkouts splashed
across the region. L.A. Police Chief Tom Reddin and Governor
Ronald Reagan denounced the walkouts as the handiwork of
outside agitators, blaming most prominently the Brown Berets,
who catapulted into the spotlight as a militant nationalist front.[34]

Closer to home, the Los Angeles School Board called a special
meeting for Monday, March 11. Acquiescing to the students' demands, the meeting was convened not at the comfortable headquarters of the board but at Lincoln High, the most deteriorated
school campus on the Eastside. At this meeting, the students se-

cured promises that the board would not discipline strike participants and would fully consider their demands. While many protesters hoped the school board would do more than "consider"
demands, other parties, including some members of the Mexican
community, criticized the board for capitulating to student pressure.[35] Nevertheless, a committee of parents, UMAS members,
educators, and other professionals came together under the
name of the Educational Issues Coordinating Committee (EICC)
to further develop community plans for the East Los Angeles
schools and to pressure the school board for reform.[36] No further
student strikes occurred that spring, as the students and the
EICC together sought to pressure the school board to quickly improve school conditions.

For many people in East Los Angeles, the student strikes sym-
bolized the awakening of Mexican youth to a political consciousness of themselves and of their ability to fight for equal treatment. Many adults, rather than viewing the students in negative
terms, felt proud of their efforts at self-determination. A community long considered pliant saw their youth rise up in protest, and
hoped that positive improvements in the community might grow
out of these young protesters' actions.

For others, though, the walkouts seemed a grossly inappropri-
ate response to school conditions, a contribution to the problem
rather than to the solution. Lincoln High School teacher Richard
Davis opined in an open letter to the community that the real issue was the Mexicans themselves:

> Most of the Mexican-Americans have never had it so good. Before
> the Spanish came, he was an Indian grubbing in the soil, and after the
> Spaniards came, he was a slave. It seems to me that America must be
> a very desirable place, witness the number of "wetbacks" and mi-
> grants both legal and illegal from Mexico. Yes, I agree that he sees
> himself as a "passive object." And therein lies the whole problem as
> well as the answer. When it comes to going to school—free and the
> best in the world—he is passive. Absenteeism is his culture, his way

of life—always mañana; maybe he will get an education—mañana; when it comes to repairing his home, controlling child birth, planning for tomorrow, he is passive.[37]

Another educator sought to ameliorate the harm done by Davis's remarks, but he did so in a letter that generally confirmed the prevalence of Davis's views:

> Being a Gringo I see and hear things that Mexican teachers and parents do not. We are not educating your children as we should and as we can . . . I stopped using the cafeteria and teachers' lounge a long time ago. I don't want to listen to teachers discuss your children—"I give up on these dumb Mexicans." "Felipe is so dirty I can't stand him." "These damn parents should go back to Mexico." "These parents are as dumb as their kids." "I went to Juan's house; what a smell!" "I've never seen such lazy children."[38]

The letter closed: "Parents, there are good teachers who do not think this way. They want to do a good job."[39]

Such letters illustrate an important source of the grievances that fueled the student walkouts. The East Los Angeles schools reflected, and in turn perpetuated, the degraded status of Mexicans in California. Long a source of community concern, horrendous school conditions served as a flash point. Reverberating with calls for "Chicano Power," the school demonstrations marked urban Mexican youth's entrance into the struggle for equal treatment in the United States. They signaled as well the dramatic rise of a new racial and political identity among the residents of East Los Angeles. There was a price for this new militancy, however. Within a few months of the walkouts, indictments and arrests cast the Chicano movement into a new trajectory of violence and confrontation with the courts and police.

INDICTMENTS AND ARRESTS

Immediately after the walkouts, prosecutors in Los Angeles began calling witnesses before the grand jury, which soon handed down multiple indictments. On the night of Friday, May 31,

1968, the police swept through East L.A. armed with arrest warrants for thirteen individuals. Plainclothes and uniformed officers burst into the offices of *La Raza*, where they handcuffed and arrested Eliezer Risco and Joe Razo.[40] *La Raza's* founder and lead editor, Risco, 31, had just served for two years as an organizer with Cesár Chávez's farm workers' movement.[41] Razo, 29, was an editor at *La Raza* and held a master's degree in psychology; he also worked for a community group funded under President Lyndon Johnson's War on Poverty.

Raiding the Brown Berets' headquarters next, the police picked up David Sánchez, 19, the Brown Berets' prime minister. Born and raised in East Los Angeles and a Roosevelt High School graduate, Sánchez had recently chaired Los Angeles Mayor Samuel Yorty's Youth Advisory Council.[42] As at the *La Raza* offices, the police confiscated subscription and membership lists, telephone numbers, and various publications from the Berets' headquarters. They also removed thousands of pamphlets and leaflets intended for use in a campaign to oppose a police bond measure up for a vote the following Tuesday.[43]

Continuing the roundup, the police found and arrested Brown Beret officer Gilbert Cruz Olmeda and UMAS leader Moctezuma Esparza in front of the Hollenbeck police station, where the two were protesting police harassment.[44] Cruz Olmeda, 23, was chairman of the Brown Berets and a decorated Vietnam War veteran employed by VISTA, Volunteers in Service to America. He held a scholarship to the University of California at Irvine for the fall.[45] Esparza, 19, was a student at the University of California, Los Angeles, where he chaired the UMAS chapter and also held the office of executive vice chairman for UMAS in California.[46] He was an honor graduate of Lincoln High School and another former member of the Mayor's Youth Advisory Council.

The police arrested Lincoln High School teacher Sal Castro, 33, in his home late that night, pausing long enough to search for "subversive literature."[47] Born and raised in East Los Angeles

and a Korean War veteran, Castro had attended college in Los
Angeles on the GI Bill and had chaired the Southern California
branch of Students for Kennedy.[48] In the dark hours before dawn
on Saturday, the police also arrested UMAS activist Carlos
Muñoz, 24. Searching his residence, the police confiscated not
only his college course books but the term paper he had just completed for class.[49] Raised in Los Angeles and a Vietnam War veteran attending college on the GI Bill, Muñoz was the president of
a local UMAS chapter and planned to begin doctoral work at
Stanford University in the fall.[50]

The police failed to arrest six of the East L.A. Thirteen during their weekend raids. Henry Gómez and Fred López surrendered on Monday morning.[51] Gómez, 20, was a Lincoln High
School graduate and a hospital laboratory technician as well as
a student at East Los Angeles College.[52] López, 20, served as
the Brown Berets' minister of communication and was enrolled
in the University of Southern California's teacher training
program.[53]

Patricio Sánchez and Richard Vigil turned themselves in on
Wednesday.[54] At age 41, Sánchez was the oldest of those in-
dicted. He worked as an engineer in the local aerospace industry
and was active in community politics, chairing the local Mexican
American Political Association chapter, as well as the Hollenbeck
Democratic Club.[55] Vigil, a former paratrooper, was a college
student who worked with community youth groups in East Los
Angeles.[56]

Carlos Montes and Ralph Ramírez surrendered much later,
after they returned from Washington, D.C. Both had been participating in Martin Luther King Jr.'s Poor People's March on
the nation's capitol.[57] Montes, 20, was the student vice president
at East Los Angeles College and a Garfield High School graduate; he was also the Brown Berets' minister of public relations.[58]
Ramírez, 19, who like most of the others was born and raised in
East Los Angeles, was the Brown Berets' minister of discipline.[59]

Initially, bail was set at $10,000, an amount which ensured that those arrested would spend the weekend in jail. That sum greatly exceeded normal bail amounts; it represented ten times the bail usually imposed on those charged with burglary and twice the sum typically required in cases of assault with a deadly weapon.[60] On Monday, June 3, the defendants were arraigned before a magistrate who reduced bail to $250 for each of the defendants, except for David Sánchez. The magistrate imposed a bail of $1,000 on Sánchez because he had allegedly attempted to flee when approached by the police and because officers claimed that they found bomb-making plans in the Brown Berets' office when they arrested Sánchez.[61] The defendants posted bond and were released. When Sal Castro attempted to return to his teaching duties the next morning, the principal told him to report to the Board of Education, which in turn informed Castro that he had been reassigned to non-teaching duties because of the felony charges against him.[62]

The March demonstrations were repeated in early June, but now protesters focused on the arrest and prosecution of the Thirteen. In part, the mass arrests themselves spurred the renewed protest, but the charges against the defendants provided a special impetus. The indictments charged the Thirteen with multiple counts of disturbing the peace, failing to disperse, and trespassing on school grounds, all misdemeanors.[63] Far more ominous, however, were felony charges of conspiracy to commit those crimes. Because of the conspiracy charges, each of the defendants faced a possible 45-year sentence. The late night arrests, the high bail, the multiple felony counts, and the possibility of long sentences infuriated the community. During the first weekend after the arrests, East Los Angeles community members demonstrated on the streets in front of the L.A. Police Department, and some incarcerated defendants began a hunger strike to protest their arrests as political persecution.[64] In addition, they made the fateful decision to engage Oscar Acosta as their lead defense attorney.

OSCAR ACOSTA, ESQ.

Oscar Acosta was born in 1935 in El Paso, Texas, to Mexican immigrant parents. In 1940 he moved with his family to River-bank, California, in the heart of the Central Valley, where his parents hoped to survive the waning years of the Great Depression as field workers.[65] Acosta was the second of five children, and in his youth he helped the family pick peaches.[66] Acosta's father, Manuel Juan Acosta, pushed his son hard to succeed. "My father was a little different than the other people where we lived," recalled Acosta in an autobiographical essay written in 1971.[67] "He wanted me to compete more than anything else, so he pushed me into competition with himself. When I was five he encouraged me to argue and fight with him, which is unusual in a Mexican family. I guess that is where I became as nasty as I am."[68]

Acosta excelled in school and was popular with his peers, so much so that his high school classmates elected him president.[69] Turning down a music scholarship to the University of Southern California, Acosta joined the Air Force after high school. There, he found God among the Baptists, and, as he explains, "being the fanatic that I am, I became a preacher immediately."[70] After a couple of years, however, Acosta suffered a crisis of faith, in his words "going crazy" and "preaching and teaching shit that I didn't believe."[71]

Leaving both God and the Air Force at roughly the same time produced what Acosta described as "the second big trauma of my life" (the first having been the end of a high school romance).[72] After attempting suicide in New Orleans in 1956, Acosta began ten years of psychiatric treatment.[73] He also returned to school as a student at San Francisco State University, before leaving abruptly in 1960 to work on a novel and to help with John F. Kennedy's presidential campaign. When several publishers rejected Acosta's first novel—"a Romeo and Juliet story of Okies and Chicanos in the valley"—Acosta decided to go to law school and pursue a career in civil rights.[74]

In 1965 Acosta graduated from San Francisco Law School. *La Voz Latina,* a Spanish-language paper in the Central Valley, published a picture of the stern-looking young Acosta wearing a dark suit and reported with pride his accomplishment.[75] But neither civil rights work nor lawyering proved to be the rewarding endeavors Acosta envisioned. "I got involved in the black civil rights movement for . . . four years in San Francisco [while attending law school], but it wasn't really me," Acosta wrote. "I told people that it wasn't just black and white, that there were Chicanos, too, and they laughed at me so I told them to go fuck themselves and they split."[76] After law school, Acosta worked briefly as a legal aid lawyer in Oakland but felt frustrated by the powerlessness of the position. "I hated it with a passion," he exclaimed. "I'd wake up in the morning and throw up. All we'd do was sit and listen to complaints. There were so many problems and we didn't do anything. We didn't have a direction, skills or tools."[77]

After a year or so, Acosta quit and, in keeping with the times, dropped out. Acosta eventually ended up in Aspen, Colorado. "I started dropping acid and staying stoned most of the time and doing all kinds of odd jobs—construction work and washing dishes—and, within about three months my head was clear."[78] During this period, Acosta became friends with the writer Hunter S. Thompson, with whom he traveled and caroused; Thompson later drew upon their "gonzo" adventures in his book *Fear and Loathing in Las Vegas,* in which Acosta figures as the "Samoan" lawyer.[79] Acosta resurrected his dream of writing the great American novel and decided to go to Los Angeles, where he hoped the nascent Chicano movement would inspire him and provide material. He arrived in Los Angeles in February 1968, with the intention of staying for just a few months. The blowouts and arrests changed his plans.[80]

In Acosta, the East L.A. Thirteen found a most unlikely advocate. A volatile person, Acosta suffered from severe mood swings, psychological instability, drug and alcohol abuse, and the certainty that he was destined to change history. Possibly worse, he had little experience as a lawyer—indeed, *East L.A. Thirteen* was Acosta's first major criminal trial.[81] Other than his brief stint as a legal aid attorney, Acosta had no practical legal training. And what little lawyering he had done had instilled in him a deep loathing for legal practice.

Nevertheless, Acosta proved to be an ideal attorney for the militants. His psychological instability coexisted with brilliance, creativity, energy, and enthusiasm. His emotional volatility gave him a fierce passion for justice and morality. His lack of legal training and his intention to pursue a writing career liberated him from the strictures of professional deportment in his approach to lawyering. Having dropped out of the establishment himself, he readily identified with his activist clients. And finally Acosta's dislike of the law mirrored the defendants' own disdain for the legal system. Acosta may have seemed ideal to some of these insurgents for many of the reasons that he was unsuited to more typical legal practice. No doubt with his special qualities firmly in mind, Acosta liked to describe himself as "the only militant Chicano lawyer in the country."[82]

Consumed by a hatred of the courts and committed to the Chicano struggle, Acosta became the lead attorney for the Chicano movement in Los Angeles. Naturally, he also collected material for the novel that had brought him to Los Angeles in the first place, and in 1972 and 1973 he finally published the books he had always dreamed of writing.[83]

Many other lawyers fought alongside Acosta in the two Chicano cases. The National Lawyer's Guild and the American Civil Liberties Union both helped on *East L.A. Thirteen*, especially on the First Amendment issues in that case.[84] Acosta also drew on law students affiliated with the newly created La Raza Law Students Association.[85] Acosta took pains to acknowledge the contributions of the other attorneys. "For them," he wrote, "it has been a labor of love."[86]

But lawyering requires money as well as love. For fundraising purposes, Acosta established the Chicano Legal Defense Fund.[87] The sponsors of the fund included the prominent politicians Edmund G. Brown and Thomas Bradley, as well as César Chávez, Bert Corona, Rodolfo Acuña, and other leading figures in the Mexican community.[88] In his courtroom battles, Acosta often had important legal, financial, and moral assistance.[89] Given the array of charges and the number of defendants facing jail, Acosta and the activists needed every bit of help they could get.

EAST L.A. THIRTEEN

Free on bond, many of the Thirteen joined with Acosta and others protesting the indictments by participating in marches and giving speeches. At the same time, they also protested in the courthouse and, not infrequently, in the courtroom. Irrespective of the actual issue's significance, an atmosphere of political theater often marked many of the hearings, especially those in the summer and fall of 1968. For instance, at a hearing regarding the scheduling of a defense motion to quash the indictments, picketers handed out leaflets, and protesters packed the courtroom to overflowing. Some defendants entered the courtroom wearing brown berets, while others came garbed in what a local columnist described as "Mexican costumes." Asked by the court to introduce themselves, the defendants emphasized the Spanish pronunciation of their names.[90]

Substantively, the defendants advanced three distinct defenses: first, that insufficient evidence existed to sustain the conspiracy charges; second, that the charges violated their First Amendment rights of free association and free speech; and third, that the absence of Mexicans on the indicting grand jury resulted from discrimination and thus violated the Equal Protection clause of the Fourteenth Amendment.

At least initially, in both their court papers and their public speeches, the activists stressed the free speech defense. For example, a July 1968 *La Raza* article stated that the indictment "is plainly another way in which the establishment is strangling the right of the Chicano community to voice its opinion; a constitutional right."[91] In presenting the First Amendment defense, the ACLU played an important role, submitting briefs and arguing before the court. Nevertheless, by the end of the summer, Acosta and the defendants had shifted their emphasis to the Equal Protection claim. They did not favor this defense because it was the most likely to produce an acquittal. The free speech arguments held greater promise and, indeed, after a two-year delay engendered partly by the Equal Protection challenge, the defendants ultimately prevailed on First Amendment grounds.[92] Rather, the attractiveness of the discrimination claim lay in the political message and explosive impact it promised to deliver.

The discrimination claim boiled down to a charge of racism against the Los Angeles Superior Court judges, who nominated all grand jurors. To support their claim, lawyers for the Thirteen cited statistics showing that in the ten years leading up to and including 1968, 178 judges had nominated a total of 1,501 jurors, of whom only 20 were Mexican (1.3 percent); of these, only 4 had actually served, out of 210 grand jurors for that period.[93] In a county where, during the 1960s, the Mexican portion of the population grew from 10 percent to 18 percent, persons from that group accounted for less than 2 percent of all grand jurors during that period.[94]

Numbers, however, constituted only a small part of the defense strategy. Much more dramatically, defense lawyers directly questioned the Superior Court judges themselves to demonstrate that they were prejudiced against Mexicans. With his unerring sense for spectacle, Acosta called to the stand dozens of judges in order to prove through direct examination their anti-Mexican bias.[95] If the legal issue in the courtroom revolved around discrimination in grand juror selection, the larger question emphasized on the street was judicial racism. As Acosta explained in the pages of *La Raza* in September 1968, in *East L.A. Thirteen* he would show "that the Judges themselves are the bigots."[96]

Acosta later attributed the boldness of his defense strategy to drugs. "I think psychedelic drugs have been important to the development of my consciousness," Acosta wrote in 1971, explaining, "Most of the big ideas I've gotten for my lawyer work have usually come when I am stoned. Like the Grand Jury challenge was the result of an acid experience."[97] Whatever the role of drugs, this strategy also resulted from the militancy of Acosta and the defendants. Reflecting on its implications, Acosta noted that no lawyer before him had attempted the grand jury discrimination argument. "Perhaps the most compelling reason for their failure to raise the issue is that ultimately what the lawyer says in such a motion is an indictment of the profession which he professes and a castigation of the society to which he belongs."[98] Acosta, as much if not more than the defendants themselves, was ready to indict and condemn not only his profession and society but, perhaps most of all, the courts.

RISING TURMOIL IN EAST LOS ANGELES

While *East L.A. Thirteen* dragged on with procedural sparring through the fall of 1968, political activism in the community accelerated. The need for improvements in the East Los Angeles schools continued to be a major issue, crystallized for the community not only by the prosecution of the Thirteen but also by the refusal of the Board of Education to reconsider its decision to remove Sal Castro from the classroom. The board's decision incensed the community all the more because the board took no action against Lincoln High School teacher Richard Davis, who in the walkout's aftermath had written the letter describing "the Mexican" as "an Indian grubbing in the soil" and "a slave."[99]

These concerns provoked members of UMAS, the Brown Berets, *La Raza,* the Educational Issues Coordinating Committee, and others to occupy the Board of Education headquarters for a week at the end of September 1968.[100]

Increasingly, though, police brutality emerged as the Chicano community's principal concern. The mass arrests of the Thirteen and the long sentences they faced shifted attention from school board intransigence to law enforcement abuse. Several dramatic incidents of police brutality in the fall also put a spotlight on police malpractice. In one of the most publicized instances, fourteen police officers severely beat Jesús Domínguez, an established member of the East Los Angeles community, after he asked several officers for help in locating his teenage children.[101] The beating of Domínguez and the subsequent efforts of the district attorney's office to convict Domínguez for assault on police officers received extensive coverage in the pages of *La Raza.*[102]

Law enforcement agencies responded to the East Los Angeles Mexican community's increasing mobilization by identifying specific groups there as special threats warranting close scrutiny. During this time, law enforcement agencies nationwide monitored political activity in minority communities. On March 4, 1968, the day before the school walkouts began in earnest, FBI Director J. Edgar Hoover issued a memo to law enforcement officials across the country urging them to give top priority to disrupting nationalist movements in minority communities.[103] Although Hoover probably had black nationalist organizations principally in mind, when the walkouts occurred the next day, FBI headquarters in Washington, D.C., sent a memo under Hoover's authority to the Los Angeles field office chastising them for laxity in monitoring the Brown Berets.[104]

Los Angeles District Attorney Evelle Younger, himself a former high official in the FBI, interpreted Hoover's directive to apply to the groups emerging in East Los Angeles.[105] A unit of the Los Angeles Police Department dedicated to "public disorder intelligence" undertook to investigate these "Brown Power"

groups. By the fall of 1968, law enforcement agencies were culti-
vating informants and placing undercover officers within the
ranks of various community organizations, including UMAS and
the Brown Berets.[106] One of those who spied for the police was
Fernando Sumaya. The day after graduating from the Los Angeles Police Academy, Officer Sumaya went undercover.[107] Operating under the supervision of Sergeant Joe Ceballos, Sumaya attempted to infiltrate the UMAS chapter at San Fernando Valley
State College (now California State University at Northridge),
but the group excluded him because no one there knew him. His
technique refined, Sumaya successfully infiltrated the Brown Berets in East Los Angeles in November 1968.[108]

Against this background of increased Chicano militancy and
heightened police intelligence activity, the California Department
of Education hosted a conference in late April 1969 at the
Biltmore Hotel in downtown Los Angeles to discuss educational
issues affecting the state's Mexican communities.[109] In the keynote address, Governor Ronald Reagan delivered remarks at a
formal banquet on Thursday, April 24. As he rose to speak, a
fire broke out in a linen storage area on the tenth floor. Within
minutes, new blazes erupted on the ninth, fourth, and second
floors, as well as in the ballroom adjacent to where Reagan was
speaking. Firefighters extinguished the fires, which had been set
with emergency road flares, and no one was evacuated from
the hotel.[110] Unaware of the commotion, Reagan continued his
speech.

As Reagan spoke, a dozen Chicano demonstrators in the audience took to their feet, shouting, stomping, and clapping in an effort to drown him out. Almost immediately, police rushed the
protesters and hustled them from the room. After the police intervention, the audience stood to cheer Reagan. He then resumed
his speech, calling on Mexicans to tell the government "what we
can do to help . . . preserve the best of Spanish cultural influence
on your young people, yet teach them how to adjust to the com-
petitive, English-language society."[111]

BILTMORE SIX

Six weeks after the fires at the Biltmore Hotel, the Los Angeles Grand Jury handed down indictments against ten persons for arson, burning personal property, burglary, and malicious destruction of electrical lines, as well as conspiracy to commit those felonies.[112] Eventually, six defendants stood trial. Among them were three of the defendants in *East L.A. Thirteen:* Brown Beret leaders Carlos Montes and Ralph Ramírez and UMAS officer Moctezuma Esparza.[113] The defendants faced possible life sentences.[114]

Undercover police officer Fernando Sumaya immediately emerged as the key witness for the state. He testified before the grand jury that he had infiltrated the Brown Berets and had been present at the time the fires were planned, as well as when they were set.[115] Acosta immediately accused Sumaya of fabricating evidence. According to the *Los Angeles Times,* "Acosta said Sumaya 'was lying.' Asked why Sumaya would have lied, Acosta answered, 'Why? Because he worked for the Police Department.'"[116] The trial promised a dramatic confrontation between Sumaya and the activists. The case ultimately fell to Superior Court Judge Arthur Alarcon, one of four Mexican judges on the 134-judge Superior Court bench.[117] Judge Alarcon probably agreed to take the case to help defuse potential claims of judicial bias.[118]

As in *East L.A. Thirteen,* Acosta assumed the role of lead defense attorney in *Biltmore Six,* and again he defended the activists by filing Equal Protection pretrial motions and by publicly challenging the racial composition of the grand jury.[119] In *Biltmore Six,* though, this defense was both more critical to the fate of the defendants and more difficult to argue convincingly. Unlike in *East L.A. Thirteen,* no other pretrial defenses were available to Acosta; he could not argue that arson and burglary somehow fell within the scope of protected speech. Simultaneously, the effort to show racial bias in the justice system faced a greater hurdle in the *Biltmore* case, at least on the symbolic level, because the principal witness against the Chicano militants and the judge trying the case were both Mexicans. Nevertheless, having no other pretrial defense and wishing to present a political response to the prosecution, Acosta pressed the claim that the Superior Court judges discriminated against Mexicans when nominating grand jurors.

Initially, Judge Alarcon refused Acosta's request to call Superior Court judges as witnesses. On appeal, however, Acosta won an order enjoining further prosecution of the Biltmore Six until Acosta had a chance to fully present his claim of jury discrimination, including by directly questioning Superior Court judges.[120] With a court order in hand, Acosta proceeded to call 109 Superior Court judges to the witness stand, interrogating each in detail about his acquaintanceship with Mexicans and his criteria and approach in nominating grand jurors.[121] Acosta even called into the witness box Judge Alarcon himself.[122]

Acosta later described these proceedings as follows:

> Then, one at a time, the judges stumble into my lair. They trickle in through the back door in their business suits. In civilian clothes they look like ordinary men. Without their black robes and their high benches, they walk and sit and talk just as most tired older men of America do . . . When I see them sitting on the slat benches outside the courtroom, when I pass and see the long thin silk socks and watch them smoke Tareytons just like me, I don't despise them then. It is only when I think about what they *say* and *do* that the acids begin dripping in my brain. But I go on and snap for their throats with a smile, a slight twist of the eyes.[123]

After six weeks of such hearings, Acosta finished presenting his judicial discrimination claim. Judge Alarcon promptly ruled against the defendants and, for good measure, chastised Acosta for failing to argue "before this Court in a consistent and lawyer-like manner."[124] With their judicial discrimination claim defeated, nothing stood between the defendants and trial.

The trial on the substantive charges commenced in August 1971, more than two years after the Biltmore protests.[125] During the trial, tensions soared. Officer Fernando Sumaya quickly emerged as the state's star witness. Sumaya testified at length and in detail: he alleged that in a meeting in the Biltmore Hotel earlier in the evening before Governor Reagan spoke, activists discussed various methods to disrupt his speech, including cutting the microphone wires; he described another gathering that day as "a guerrilla warfare meeting"; he testified that Moctezuma Esparza planned to let in protesters by opening the banquet hall doors while the governor spoke; he told of meeting Carlos Montes in a hallway of the Biltmore, whereupon Montes said "Well, that's one fire"; and he recounted accompanying Montes as he started another fire in a hotel bathroom.[126]

Acosta and the defendants, in contrast, sought to show that Sumaya acted as a provocateur, planning and committing whatever crimes took place at the Biltmore Hotel during Governor Reagan's speech. Acosta, for instance, asked Sumaya: "Did you admit to Ralph Ramirez at that point about you and Carlos setting that fire in the restroom?"[127] When the judge sustained the prosecutor's objection to that question for misstating the testimony, Acosta nevertheless asked it again, though more pointedly: "Did you admit to Ralph Ramirez at that point that *you* had set fire to the restroom?"[128] The prosecutor intervened with another "Objection," which Judge Alarcon sustained.[129]

Adding to these clashes, Judge Alarcon twice jailed Acosta for contempt of court. In one exchange, on Tuesday, August 10, Acosta objected to testimony elicited from Sumaya by the district attorney and then protested vehemently when Judge Alarcon allowed the testimony. Judge Alarcon responded by jailing Acosta for two days, describing Acosta's behavior as "rude, insolent, and contemptuous."[130] When Acosta returned to court on Thursday the pyrotechnics continued. Judge Alarcon again ordered Acosta jailed, this time for five days for "improper and disruptive" behavior.[131]

All of the defendants eventually walked away free from *Biltmore Six,* though not before the arrests and trial consumed several years of their lives. Of the six, Judge Alarcon initially dismissed charges against Juan Rojas, citing insufficient evidence.[132] In September 1971, upon the conclusion of the trial, the jury acquitted Rene Nuñez and Moctezuma Esparza, and Judge Alarcon declared a mistrial with respect to Ralph Ramírez and Ernest Eichwald Cebada.[133] Acosta subsequently withdrew as their attorney.[134] In May 1972, after a second trial, a judge acquitted Ramírez and Eichwald Cebada after ruling that the prosecution had not produced sufficient evidence to send the case to the jury.[135] The remaining defendant, Carlos Montes, had fled prosecution in January 1970. Upon his return to Los Angeles, he was tried and, in 1979, acquitted of the charges stemming from his role in the Biltmore protests.[136] Of the ten people initially indicted on the most serious charges, and of the six who eventually stood trial in the Biltmore case, no one was convicted.

East L.A. Thirteen and *Biltmore Six* were not the only significant cases in the legal history of the East Los Angeles Chicano movement. In another important case, Acosta secured the acquittal of a group of activists, Catolicos por La Raza, on charges stemming from their 1969 Christmas Eve demonstration at downtown Los Angeles's St. Basil's Cathedral. The activists had hoped to highlight the Catholic Church's disregard for Mexican parishioners by forcing their way into midnight mass.[137] Acosta also defended Chicano leader Corky Gonzales when he was tried in Los Angeles on a concealed weapons charge.[138] In both cases, Acosta approached the bench with his characteristic aggressiveness and flamboyance, as well as his trademark hostility to the courts.

In the St. Basil's case, Municipal Judge Irwin Nebron ordered Acosta jailed for three days for what the prosecutor described as "the most shocking and insolent conduct" he had ever observed in a courtroom.[139] In the Gonzales case, Municipal Judge Joseph Grillo jailed Acosta for twenty-four hours apparently because

Acosta ignored the judge's order that he desist from questioning prospective jurors about any potential racial bias.[140] At another point in that case, to explain inconsistencies in witness testimony, Acosta picked up one of the weapons allegedly found in Gonzales's possession and brandished it in the jurors' faces while pacing before the box yelling at them. Setting the weapon down, Acosta challenged the wide-eyed jurors to recollect exactly what the judge and prosecutor had been doing while Acosta had waived the gun about. How could they expect that all of the witnesses would have exactly the same recollections, Acosta then asked the jurors, when there had been "loaded pistols and shotguns pointed at [the witnesses] by angry and excited policemen during the arrests."[141]

The late 1960s and early 1970s marked a politically and culturally contentious period, and Acosta and the Chicano movement carried that tumult into the courtrooms of Los Angeles. But *East L.A. Thirteen* and *Biltmore Six* provide insight into more than just the chaos of the times. The cases provide a magnifying lens through which to examine the rapid transformation of Mexican racial identity that occurred over those few years. Although neither *East L.A. Thirteen* nor *Biltmore Six* ultimately turned on the Equal Protection defense, this defense and the accompanying strategy of interrogating Superior Court judges nevertheless formed the heart of both cases. Acosta and the defendants conceived of these cases as vehicles to promote the Chicano movement, and they attempted to use the courts as a stage upon which to unmask judicial bias against Mexicans. Even more basic than this, however, the defendants, first and foremost, would seek to prove through their trials that Mexicans existed as a subordinated group in the American Southwest. In the end, whether they convinced the judges who sat over them mattered less than whether they convinced the Mexican community as a whole, and themselves in particular.

PROVING MEXICANS EXIST

More than a decade before the acceleration of protest that led to the Chicano cases in East Los Angeles, the United States Supreme Court declared that the Fourteenth Amendment prohibited Texas from excluding Mexicans from grand juries. Decided in 1954, *Hernandez v. Texas* was the first Supreme Court case to extend constitutional protections to Mexicans.[1] Issued just two weeks before *Brown v. Board of Education* declared school segregation unconstitutional, *Hernandez* and *Brown* were companion cases by a Court unified under the leadership of Chief Justice Earl Warren to end the reign of "separate but equal."[2] In a crucial respect, however, *Brown* and *Hernandez* were mirror opposites. In *Brown,* the Court accepted without question that the Fourteenth Amendment protected African Americans but struggled over whether to prohibit school segregation. In contrast, in *Hernandez* the Court recognized that the Constitution barred discrimination in jury selection but wrestled with whether Mexicans constituted a protected group.

The Court in *Hernandez* implied that Mexicans did not deserve constitutional protection as a racial minority but might merit protection if they formed a distinct class. "Throughout our history differences in race and color have defined easily identifiable groups which have at times required the aid of the courts in securing equal treatment under the laws. But community prejudices are not static and from time to time other differences from the community norm may define other groups which need the same protection."[3] According to the Court, race and color did not set Mexicans apart, but "other differences from the community norm" perhaps did so. Thus, before the petitioner could prove his discrimination claim, the Court required him "to prove that persons of Mexican descent constitute a separate class."[4] The Court suggested that "whether such a group exists within a community is a question of fact," one that "may be demonstrated by showing the attitude of the community."[5]

Hernandez necessarily figured prominently in the East L.A. Thirteen argument over whether Superior Court judges had unconstitutionally excluded Mexicans from grand jury service.[6] Yet Hernandez both helped and hindered the defense: it established clear precedent for applying the Fourteenth Amendment to prohibit discrimination against Mexicans, but it did not recognize Mexicans as a racial group. Instead, Hernandez required that Mexicans prove their existence as an identifiable class in every case. According to Hernandez, whether Mexicans were a group depended on their situation "within a community" and turned on local "attitude." Thus, simply by invoking the Constitution to vindicate their rights, the East L.A. Thirteen defendants moved Mexican identity to center stage.

WHITE PERSONS OF SPANISH SURNAME

Faced with the need to prove that Mexicans met the threshold definition of a distinct group in Los Angeles, Acosta first relied on expert witnesses, including demographers from the Los Angeles County Regional Planning Commission, staff from the Los Angeles Commission on Human Relations, and sociologists from the University of California campuses at Los Angeles and Riverside.[7] The defendants' principal expert was Joan Moore, then an associate professor of sociology at UC Riverside and the co-director of a just-completed five-year UCLA study of Mexicans, at that point the most significant study of its kind.[8]

Drawing on census data and information from the UCLA study, Moore defined Mexican group identity along four axes: group distinctiveness as recognized by society as a whole; concentrated socioeconomic patterns; shared cultural traditions; and intergroup relations, in particular intermarriage. On the first axis, Moore testified that the tendency of state institutions through the early 1960s to collect statistics on "Mexicans" typified the widespread social perception that Mexicans constituted a distinct group. So too did the census bureau's efforts to track this group.[9] Regarding socioeconomic patterns, Moore noted that census data showed "distinctive differences in almost all measures of social welfare" as compared with Anglos: higher proportions of Mexicans with little or no education and lower proportions with any college education; far higher numbers at or below the poverty level; a surplus of unskilled laborers and relatively few professionals; and acute housing problems, including overcrowding and high rates of segregation, particularly in Los Angeles.[10] With respect to cultural continuity, Moore cited Catholicism's prevalence among Mexicans as well as the maintenance of Spanish fluency by roughly 85 percent of the community.[11] Finally, Moore testified that low marriage rates outside the group reflected the cultural, economic, and residential isolation of Mexicans. She explained that only one in four Mexicans in Los Angeles County married a non-Mexican, an exogamy rate far lower than that of most other groups.[12]

If these statistics helped the defendants' case, they also presented a problem: Moore, like the other experts Acosta called, relied on census data, where the 1960 census enumerated not "Mexicans" directly, but instead "white persons of Spanish surname."[13] This statistical category undermined Acosta's effort to establish the group distinctiveness of Mexicans. First, by referring to "white persons," this taxonomy implied a racial congruence between Mexicans and Anglos. Second, by purporting to measure group difference by reference to surnames, it promoted a superficial distinction.

In oral arguments on the Equal Protection challenge, Acosta tried to minimize the troubling implications embodied in references to white persons of Spanish surname. Before asking Professor Moore to testify regarding Mexican group identity in Los Angeles, Acosta asked her to justify the census category.[14] Moore explained that, while the 1930 census used "Mexican" as a racial designation, in 1950 the census bureau introduced "white persons of Spanish surname" in order to respond to perceived problems with the "Mexican" label.[15] Moore testified that "Mexican" carried pejorative connotations as a "dirty word," and she observed that the new census category partly resulted from political pressure by the Mexican community for a term denoting a white identity.[16] Acosta allowed that last point to remain undeveloped, but asked Moore whether white persons of Spanish surname basically encompassed persons of Mexican descent. Moore testified that the census bureau intended this, and also informed the court that the census employed this category only in California, Texas, Arizona, Utah, and New Mexico, thereby ensuring that members of other Latino groups such as Puerto Ricans and Cubans were not counted by virtue of their relative absence from the Southwest.[17] Faced with the need to rely on census data to build his case for Mexican distinctiveness, Acosta initially hoped to establish that the "white persons of Spanish surname" category posed no impediment to his arguments.

But District Attorney Richard Hecht refused to accommodate Acosta. In cross-examining Moore, Hecht pushed her to compare the Spanish-surname classification's "strength" with that of another category, "[a] group that we can call Negroes."[18] When Moore balked at the ambiguous nature of the term "strength," Hecht made his concerns explicit: "When I speak to the strength or weakness of a classification, I have reference to the fluidity of the members of that group to voluntarily or involuntarily associate or disassociate themselves from that particular group."[19] Moore responded that internal boundary-setting processes and

social prejudices established group membership, but Hecht ignored this response and asked instead about a hypothetical
"Mary Gonzales," who in marrying "a non-Spanish-surnamed
person . . . would have disassociated herself from that particular
group."[20] Hecht apparently hoped to demonstrate that the defense rested its case on an arbitrary counting device. By emphasizing the "fluidity" of the classification and by contrasting Mexicans and blacks, Hecht intended to show that the Spanish-
surname category lacked the innate distinctions that presumably
defined racial groups.

Ironically, Acosta and the defendants shared Hecht's disdain
for the census category. Their hostility arose, however, not because they doubted that Mexicans could be defined as a group
but because they increasingly believed that Mexicans were innately distinct. If allusions to surnames troubled Hecht, references to white persons antagonized the Chicano militants. In the
court proceedings, the defense almost uniformly abbreviated references to the census category to "persons of Spanish surname"
or simply to "Spanish-surnamed persons." For convenience—
but also to avoid its racial implications—references to Mexicans
as white persons disappeared from the defense's vocabulary.

QUESTIONING THE JUDGES
In addition to calling experts, Acosta used the Superior Court
judges' testimony to establish Mexican group identity. But as had
the experts, the judges often implied that Mexicans were white,
making direct questions regarding whether a judge considered
Mexicans distinct a risky approach. Acosta's examination of
Judge Robert Feinerman exemplifies the problem:

Q. Do you consider Mexicans, Mexican-Americans, Latin-Americans, members of a different ethnic or cultural group than your
own? . . .
A. No. I—Again, the classification Mexican-Americans is within the

white racial group . . . they are classified as a subdivision from the Anglos in the white category, so you would have Mexican-Americans and Anglos in this community at least.[21]

Despite the attraction of a direct approach, the exchange with Judge Feinerman demonstrates that this line of questioning proved tricky for Acosta. While on the one hand judges often acknowledged a distinct Mexican identity, on the other hand they frequently located Mexicans within the white race. Most likely to prevent judges from characterizing Mexicans as white, Acosta confined himself largely to asking judges whether they personally knew any Mexicans and, if they did, whether they could name their acquaintances. Acosta probably hoped to demonstrate that the judges recognized Mexicans as a distinct group but did not associate with them.

Judges typically responded to Acosta by claiming to have many Mexican acquaintances. Nevertheless, almost invariably those judges, when pressed, could not name particular individuals. Judge Benjamin Landis certainly struggled to name the Mexicans he claimed to know:

Q. Do you know any persons who are of Mexican descent?
A. Oh, I'm sure I know some. But if you asked me to name them, I couldn't right now.
Q. Can you think of any one person at all?
A. Are you particularly interested in people who would qualify for the Grand Jury, or just generally?
Q. Generally, first. What I really want to know is your familiarity with persons of Spanish surnames, of Mexican descent, Latin descent?
A. Well, I can't name them specifically right now . . . If you ask me specifically to name a Mexican-American that I know, I can't name one right now, I can't name one right now, so I am speaking very generally, but it is inconceivable that I don't know several of them,

that I must know over the years that I have met, but they are not close friends of mine.[22]

The many judges who testified similarly did little to establish the existence of Mexicans as a distinct group. They largely averred that they knew some Mexicans and understood that Mexicans and Anglos differed, but usually they could not specify how, and frequently they suggested that both groups were white. These judges seemed downright helpful to Acosta, however, when compared with the numerous judges who testified that no basis at all existed for distinguishing Mexicans. Acosta's exchanges with these judges produced some absurd courtroom drama. The colloquy with Judge Bayard Rhone, a former California deputy attorney general, stands out.[23]

Q. Do you know any Mexican-Americans?
A. I assume I do. I don't think of them as such.
Q. Then you don't know whether you in fact know any Mexican-Americans?
A. I'm sure I do, but I don't discriminate one way or the other, so I just don't give any thought to that . . .
Q. Do you know the names of these persons that you suspect might be of Mexican descent?
A. I don't even suspect. I mean I just don't give it any thought.
Q. Well, who are these persons you are referring to that you said might be?
A. They are a vague group of people that I think you are referring to, and I just don't classify them in any particular way like you are trying to classify them.
Q. I am trying to determine whether or not you in fact know any Mexican-Americans?
A. I suspect I do, but I don't classify them just that way.
Q. Well, what are the names of these persons?
A. I can't give them to you.

Q. Can you think of one Mexican-American that you know by name?

A. If you want somebody with a name like Garcia, I don't know anybody else with a similar name.[24]

At this point, Acosta changed his tack and attempted to draw Judge Rhone into a conversation about the few Mexican Superior Court judges with whom he shared the bench.

Q. Do you know a Judge Teran?
A. I do.
Q. Do you know whether or not he has a Spanish surname?
A. I rather assume he has, but I'm not sure.
Q. What do you base this assumption on?
A. I don't have anything to base it on at all.
Q. Does it have something to do with the way he looks or the way he talks?
A. I can't answer that; I don't know.[25]

Acosta tried again:

Q. Do you know a Judge Sanchez?
A. I do.
Q. Do you know whether or not Sanchez is a Spanish surname?
A. I think it is.
Q. Do you have an opinion as to whether or not Judge Sanchez is a person of Spanish or Mexican or Latin descent?
A. I assume he is, but I have never given it any thought.
Q. What do you base that assumption on?
A. I don't think I can answer that one, either.[26]

And so the exchange continued, even after Acosta changed tack again:

Q. Of your nominees, Judge, were any of these persons Negroes, to your knowledge?
A. No.

Q. Were any of these persons Orientals, to your knowledge?
A. No.
Q. Were any of these persons Mexicans, to your knowledge?
A. Not that I know of.
Q. Would you be able to tell if they were?
A. I don't know as I would.[27]

Judge Rhone readily distinguished between Mexicans and non-Mexicans. He easily categorized his Mexican colleagues and quickly admitted that none of his grand jury nominees were Mexican. But fearing to engage in what he termed "discrimination," Judge Rhone refused to acknowledge that he could distinguish Mexicans or that Mexicans even existed. Judge Rhone's testimony, like that of the numerous judges who adopted a similar stance, not only frustrated Acosta but made it very difficult for him to prove that Mexicans were a distinct group.

Nevertheless, a few judges both recognized Mexican distinctiveness and assigned it social importance. Notably, these judges identified Mexicans as a race. Even here, however, Acosta confronted problems in establishing the terms of Mexican identity. Among these judges, some viewed the community as a racial minority deserving legal protection, but others simply endorsed stereotypes.

Judge Ralph Nutter, a relatively young judge who joined the bench in 1961, testified that he had specifically attempted to nominate persons from the Mexican community and that his interest in that community stemmed from the 1950s, when he had worked as an attorney for a Mexican civil rights group.[28] Acosta sought to draw out Judge Nutter's position on nominating minorities to the grand jury:

Q. Your Honor, you said you took an affirmative effort to seek out minority persons. Are you referring generally to Negroes and Spanish-surname persons?
A. Both.

Q. Does this imply then that you did in fact take race into consideration?

A. Well, if you want to put it that way, you could call it that. I would say this: I felt that we should try to get a more representative Grand Jury, and one of the ways of getting a more representative Grand Jury would have to be to have more minority races.[29]

At least some judges sought to increase Mexican representation on the grand jury out of a belief that diversity was important.[30] More pertinent to the discussion here, Judge Nutter's testimony demonstrates that some judges recognized Mexicans as a distinct racial group.

Other judges also recognized Mexicans as a race, though they did so in terms of romantic stereotypes. Judge George Dockweiler, who retired in 1968 after thirty-one years on the bench, expressed this outlook. Although he failed to name more than a few Mexican acquaintances, he nevertheless sought to reassure defense counsel that this reflected no ill will on his part; indeed, just the opposite. Thus, near the end of his testimony, Judge Dockweiler stressed his fondness for the Mexican people:

> It just seems to me that I have just been around with everybody other than the Spanish and the Mexican group, and there is no more colorful group than the Spanish and Mexican people.
>
> I am very much in love with the race as a whole, and as I say, I, my taste for Spanish, usually I satisfy that with at least one night out for a Spanish dinner, or Mexican dinner, or whatever it may be, but I think the Spanish people and the Mexican people have made a very splendid contribution to this area here.[31]

Perhaps to solidify his claim to warm feelings for Mexicans, at the end of his testimony, Judge Dockweiler asked in Spanish "*Bastante?*" Enough?[32] Acosta did not respond, at least in any manner captured by the transcript.

RACE IN EAST L.A. THIRTEEN

After weeks of testimony, the judge presiding over *East L.A. Thirteen* accepted the defense's argument that Mexicans constituted a distinct class, ruling that they had overcome that threshold issue in their discrimination claim. But Judge Kathleen Parker's oral disposition was not a clear triumph for Acosta and the defendants. Judge Parker ruled for the defense in a tentative manner that further demonstrated the sorts of challenges they faced in attempting to convince Anglo judges that Mexicans suffered discrimination. According to Judge Parker, Mexicans probably segregated themselves and, in any event, surnames provided a suspect basis for grand jury selection:

> When we first started on this motion, the fact that names could become a classification or group didn't occur to the Court. I would, I think, almost have assumed that the Mexican-Americans, perhaps through their own choosing rather than the choosing of the community, have segregated themselves more or less in a certain part of the community, and have different problems than other parts of the community, and I would not have thought that so difficult to establish, but the fact that somebody should sit on the Grand Jury because they bear a Spanish surname didn't occur to me.
>
> After hearing the defendants' witnesses, I am still not so sure that his is a classification which can be recognized for this purpose, although it may be, and I am assuming that the defendants have established that fact.[33]

Judge Parker's ruling suggests that, at least before the trial commenced, for her Mexicans existed as a people who kept themselves apart, not as a group subject to rampant prejudice. It also suggests that the expert testimony confused Judge Parker about the basis of Mexican identity. Rather than understanding that the census category offered only a taxonomic device for gathering statistics and generalizing about Mexicans, she seemed to conclude that surnames provided the foundation for Mexican group identity. In expressing her concern that surname alone might justify inclusion on the grand jury, Judge Parker substituted the categorical device for the social reality. Judge Parker's courtroom proved a difficult arena for the defendants as they labored under the legal burden of proving their own existence.

The Supreme Court in *Hernandez* required that Mexicans seeking constitutional protection prove on a case-by-case basis that they existed as a distinct group. To do so in *East L.A. Thirteen,* the defendants had to rely on a census category that both explicitly categorized Mexicans as white and implied that the differences between Mexicans and Anglos boiled down to surnames. The reasoning in *Hernandez* together with the census's taxonomic approach preempted arguments that Mexicans constituted a distinct *racial* group. For the most part, Acosta acceded to this, and in *East L.A. Thirteen* did not emphasize that Mexicans were a separate race. Nevertheless, race continued to surface in the defendants' arguments, and with it arose a strong current of confusion about whether, and how, Mexicans might actually be racially different.

Acosta often invoked race in his arguments, but he did so in a manner that suggested at least three different understandings: race was by turns rooted in descent, physical features, or group culture. The descent understanding emerged in an exchange between Acosta and District Attorney Hecht when the D.A. sought to question a jury commissioner on whether any African Americans sat on the 1968 grand jury. Acosta immediately objected that the jury commissioner was not qualified to testify as to the racial or ethnic characteristics of a person because "there are many persons who have one-fourth Negro blood or one-eighth Negro blood, and we cannot tell, and certainly he cannot tell."[34] Hecht responded that racial differences are readily observed, but Acosta continued arguing that race was a matter for experts:

> *Mr. Hecht.* I think, Your Honor, that when something is a matter of common observation, the witness is qualified to answer.

PROVING MEXICANS EXIST   53

Mr. Acosta. I would disagree very strongly with this common obser-
vation. This is one of the mistakes many people of the Anglo race
make, that certain racial groups all look alike. It is quite obvious
there are many people within the Negro race, as well as within the
Mexican race, that do not have the same characteristics. We look
different.[35]

The judge sustained Acosta's objection, closing that line of questioning.

In this exchange Acosta seemed confident that blacks and
Mexicans were distinct races by virtue of blood and thereby descent. Acosta's references to "one-fourth" and "one-eighth Negro blood" invoked a conception of race as biological inheritance. In doing so, Acosta downplayed the importance of
physical appearances. Though he probably would have conceded
that ancestry influenced physiognomy, Acosta emphasized that
descent and not features ultimately determined racial identity.
His insistence that only experts could properly weigh fractions of
"Negro blood" or spot specific "Mexican characteristics" con-
tradicted his demands that the judges racially identify their acquaintances and nominees.[36] It seems likely that Acosta did not
actually believe that only experts could recognize racial differences, and that he made this argument largely to frustrate the district attorney. Nevertheless, it bears noting that in this exchange,
Acosta presented race as a fundamentally biological phenome-
non, not a matter of mere appearances.

Acosta expressed this certainty regarding race's biological nature early in *East L.A. Thirteen*, before either his experts or the
judges had testified. As Acosta called more and more witnesses,
however, he came to treat race not only as a matter of descent but
also as a question of features and culture. Acosta consistently
took umbrage when judges implied that Mexicans were white,
and in several outbursts Acosta revealed his increasingly complicated understanding of race. When Judge Rhone suggested that
"Orientals have different features, but . . . Mexicans are classi-

fied as Caucasians," Acosta brusquely shot back "So they tell me."[37] Acosta's annoyance suggests that he believed physical appearance—the criterion he had earlier questioned—could mark Mexicans as a separate race. In contrast, when questioning another judge, Acosta asked directly, "Do you consider Mexicans, Mexican-Americans, Latin-Americans, members of a different ethnic or cultural group than your own?"[38] When the judge responded that Mexicans were not racially different while blacks were, Acosta bristled, asking him whether he believed only two races resided in the county.[39] Acosta here seemed to understand race as also involving ethnicity and culture.

In court Acosta confronted a formal presumption, rooted in the logic of the census bureau, that Mexicans were white. Rather than attempt to overcome this presumption, Acosta sought to demonstrate that Mexicans existed as a *socially* defined group. From our vantage point today, we know that no sharp line separates social from racial distinctions: racial ideas are irreducibly cultural. For Acosta and the defendants, however, race was not socially constructed but physically real, something fixed by nature. Thus, although Acosta repeatedly referred to Mexicans as a distinct race and took offense when someone suggested that they were white, the constant insistence in the courtroom that Mexicans socially define themselves undoubtedly abraded Acosta's understanding of Mexican racial identity. Acosta's recourse to shifting racial conceptions intimates a certain confusion regarding the nature of racial identity, an insecurity that the judicial proceedings amplified.

The courtroom arguments about Mexican identity took their toll on Acosta's understanding of race. Before his experts had testified, Acosta boldly insisted that race turned on "blood." In contrast, when he stood to summarize his discrimination argument, he conceded that he no longer knew what race was: "The one Judge whose comment about that we—he did not consider us a separate race, well, perhaps technically that's right. I don't know that Spanish-surnamed persons or Mexican persons are a race. I don't even know what the word 'race' really means, but that we are an identifiable group cannot be denied in this courtroom."[40]

Handicapped by *Hernandez* and hamstrung by surnames, Acosta had no choice but to insist that Mexicans formed an identifiable and distinct group defined on some criteria other than race. Yet Acosta went further than he needed to, lamenting that Mexicans might not be a race "technically" and admitting that he no longer understood the word "race." As happened to Judge Parker, the experts with their mounds of social science data and their numerous demographic and sociological criteria for group identity induced in Acosta a certain vertigo regarding Mexican identity.

The courtroom battles over identity in *East L.A. Thirteen* did not explicitly turn on race, yet they often reduced to shifting definitions of that concept. Why did the judges hold such disparate views about Mexican identity? Why was race for Acosta by turns a matter of ancestry, appearance, or culture? Why did the defense repeatedly emphasize race, when the terms by which they were forced to define themselves in the courtroom precluded racial arguments? To answer these questions requires some familiarity with the history of Mexicans in the Southwest and the related history of the racial construction of Mexicans. Acosta did not have this material to assist him in presenting the defendants' Equal Protection challenge, for in 1968 neither the story of Mexican racialization nor the history of Mexicans in the United States had been written.[41] Several decades later, we are in a better position to take up these questions.

THE MEXICAN RACE IN EAST L.A.

To understand the Chicano cases, we must examine the rise of East Los Angeles as a Mexican enclave, a story that is bound up with the history of Mexicans in the Southwest and their racial construction, both by Anglos and by themselves. This story begins with Spanish conquest in the Americas.[1]

Under Spanish dominion, California society in the early 1800s divided along class and race lines. From their privileged heights, an educated, landed, and wealthy elite ruled the community. They prized their predominantly European ancestry and called themselves *Californios* or *gente de razón*—people of reason.[2] Below the Californios lived the *pobladores*, merchants and artisans as well as overseers on the large ranches. Often illiterate and comparatively poor, pobladores often had mixed European, Native American, and African ancestry, and tended to be recent arrivals from central Mexico. The Californios often referred to them as *Mexicanos*, or, using a more degrading term, as *Cholos*. Indians occupied the bottom of the social and racial hierarchy, with a further division between those in the Spanish Missions and those still living in culturally intact settings. One historian compared the racial and class structure of early California to that of the U.S. South in the same period: "The Indians were the slaves, the *gente de razon* were the plantation owners or 'whites,' and the Mexicans were the 'poor whites.'"[3] Mexico's independence from Spain in 1821 hardly changed this social and political arrangement.

Anglos arriving in California as late as the early 1840s were primarily traders who came by ship from the eastern seaboard. They largely observed the existing racial-social distinctions and allied themselves with the Californio elite, often by marriage, in allegiances that brought many Anglos great wealth and political power.[4] For Californios, close association with Anglos allowed them to further differentiate themselves from the rest of California's population. In the racial politics of the times, as one historian put it, Anglos were "*genuine* white people."[5] At least through mid-century, Mexicans in California insisted upon, and Anglos accepted, a racial hierarchy that placed Mexicans as a whole above the status of Indians, and Californios on par with Anglos.[6]

The Mexican population's status in California quickly eroded after 1848, when the United States annexed the Southwest and gold was found at Sutter's Mill. Rough frontiersmen began pouring into California from across the desert and over the Sierras in numbers that quickly overwhelmed Mexican Californians. By the end of 1849, California's population stood at approximately 100,000 Anglos and 13,000 Mexicans. Anglos predominated in the state's northern half but not yet in the southern part. Los Angeles's 5,000 residents in 1854 included about 3,500 Mexicans and 1,500 Anglos.[7] Rapid changes in northern California stripped the Californios of racial standing, social status, political power, and control over land and other resources. These changes would come, though more slowly, to southern California as well. It is a common quip in Latin America that money whitens.[8] For Mexicans in mid-nineteenth century California, Anglo ascendancy proved certain corollaries: darkness impoverishes, and poverty darkens.

THE MEXICAN RACE

At the beginning of the 1800s, U.S. society tended to characterize
Mexican nationals primarily in terms of culture and religion, and
less so in descent-based terms.[9] During the 1830s and 1840s,
however, as conflict between the United States and Mexico deepened and war loomed, the terms that Anglos used to describe
Mexicans shifted sharply from ones accentuating perceived differences in culture, religion, and language toward ones stressing
skin color and ancestry. Three principal, mutually reinforcing aspects of Anglo racial ideology contributed to the racialization of
Mexicans.

First, whites extended to Mexicans their preoccupation with
racial mixture. Racial ideology in the United States largely
defined races according to continental geography, with Europe,
Asia, Africa, and America serving as the supposed sources of
the "great" races. By this understanding, Mexicans with their
mixed European, American, and African ancestry should have
been difficult to categorize. But notions of interracial transgression are as old as ideas of race, and U.S. society had early developed a virulent antipathy to white-black miscegenation. The
mixed origins of Mexicans proved no bar to their racialization,
for U.S. society fit them neatly into the degraded category reserved for racial mongrels. The *Southern Review* published an
editorial in 1871 that typified the horror Anglos expressed for racial mixing:

> An admixture of two unequal races is therefore a cancer, an unpar-
> donable sin against mankind and against nature, which has launched
> an ever flaming curse on all such connections; inasmuch as she lets
> the mongrels invariably inherit all the vices and evil traits of both
> races and rarely, or never, any of the good. Nature absolutely disal-
> lows the adulteration of blood; and herein she shows herself to be an
> aristocrat of the purest water. Every violation of these laws she visits
> in the most condign and pitiless manner.[10]

But for the fact that this quote comes from an article entitled "The Latin Races in America," one could be forgiven for
thinking it just another screed on the dangers of white and black
mixing.[11]
Anglos relied on the racial ideology surrounding miscegenation to denigrate Mexicans as a mixed and therefore inferior people. For example, Congressman William Wick opposed annexing
Mexican territory because, as he said, "I do not want any mixed
races in our Union, nor men of any color except white, unless
they be slaves. Certainly not as voters or legislators."[12] Senator
John Clayton similarly opposed any annexation, but in stronger
language: "Yes! Aztecs, Creoles, Half-breeds, Quadroons,
Samboes, and I know not what else—'ring streaked and speck-
led'—all will come in, and instead of us governing them, they, by
their votes, will govern *us*."[13] Congressman John Box opined
that Mexicans were a "mixture of Mediterranean-blooded Spanish peasants with low grade Indians who did not fight to extinc-
tion but submitted and multiplied as serfs."[14] Similar opinions
permeated the popular press. The *Cincinnati Herald* warned its
readers of the threat posed to U.S. society by the inclusion of millions of Mexicans, "with their idol worship, heathen supersti-
tion, and degraded mongrel races."[15] The *Augusta Daily Chronicle* saw in the Mexican population "a sickening mixture,
consisting of such a conglomeration of Negroes and Rancheros,
Mestizoes and Indians, with but a few Castilians."[16]
     The preoccupation with miscegenation included a fear that
Mexicans would facilitate racial mixing in the United States.
Their mixed origins suggested to Anglos that Mexicans had lax
standards about interracial relations which, if transplanted to
the United States, threatened racial disaster. Congressmen John
Box and Thomas Jenkins warned that "such a situation will
make the blood of all three races flow back and forth between
them in a distressing process of mongrelization. No other alien
race entering America, produces an easier channel for the inter-

mixture than does the Mongrel Mexican . . . their presence and intermarriage with both the White and Black races . . . create the most insidious and general mixture of White, Indian and Negro blood strains ever produced in America."[17]

The second aspect of racial ideology at work in Mexican racialization was the Anglo belief that non-white races would disappear before the march of civilization. In 1848 Congressman Daniel Dickson justified U.S. expansion into the Southwest by equating Mexicans with "the fated aboriginal races, who can neither uphold government or be restrained by it; who flourish only amid the haunts of savage indolence, and perish under, if they do not recede before, the influences of civilization."[18] Dickson continued, "Like their doomed brethren, who were once spread over the several States of the Union, they are destined, by the laws above human agency, to give way to a stronger race."[19] Sam Houston expressed the same sentiment, though more bluntly: "The Mexicans are no better than Indians, and I see no reason why we should not go in the same course now, and take their land."[20]

As whites spread westward, they believed that the populations they encountered were inferiors destined to fade before them, not through any Anglo fault or misdeed but by the laws of nature. Westward expansion was the white man's manifest destiny, to use the then increasingly popular phrase, and purported racial characteristics were thought to seal the fates of America's various peoples. Thomas Jefferson Farnham, a booster of Anglo expansion into California, promoted U.S. conquest by emphasizing Mexican racial failings: "No one acquainted with the indolent, mixed race of California, will ever believe that they will populate, much less, for any length of time, govern the country. The law of Nature which curses the mulatto here with a constitution less robust than that of either race from which he sprang, lays a similar penalty upon the mingling of the Indian and white races in California and Mexico. They must fade away."[21]

The belief by whites that inferior races would fade before

them corresponded with the certainty among whites that they were racially destined for greatness. Farnham, like many, joined to his indictment of Mexican inferiority a celebration of Anglo-Saxon superiority:

> The mixing of different branches of the Caucasian family in the States will continue to produce a race of men, who will enlarge from period to period the field of their industry and civil domination, until not only the Northern States of Mexico, but the Californias also, will open their glebe to the pressure of its unconquered arm. The old Saxon blood must stride the continent, must command all its northern shores, must here press the grape and the olive, here eat the orange and the fig, and in their own unaided might, erect the altar of civil and religious freedom on the plains of the Californias.[22]

Whites' conviction that race made them superior supplied the third aspect of Anglo racial ideology that shaped Mexican racialization. The clash with Mexico came at a critical historical juncture for the United States, just as Romantic ideals of national particularism combined with an emerging natural-science approach to the study of race. The result was a volatile ideology of white superiority supposedly rooted in nature and revealed through physical differences. Conflict with Mexico fueled this unstable mixture, as Anglos struggled to define not only what made their enemies weak and base but what made themselves strong and just.[23] To know themselves as an innately superior people destined to rule the continent required that Anglos construct Mexicans as a people doomed to defeat by history and blood.

As Anglos in the mid 1800s pushed into California, they brought three closely related racial impulses: a preoccupation with racial mixing, a conviction that race destined certain peoples to inferiority and even oblivion, and a belief in their own specifically racial greatness. This racial ideology presented the land-hungry United States with a conundrum upon the defeat of Mexico: whether to take Mexican land and rule its residents in an imperial manner—a resolution anathema to those who still harbored deep suspicions about the politically corrupting nature of empires—or rather to grant the residents of acquired territories the status of citizens, thus treating "racial inferiors" as political equals. The 1848 Treaty of Guadalupe Hidalgo represented a compromise. By taking the sparsely populated northern third of Mexico and granting citizenship to its residents, the United States claimed "the largest possible area from Mexico with the least number of Mexicans," according to the historian Reginald Horsman.[24] Whether a compromise, the United States did grant citizenship to Mexicans in the now American Southwest. In social, economic, and political relations, however, Mexicans remained a non-white group marked by a host of degraded traits.

DARK, DIRTY, LAZY, COWARDLY, AND CRIMINAL

In positioning Mexicans as an inferior race, whites imputed to that group numerous faults. These pernicious myths did their principal work not simply by highlighting physical features but by tying to them failings of character, temperament, and will.

After the mid 1800s Anglos routinely found evidence of Mexican racial inferiority in skin color. Remarks about the dusky tones, tawny complexions, dirty colors, and filthy hues of Mexicans were common. During this period Anglos also referred to Mexicans as "greasers," a racial slur typically spat out with contempt. From the very beginning, "greaser" linked skin color to character. One early source stated that a "'greaser' was a Mexican—originating in the filthy, greasy appearance of the natives."[25] The association of dirtiness with the skin color supposedly typical of Mexicans created one of the most enduring stereotypes associated with that group. For many decades, the term "dirty Mexican" functioned virtually as a single word, a marker of the racial opprobrium affixed to that group.[26]

Nineteenth-century Anglos attached other negative stereotypes to Mexican identity as well. For instance, whites frequently criticized the indolence of Mexicans, seeing in this trait yet further evidence of, and reason for, Anglo ascendancy in the Southwest.[27] U.S. writers often expressed prejudiced views about lazy Mexicans. "Give them but tortillas, frijoles, and chile colorado to supply their animal wants for the day, and seven-tenths of the Mexicans are satisfied; and so they will continue to be until the race becomes extinct or amalgamated with Anglo-Saxon stock; for no political change, no revolution, can uproot that inherent indolence and antipathy to change, which in this age of improvement and advancement must sooner or later work their ruin and downfall."[28] In the view of another nineteenth-century writer: "All day long they sit by the doors of their filthy little adobe huts, smoking cigarritos and playing cards. I fancy they like it better than working. At least they live by idleness. Industry would kill them. When these mixed races are compelled to work, they sicken and die."[29] Richard Henry Dana observed in his classic account of Mexican California *Two Years before the Mast* (1835) that laziness is the "California fever" and that "Californians are an idle, thriftless people, and can make nothing for themselves."[30]

Anglos saw cowardice as another defining element of Mexican character.[31] Thus, one writer said of the eagle on the Mexican flag: "The Mexican eagle is a dirty, cowardly creature that feeds on carcasses, and will hardly attack a live rabbit—a perfect buzzard. And there is such close affinity between their habits and the Mexican character, that I don't wonder at their hoisting a carrion-bird upon their national standard."[32] Another gave this account of Mexican courage: "I have no faith in the courage of these people, except where they have greatly the advantage, or can kill in the dark, without danger to themselves."[33]

Finally, Anglos frequently depicted Mexicans as innately criminal—"the sort of people who would steal anything not nailed down."[34] Thievery formed only one facet of Mexican criminality, however. One nineteenth-century romance described a generic greaser as someone who "would murder a brother for a peso, and betray anything but his priest for half the money."[35] The image of the Mexican *bandidos* as "murdering, throat-cutting, bloodthirsty, thieving outlaws" became stock characters in early Hollywood cinema.[36] In films such as *Licking the Greaser* (1910) and *Guns and Greasers* (1918), indolence, cowardice, and villainy marched together under the bandido's tattered sombrero as the epitome of Mexican character.[37]

To be sure, Anglos sometimes described Mexicans in other terms as well. For instance, in debates in the 1920s over immigration, agricultural interests insisted that Mexicans were especially suited for stoop labor, could easily withstand high temperatures in the field unbearable to white workers, and were easily managed owing to their childlike demeanor. In the praise offered by one grower, the Mexican is "just like a dog; slap him and he'll lick your hand."[38] Continuing to analogize Mexicans to dogs, another proponent of Mexican labor testified before Congress that "the Mexican is a quiet, inoffensive necessity in that he performs the big majority of our rough work, agriculture, building, and street labor. They have no effect on the American standard of living because they are not much more than a group of fairly intelligent collie dogs."[39]

Those who opposed immigrant labor from Mexico resorted to the more common stereotypes. In 1930 an economist testifying before the House Committee on Immigration raised all the standard calumnies, plus some:

> In every huddle of Mexicans one meets the same idleness, hordes of hungry dogs and filthy children with faces plastered with flies, disease, lice, human filth, stench, promiscuous fornication, bastardy, lounging, apathetic peons and lazy squaws, beans and dried chili, liquor, general squalor, and envy and hatred of the Gringo. These people sleep by day and prowl by night like coyotes, stealing anything they can get their hands on, no matter how useless to them it may be. Nothing left outside is safe unless padlocked or chained down.[40]

The characteristics imputed to Mexicans varied by historical context and region. Similarly, the stereotypes Anglos applied to Mexican individuals differed according to their physical features, class, and gender. The darker-skinned and poorer suffered from more virulent racism than the lighter-skinned and wealthier, who were more likely to be racialized as white or close to it.[41] Similarly, the identities imposed on Mexican men and women often differed. Some stereotypes carried meanings closely bound up with gender. Mexican men more than women were demeaned by allegations of cowardice, for instance, as that trait stood in counterpoint to the manly virtue of courage. Other stereotypes, such as dirtiness, were less gendered and applied indiscriminately to men and women. In addition, white men routinely saw Mexican women as willing sex partners. Again, class and racial appearances made a difference, with well-off and fair-featured women more likely to be considered for marriage. White men nevertheless stereotyped most Mexican women as having loose morals and a special eagerness for Anglo partners that justified constant sexual predation.[42] An Anglo miner's 1850 letter to a California paper, the *Stockton Times*, made this viewpoint abundantly clear: "Mexicans have no business in this country . . . The men were made to be shot at, and the women were made for *our* purposes."[43]

Although negative stereotypes varied, the attributes of filth, indolence, cowardice, criminality, and dark skin emerged as the principal ones Anglos assigned to Mexicans during the first century of intense contact. Anglos attributed these characteristics to Mexicans as a supposed matter of nature: Mexican vices were rooted in Mexicanness itself. In the Anglo view that developed during the 1800s and to some extent carries forward to today, Mexicans constituted a mongrel race stamped by ancestry with dark skin and an inferior and unalterable character.

THE CONQUERED GENERATION

The new State of California degraded Mexicans almost immediately in both legal statute and practice. In 1850 the newly established state legislature imposed a Foreign Miners Tax on Mexican and Chinese miners to increase the costs of, and thereby hinder, their participation in gold mining; Anglo mobs quickly usurped this law to legitimize their own claims to California's gold and to justify vigilante violence against non-white miners.[44] In 1855 the legislature again targeted Mexicans, this time through An Act to Punish Vagrants, Vagabonds and Dangerous and Suspicious Persons. This vagrancy law became popularly known as the Anti-Greaser Act because it singled out for special concern "all persons who are commonly known as 'Greasers' or the issue of Spanish and Indian blood who . . . go armed and are not peaceable and quiet persons."[45] The act imposed imprisonment under hard labor with ball and chain on hapless offenders. These statutes not only informed but also affirmed the most negative Mexican stereotypes: Mexicans were foreigners and greasers—dirty, violent, and indolent vagrants best removed from the streets and punished by harsh and humiliating treatment.

Mexicans' declining racial status found expression not only in statutes but also in evolving legal practices. In one particularly telling example, Manuel Domínguez, a wealthy landowner and member of the Californio elite, sought to appear as a witness in a case being heard in San Francisco in April 1857. Domínguez had been a delegate to California's constitutional convention less than a decade before and a signatory to California's constitution; at the time of the trial, he sat on the Los Angeles County Board of Supervisors. Before he could take the stand, however, the judge ruled that, because Domínguez had mixed ancestry, he was barred from testifying under a recent statute that prohibited testimony by Indians and blacks in any case involving a white person.[46]

This incident captures the remarkable slide in racial status experienced by Mexicans in northern California in the decade immediately following statehood. Although Mexicans were not explicitly subjected to all of the legal disabilities imposed on blacks or Native Americans, in practice the legal system often mistreated Mexicans similarly. Nevertheless, Mexicans in California generally escaped the full weight of racial oppression imposed on

Native Americans, a racial oppression so severe in the four decades following statehood that it virtually amounted to genocide.[47]

The changing racial and social hierarchy of northern California eventually spread south. The practice of lynching Mexicans that developed quickly in northern mining areas also appeared in southern California. While no firm numbers exist, Carey McWilliams reports that in 1857 alone, Anglo mobs lynched eleven Mexicans in Los Angeles, with another four victims in neighboring El Monte, home to a large community of Anglo Texans.[48] Even so, Los Angeles remained a predominantly Mexican town into the 1860s, and Mexicans retained a fair degree of social standing and political power.[49]

In the 1860s, though, the Anglo population began to rise steadily while the Mexican population leveled off. In 1850 three out of every four Angelenos were Mexican; by 1880 that number had dropped to one in five.[50] Over the same years, Mexicans in Los Angeles suffered a dramatic decline in property ownership. In 1850 three-fifths of Mexican families in the city owned property, with the average property value standing at $2,105. By 1870 only one-fifth of the families owned city property, and the average value had fallen by half.[51] Moreover, Mexican property disenfranchisement accompanied an increasing spatial segregation, with the majority of Mexicans being concentrated into the area around the old plaza and to the immediate south of the city center. By 1880, 83 percent of the property held by Mexicans was located in this area and 70 percent of the Mexican population resided there.[52]

The demographic, economic, and spatial collapse of the Mexican world produced profound social changes in the cultural identity of Los Angeles's Mexican residents. No longer in their own dominion, Mexicans became an embattled minority, increasingly isolated linguistically, politically, and economically. They were residents of an adobe town encircled by a wood and brick city that disdained them, members of what one historian

terms a "conquered generation."[53] Nevertheless, Mexicans in
Los Angeles were not utterly defeated or immobilized. As the loss
of political power and the increasing segregation forced them together geographically, the Mexican community adopted a more
self-conscious group identity.[54] The Spanish-language press began to write about *una Raza,* one people sharing both a cultural
and racial identity, and also referred to the Mexican section of
Los Angeles as a *barrio,* a small city within a city.[55]

CROSSING THE LOS ANGELES RIVER

After a long period of steady numbers, L.A.'s Mexican population grew dramatically for roughly thirty years, from 1900 until
the onset of the Great Depression. In just the last decade of this
period, the Mexican population in Los Angeles more than tripled
to 97,000 residents.[56] The rapid influx of Mexican immigrants
reflected rising turmoil in Mexico combined with an increasing
demand for labor by new large-scale agricultural and industrial
enterprises in the Southwest. In 1917 hysteria against communism in the United States metamorphosed into a "brown scare"
that targeted Mexican nationals and temporarily slowed immigration, but high levels of Mexican migration resumed in the
1920s.[57]

Nevertheless, Mexicans did not regain numerical dominance
in Los Angeles. Their influx formed part of a larger migration
pattern that between 1890 and 1930 saw the county's population explode from 101,000 to 2.2 million.[58] Most of the new immigrants were native-born whites moving to southern California
from elsewhere in the United States. The relative absence of the
eastern and southern European immigrants who were then transforming cities on the eastern seaboard allowed Anglos in L.A. to
view their metropolis as a white city. While East Coast cities
grappled with the racial identity of the most recent European immigrants, Los Angeles boosters took pride in calling their home
"the last purely American city in the nation" and "more Anglo-
Saxon than the mother country today."[59] Nonetheless, among

the nation's largest cities, only Baltimore exceeded L.A. in the percentage of non-whites in the population (14 percent, including Mexicans).[60]

Anglos kept L.A. white, at least as far as they were concerned, by rendering invisible those they considered non-white. White Angelenos partly accomplished this trick by depicting Mexicans as a feature of the California landscape. One Los Angeles Chamber of Commerce member insisted that Mexican workers were not southern California residents but temporary sojourners little different from "swallows at the old mission. They come and go at about the same time every year," presumably in natural harmony with their employers' cyclical needs.[61]

In greater measure, though, Los Angeles maintained a white identity by segregating Mexicans.[62] The Los Angeles School District justified separate schools for Mexicans by insisting that they exhibited "different mental characteristics," were "primarily interested in action and emotion but grow listless under purely mental effort," and "introduced diseases to the schools."[63] Residential segregation by and large reserved the western and northern parts of Los Angeles for Anglos, with one community boasting to the Los Angeles Chamber of Commerce in 1927 that it "had no negroes or Mexicans" and another crowing in 1930 that "Lynwood, being restricted to the white race, can furnish ample labor of the better class."[64] In contrast, Mexicans continued to be forced into the plaza area, which served as the gateway for many new immigrants, not only those from Mexico.[65]

As the plaza area grew more crowded and dilapidated, those who could do so began to move out, with many heading east across the Los Angeles River.[66] The more prosperous families fled first, settling the new neighborhoods around Boyle Heights immediately across the river. Still further east lay the town of Belvedere, only three or four miles from the city center but nevertheless an unincorporated part of the county where housing costs were lower.[67] Although Mexicans predominated among those who jumped to East Los Angeles, they were joined by other recent immigrants, including Jews, Japanese, Italians, Russians, and Armenians.[68] Eastside barrios provided their Mexican residents a sense of community and a safe cultural space; yet, these neighborhoods were also shaped by the forces of racial segregation. Indeed, in 1939, the Federal Housing Agency redlined Boyle Heights and surrounding areas, refusing to issue federally supported loans in what the agency perceived as "a 'melting pot' area literally honeycombed with diverse and subversive racial elements."[69]

FROM IMMIGRANTS TO MEXICAN AMERICANS

After several decades of high immigration, by 1930 five out of six Mexican families in Los Angeles were headed by foreign-born individuals.[70] Over those same decades, the political imagination of Los Angeles's Mexican community had increasingly looked southward. By 1930 community leaders identified more with Mexico than the United States.[71]

As the Great Depression set in, though, Los Angeles suffered a severe decline in real wages and a dramatic increase in unemployment.[72] The economic crisis inflicted particular hardship on the Mexican community, forcing Mexicans to compete for work and government assistance with newly desperate Anglos. Employers and government relief agencies turned away otherwise qualified Mexicans, favoring whites.[73]

The deepening economic misery sparked a public clamor for the expulsion of Mexicans. In Los Angeles, officials in the national, state, and local governments seized on Mexican repatriation as a popular response to the spreading distress.[74] Los Angeles County offered to pay the passage for persons desiring to return to Mexico, and the first trainloads of county-sponsored repatriates left in spring 1931. Many who departed early still had strong cultural and political connections to Mexico. As the Depression wore on, though, many other Mexicans found themselves pushed into repatriation—partly by dire circumstances but also because local government agencies pressured Mexican nationals as well as U.S. citizens of Mexican descent to leave the country. The Los Angeles police and sheriff's departments intimidated many Mexicans into leaving: law enforcement officials staged mass roundups and interrogations, publicly proclaimed their intention to stop all persons who "look like Mexicans," and threatened that "attention will be paid not only to the person under arrest, but to all members of the family."[75] Under these circumstances, the deportation efforts of 1933 and 1934 took a tremendous toll on the Mexican community, which lost one-third of its members.[76] By 1935 the federal government had deported approximately half a million Mexican nationals and U.S. citizens.[77]

The mass deportations transformed the composition and consciousness of Los Angeles's Mexican community. Those who remained tended to have strong ties to the city, including bonds of long-time residence, property ownership, and membership in settled families.[78] The community's cultural and political focus returned to concerns shared by those planning to remain in the north. The community shifted from one that dreamed of Mexico to one that identified with the United States, and Mexicans increasingly carved out a course of assimilation for themselves and their community. Calling themselves "Mexican Americans," this generation dedicated itself to the struggle for full inclusion in U.S. society, although on terms that respected Mexican heritage.[79]

The shift from an immigrant to a Mexican American identity spurred the rise of new civic associations within the Mexican community. The League of United Latin American Citizens (LULAC), formed in Texas in 1929, stands out as the archetype of such new organizations. LULAC emphasized the importance of U.S. citizenship, advocated pride in Mexican origins, and orchestrated a civil rights campaign that included *Hernandez v. Texas,* the landmark 1954 jury discrimination case.

In East Los Angeles, the new political and social zeitgeist produced the Mexican American Movement (MAM) in 1934 and the National Congress of Spanish Speaking Peoples, known more often as *El Congreso*, in 1938.[80] High school students organized MAM, though it gradually evolved into an association primarily made up of older middle-class members.[81] Until its demise in 1950, MAM consistently stressed education as the key to social advancement for individuals as well as for the community. According to a MAM newspaper article, "Education is the only tool which will raise our influence, command the respect of the rich class, and enable us to mingle in their social, political and religious life."[82] Another article stressed that educational success proved that Mexicans "are as good a race as any other—artistically, mentally and physically."[83]

If MAM spoke for the more economically successful members of the community, El Congreso sought to organize the working class. Typical of Mexican American groups from this era, El Congreso urged immigrants to seek U.S. citizenship and to participate in the political system. It also worked for civil rights and pursued educational reforms, including a campaign to initiate bilingual education.[84] Reflecting its working-class orientation, El Congreso also encouraged solidarity between recent Mexican immigrants and long-term Mexican residents. It promoted participation in local labor unions and cooperation with the domestic Communist Party.[85] El Congreso, MAM, and LULAC involved different sectors of the Mexican community and carved out distinct political agendas. Nevertheless, all three organizations evince the hallmark of the Mexican American era: a commitment to full participation in U.S. society for people of Mexican descent.

THE CHALLENGE OF ASSIMILATION

World War II strengthened the Mexican American generation's political and social aspirations. Responding to the war crisis, Mexican American organizations, including MAM and El Congreso, largely suspended their activities, believing that national salvation depended upon the complete cooperation of the citizenry.[86] Meanwhile, many young Mexicans joined or were drafted into the armed services. In all, 400,000 Mexicans served in the U.S. military during World War II.[87] Mexicans received seventeen Medals of Honor, more than any other group. But they also died at a disproportionately high rate. In Los Angeles, Mexicans accounted for one-tenth of the population but comprised one-fifth of the war dead.[88] Partly because of such sacrifices, the war brought optimism to Mexicans. Mexican Americans believed that their evident patriotism ensured the recognition and fair treatment the community deserved.

Rather than fostering increased good will toward the Mexican community, however, the war exacerbated white antipathy toward minority communities. The first victims were the Japanese, including East Los Angeles residents who were among those uprooted from their homes in 1942 and interned in distant concentration camps.[89] That same year, the Los Angeles press ran a series of articles playing up the threat posed by "Mexican" crime and "Mexican" delinquency.[90] Anti-Mexican attacks in 1942 and 1943 beset the East Los Angeles community, particularly during two troubling episodes: the *Sleepy Lagoon* case and the zoot suit riots.

On August 2, 1942, a young man, José Díaz, died near a gravel-pit swimming hole frequented by Mexicans excluded from the public pools, a swimming place the press later dubbed Sleepy Lagoon.[91] His skull had been fractured sometime after he left a party at a nearby house, although how this occurred was not known.[92] Nevertheless, the press pointed to Díaz's death as evidence of a Mexican crime wave. The police rounded up and beat, some quite severely, twenty-four Mexican boys and young men, members of an alleged gang who had attempted to crash the party Díaz attended.[93] The prosecutors convinced the Los Angeles grand jury to indict these youths for felony murder—a charge that applies when a death occurs, even by accident, during the commission of a felony. In a striking parallel to the charges in *East L.A. Thirteen,* the underlying felony was a supposed conspiracy to commit misdemeanor trespass—that is, crashing the party.[94] In other words, the twenty-four young men faced murder charges because they allegedly conspired to crash a party, thereby committing a felony sometime during which Díaz had somehow died.

The charging irregularities presaged serious errors in the trial's conduct. Among other things, for weeks Los Angeles Superior Court Judge Charles Fricke forbade the defendants to cut their hair or change clothes, forcing the defendants to face the jury while ill-kempt and filthy.[95] The jury convicted seventeen of the young men, nine for murder and the remainder on lesser charges.[96] Sentenced to long prison terms and unable to raise bond money to secure their release during the appeal process, the convicted men languished in jail nearly two years, until in October 1944 an appeals court reversed the convictions and castigated the trial court for its egregious conduct.[97]

Sleepy Lagoon exacerbated rather than calmed hysteria concerning the "Mexican menace." As the trial unfolded, the volume and virulence of anti-Mexican propaganda increased. The Los Angeles County sheriff's department greatly contributed to the growing uproar. Soon after Díaz's death, a special grand jury committee investigating the "awful" situation of "Mexican juvenile delinquency" heard testimony from the chief of the sheriff's Foreign Relations Bureau—a telling name for an office assigned to monitor Los Angeles's Mexican population.[98] Captain Edward Duran Ayres, a member an old Los Angeles Californio family, submitted a gripping report regarding the inherently violent nature of Mexicans.[99] All the "Mexican element" knows or feels, Ayres testified, "is a desire to use a knife or some lethal weapon. In other words, his desire is to kill, or at least let blood . . . When there is added to this inborn characteristic that has come down through the ages, the use of liquor, then we certainly have crimes of violence."[100]

Displaying its wartime origins and California's preoccupation with the Pacific war theater, the report placed Mexicans within a larger racial context that focused on the malevolent characteristics of "Orientals." Arguing that "the Mexican Indian is mostly Indian," Captain Ayres explained that "the Indian, from Alaska to Patagonia, is evidently Oriental in background—at least he shows many of the Oriental characteristics, especially so in his utter disregard for the value of life."[101] It could not have been lost on Mexican Americans that the lead law enforcement agency in Los Angeles County identified them as *innately* predisposed to violence—possessing, as the report said, an inborn desire to let blood and kill that had come down through the ages. Nor was this conclusion lost on a taut and anxious Anglo community.

Anti-Mexican hysteria in Los Angeles peaked in the summer of 1943. During that winter and spring, the Los Angeles press had replaced general tirades against "Mexicans" with a more focused campaign against "zoot-suit hoodlums," a reference to Mexican youths and their distinctive style of dress.[102] Called drapes by the youth themselves, the trousers with pegged cuffs and high waists and the coats with broad shoulders resembled the zoot suits then worn in Harlem and in cities across the nation.[103] Stimulated into action by the press, for ten days in early June Anglo mobs led by sailors and soldiers took over the streets of Los Angeles and terrorized the Mexican population. Commandeering taxi cabs to form flying brigades, or sometimes marching hundreds abreast, the rioters scoured downtown Los Angeles and penetrated deep into East Los Angeles, pummeling and stripping the clothes from young Mexicans.[104] The police did little to stop the rioters, instead following along behind the mobs to arrest the victims.[105] Local government officials, like most Angelenos, supported the attacks.

On June 9, with the riots at their height, the Los Angeles City Council passed a resolution banning zoot suits.[106] The attacks continued until Washington, D.C., officials recognized that, by tarnishing the United States' image abroad, the violence was im-

peding the war effort, whereupon the military services declared
Los Angeles out of bounds for soldiers and sailors. No one was
killed during these riots, but this explosion of anti-Mexican violence deeply scarred the Mexican community.[107] Josefina Fierro
de Bright, the head of El Congreso, would lament forty years after the race riots, "That was the most horrifying experience of
my time. I dreamed about it for months."[108]

FIGHTING TO BE WHITE

Even in the face of these and other attacks, Mexican Americans
in Los Angeles and in the Southwest as a whole clung to the idea
that patriotism and hard work would get them full admission to
U.S. society. A renewed postwar commitment to assimilation in-
vigorated LULAC's 1940s and 1950s campaign to secure Mexican civil rights and spurred the formation of new organizations
such as American GI Forum and the Community Service Organization.[109] The American GI Forum formed after a Texas funeral
parlor refused to bury a veteran's remains because he was a
"Mexican." With the help of Senator Lyndon Johnson, the new
veterans group secured the soldier's burial at Arlington National
Cemetery with full military honors.[110] The Community Service
Organization (CSO) came together in Los Angeles after an un-
successful campaign by the prominent Mexican Edward R.
Roybal for a seat on the Los Angeles City Council.[111] Focused on
voter registration, municipal government reform, education, and
police malpractice, the CSO became an important political and
service organization in East Los Angeles and also nationally; in
1962 the CSO helped to elect Roybal to the United States Congress.[112]

Part of the fight to assimilate included a protracted effort by
Mexican Americans to establish for themselves a white identity.
LULAC incorporated this goal into its legal strategy through
what it termed the "other white" argument. Rather than challenging discrimination per se, LULAC consistently argued that
no grounds existed for discriminating against Mexicans because

Mexicans were white.[113] This strategy informed LULAC's arguments in *Hernandez v. Texas*, the grand jury case.[114] The organization's lawyers documented the oppression of Mexicans in Jackson County, where the case arose, proving segregation in schooling, civic organizations, and places of business, including one restaurant that prominently displayed a sign reading "No Mexicans Served."[115] The lawyers also showed that "on the courthouse grounds at the time of the hearing, there were two men's toilets, one unmarked, and the other marked 'Colored Men' and 'Hombres Aqui' ('Men Here')."[116] Yet, LULAC did not present this evidence to demonstrate that segregation was wrong per se. Instead, LULAC's brief to the Supreme Court argued that Jackson County violated their rights when it acted as if "the term 'white' excludes the Mexican."[117] LULAC insisted that Mexicans should be free from discrimination not because discrimination was wrong but because they were white.[118]

The effort to be white led many Mexican Americans to adopt views associated with white supremacy. This included anti-black prejudice. Thus, a LULAC official in 1936 encouraged members to "tell these Negroes that we are not going to permit our manhood and womanhood to mingle with them on an equal social basis."[119] During the 1950s, another Mexican American published a weekly newspaper in Dallas with headlines such as "conserva su raza blanca," preserve your white race, and "segregación es libertad," segregation is liberty.[120] The same paper urged its readers to join the Spanish Organization of White People, and decried "the American GI Forum, LULAC, the NAACP, chambers of commerce, and other nigger groups [for having] consistently promoted integration to raise the equality, intelligence, and superiority of the black race."[121] As the criticism of groups like LULAC and the GI Forum indicate, these views were more extreme than those held by most Mexican Americans. Nevertheless, Mexican Americans frequently supported the denigration and segregation of blacks.

White supremacist views also skewed how many Mexican

Americans understood their own mixed origins. Mexican Americans sought assimilation rather than absorption—they hoped to have equal access to all sectors of U.S. society, but not necessarily to disappear among Anglos. Many Mexican Americans took great pride in how their ties to Mexico made them a distinct and special group. But Mexican Americans thought of Mexico's culture and greatness as Spanish and therefore European in character. Mexican Americans during this period frequently called themselves Spanish, and an etiquette developed whereby Anglos who wanted to avoid offense used this term as well. While celebrating a Spanish identity, Mexican Americans downplayed their indigenous ancestry and demeaned Mexico's indigenous population. Carlos Castañeda, a historian at the University of Texas, Austin, and a leading Mexican American intellectual, devoted his career to demonstrating similarities between Anglos and Mexicans. He emphasized that both groups were European, both had pioneered new lands, and both had civilized indigenous peoples.[122] Painting Native Americans as "simple, cruel, and child-like," Castañeda celebrated the imposition of Spanish missions as tantamount to the spread of civilization, benefiting not only the colonists but also the colonized.[123]

Finally, Mexican Americans held negative views regarding other Mexicans, especially those in the working class. Community leaders stressed personal responsibility and largely ignored structural impediments to advancement. In turn, Mexican Americans often explained the marginal position of community members by invoking myths of Mexican inferiority. This pattern defines the racial uplift message frequently espoused by Los Angeles's Mexican American Movement. In a 1938 MAM paper on how to progress in society, we find this advice:

Why is it that we as Mexicans do not command respect? What can one individual do about this situation? He can uplift the Mexican name by constant work—hard work with others who have the same high ideals and aims [by] securing an education, not just high school but a college one, by being a clean-cut fellow, trustworthy and dependable with the highest moral aims. A Mexican boy can and must provide a favorable opinion wherever he goes.[124]

But MAM's encouragement of clean-cut fellows was coupled with an explicit criticism of "easy going, time wasting Mexicans":

Just realize—a Mexican did all this, a Mexican like you and me, a Mexican with the same kind of blood as you and I. You can too! You can do all these things all of these young fellows have done. All you need is encouragement, help. Don't heed the fellows loafing at street corners, wasting their time. They'll *tell you an education is worthless. Don't believe them.* They don't want you to progress. They are greedy and jealous, because you have a better chance. They want you to be like them—easy going, time wasting Mexican fellows who drag down our name.[125]

In urging the Mexican boy to be clean-cut and moral, MAM prescribed a route to success that stressed personal achievement and which suggested that those who failed were "time-wasting Mexican fellows." Using similar logic, MAM partly blamed the zoot suit riots on the Mexican community, picking out its failure "to encourage education among our youth" and its reluctance "to dismiss our cultural heritage, our Spanish language, our food habits, and the like" as reasons why "the Mexican-American has failed to improve his economic and social life."[126] For MAM, success and failure were tantamount to personal choices— and choosing not to emulate middle-class white Americans amounted to selecting failure.

CONFLICTING MEXICAN VIEWS

The claim to be white stood at the center of many Mexican Americans' self-understanding. But this does not mean that all Mexicans from the 1930s to the 1960s emphasized white identity, or that whiteness held the same importance or meaning across the Southwest. Severe Jim Crow segregation in Texas encouraged Mexicans to assert white identity more aggressively there.[127] In contrast, Los Angeles's Mexican population was more ambiguous about racial identity. Its members strongly shared the trademark Mexican American commitment to assimilate into U.S. society, as MAM's exhortations demonstrate. Yet among Mexicans in Los Angeles there were fewer efforts to openly proselytize a white identity and generally less discussion of race itself. California's Mexican American leaders accepted the argument pushed by Texas-born regional organizations such as LULAC and GI Forum that Mexicans were white. But Los Angeles leaders did not seem to place the same emphasis on whiteness. Rather, Mexican Americans in Los Angeles emphasized their group's cultural ties to Mexico, though in their view this self-conception included the belief that Mexicans were white.[128]

At the same time, the racial views expressed by mainstream Mexican American leaders should not be taken to represent the views held by every segment of the community.[129] Many LULAC and MAM members came from the relatively small Mexican middle-class. In Los Angeles during the 1940s and 1950s, somewhere between 8 percent and 14 percent of the Mexican population worked in white-collar jobs or owned small business, putting them in a superior social and economic position relative to other community members.[130] In addition, middle-class Mexicans were more likely to physically resemble Europeans; under the longstanding racial ideologies of both Mexico and the United States, European features facilitated upward economic and social mobility. Light-featured and relatively well-off Mexicans experienced race differently than other community members. For middle-class Mexicans, especially those with more European looks, claiming to be white was socially advantageous in the context of the times, and it was plausible, even if not readily accepted.

In contrast, for darker-skinned Mexicans, those in the laboring class, and those not proficient in English, the full weight of anti-Mexican hostility made any pretense to be white delusional.

Segregated in jobs, education, and housing, relegated to the margins of society, branded with a highly pejorative identity as dirty Mexicans, this segment of the Mexican population probably expended little energy arguing that they were white. A prominent Mexican American generation intellectual, the folklorist Arthur Campa, noted that "if one went to the common people one would find that they were not so obsessed with racial distinctions as were the more middle classes."[131] According to Campa, the common people "conceive of their own kin in realistic terms such as *nosotros, nuestra gente, la raza,* and *nosotros los mexicanos"*—that is, as us, our people, or we the Mexicans.[132] Campa's observations apply with particular force to laborers who had recently immigrated. Their *corridos* or songs recorded the travails of their daily lives, and in them Mexican migrants often lamented the prejudice they encountered in the North. In their corridos, however, they did not respond to racist slights by insisting that they were white but by proclaiming their pride in and allegiance to Mexico.[133] This group saw itself primarily in class and national, not racial, terms.[134]

In Los Angeles in the 1940s and 1950s, another Mexican group prominently rejected white identity. Many children of the East L.A. working class took on an identity as *Pachucos* who rejected the middle-class aspirations of racial and social assimilation. Particularly in the early 1940s, but with elements lasting until and informing the Chicano movement, Pachuco culture in L.A. was defined by a working-class youth style that involved wearing drapes or zoot suits, using Spanish and English slang, dancing everything from swing to danzón, and, most importantly, affecting alienation from mainstream U.S. culture.[135] It was Pachuco style that newspapers hysterically excoriated during the war years, and the ferocity unleashed in the zoot suit riots especially targeted Pachucos. The rebellious, suave Pachucos are often presented as the original Chicano activists, and they clearly inspired Chicanos by providing an early model of disaffected youth. Their sense of alienation, however, did not mobilize them to political action, let alone cause them to embrace a specifically racial non-white identity. Like other members of the Mexican community who rejected pretensions of whiteness, the Pachucos did so by downplaying the importance of race as a source of their identity.[136]

THE COMMON SENSE OF MEXICAN IDENTITY

By the 1950s, the frank denigration of Mexicans as a separate and inferior race had largely disappeared from public discourse. Several factors contributed to this. Beginning in the 1920s, social beliefs began to change regarding the boundaries of white identity, increasing the range of individuals and groups considered white.[137] Simultaneously, racial progressives gained ground both in their argument that race did not determine character and intellect and in their push for conceptualizing group differences in ethnic terms, thus emphasizing culture more than biology.[138] World War II contributed to these shifts as the United States positioned itself against the racial extremism of the Axis powers. Finally, Mexican American efforts to oppose discrimination and demand recognition as whites also greatly reduced public expressions of anti-Mexican prejudice.

One measure of the changing times can be found in the official categorization of Mexicans. Where the 1930 census treated "Mexican" as a race, the 1940 census classified "persons of Mexican birth or ancestry who were not definitely Indian or of some other nonwhite race . . . as white."[139] In 1950 the census promulgated the "white persons of Spanish surname" category.

Nevertheless, the official treatment of Mexicans as whites rarely brought with it meaningful equality with Anglos. To begin with, Anglo acceptance of Mexican whiteness frequently served Anglo self-interest. In *Hernandez v. Texas,* for instance, the State of Texas had agreed with LULAC that Mexicans were white, but it did so in order to argue that because whites sat on Texas juries, Mexicans were represented on such juries and suffered no discrimination by being excluded.[140]

The negative treatment of Mexicans also persisted, often by government policy. In Los Angeles, urban renewal and redevelopment disproportionately harmed the Mexican community. Los Angeles County displaced thousands of Mexican families when it bulldozed an Eastside community for the construction of Dodger Stadium. When new freeways were needed, they were located in East Los Angeles, repeatedly bisecting the community.[141] Yet another assault came from "Operation Wetback." Instigated by U.S. Attorney General Herbert Brownell in the first half of the 1950s, Operation Wetback revived Depression-era mass deportations.[142] Responding to public hysteria about the "invasion" of the United States by "illegal aliens," this campaign targeted large Mexican communities such as East Los Angeles.[143] For five years, the Border Patrol, assisted by local police forces, engaged in broad sweeps and deported over 3.8 million persons to Mexico. Only 63,515 of those deported received formal deportation hearings, and the deported included many U.S. citizens.[144]

The mass deportations conflicted with the Mexican community's belief that they were entitled to full citizenship because of their role as one of the country's founding cultures, their decades of toil, and their wartime sacrifices in the country's defense. Equally grating were the anti-Mexican stereotypes that still circulated. Mexicans continued to be widely regarded as lazy, dirty, cowardly and criminal, although such views increasingly operated in the form of general social knowledge rather than as explicit attacks.

In 1968 the critic Thomas Martínez analyzed ten contemporary advertisements featuring Mexicans. Six of these commercials—from major corporations such as General Motors, A.J. Reynolds, Frigidaire, and Frito-Lay—painted Mexicans as dirty or criminal, and another three invoked the lazy stereotype.[145] Here Martínez describes an ad for Arrid deodorant that protrays Mexicans as filthy and foul smelling: "Emerging from a cloud of dust appears a band of horse-riding, ferocious-looking Mexican banditos. They are called to a halt by their sombrero-covered, thick-mustached, fat-bellied leader, who, upon stopping, reaches with the utmost care for a small object from his saddle bags. He picks up the object, lifts up his underarm, and smiles slyly—to spray Arrid deodorant. An American Midwestern voice [says], 'If it works for him, it will work for you.'"[146] Such commercials told stock stories that at once drew upon and confirmed stereotypes of Mexican inferiority. These pervasive images formed part of the cultural patrimony of all U.S. residents.

The extent and tenor of negative beliefs regarding Mexican identity ensured that they occasionally erupted into public discourse. One volatile outburst occurred in 1969 during a sentencing hearing for a juvenile who had pled guilty to incest. (The defendant subsequently claimed that he was innocent and insisted that he had pled guilty only on advice of counsel in order to avoid trial.[147]) Superior Court Judge Gerald Chargin's tirade merits extended quotation because it captures in extreme form prevailing Mexican stereotypes, and also because his words were widely cited by and directly influenced Chicano activists.

The Court. Don't you know that things like this are terribly wrong? This is one of the worst crimes that a person can commit. I just get so disgusted that I just figure what is the use? You are just an animal. You are lower than an animal. Even animals don't do that. You are pretty low. I don't know why your parents haven't been able to teach you anything or train you. Mexican people, after 13 years of age, it's perfectly all right to go out and act like an animal. It's not even right to do that to a stranger, let alone a member of your own family. I don't have much hope for you. You will probably end up in State's Prison before you are 25, and that's where you belong, anyhow. There is nothing much you can do. I think you haven't got any moral principles. You won't acquire anything. Your parents won't teach you what is right or wrong and won't watch out. Apparently, your sister is pregnant; is that right?
The Minor's Father, Mr. Casillas. Yes.
The Court. It's a fine situation. How old is she?

The Minor's Mother, Mrs. Casillas. Fifteen.

The Court. Well, probably she will have half a dozen children and three or four marriages before she is 18. The County will have to take care of you. You are no particular good to anybody. We ought to send you out of the country—send you back to Mexico. You belong in prison for the rest of your life for doing things of this kind. You ought to commit suicide. That's what I think of people of this kind. You are lower than animals and haven't the right to live in organized society—just miserable, lousy, rotten people. There is nothing we can do with you. You expect the County to take care of you. Maybe Hitler was right. The animals in our society probably ought to be destroyed because they have no right to live among human beings. If you refuse to act like a human being, then, you don't belong among the society of human beings.

Mr. Lucero [Defense Counsel]. Your Honor, I don't think I can sit here and listen to that sort of thing.

The Court. You are going to have to listen to it because I consider this a very vulgar, rotten human being.

Mr. Lucero. The Court is indicting the whole Mexican group.

The Court. When they are 10 or 12 years of age, going out and having intercourse with anybody without any moral training—they don't even understand the Ten Commandments. That's all. Apparently, they don't want to.

Mr. Lucero. The Court ought to look at this youngster and deal with this youngster's case.

The Court. All right. That's what I am going to do. The family should be able to control this boy and young girl.

Mr. Lucero. What appalls me is that the Court is saying that Hitler was right in genocide.

The Court. What are we going to do with the mad dogs of our society? Either we have to kill them or send them to an institution or place them out of the hands of good people because that's the theory—one of the theories of punishment is if they get to the position that they want to act like mad dogs, then, we have to separate them from our society. Well, I will go along with the recommendation. You will learn in time or else you will have to pay for the penalty with the law because the law grinds slowly but exceedingly well. If you are going to be a law violator—you have to make up your mind whether you are going to observe the law or not. If you can't observe the law, then, you have to be put away.[148]

Chargin's words do not typify public comments by Superior Court judges or other government officials. Nevertheless, his outburst tells us something important about deeply ingrained anti-Mexican prejudice, even among members of the judiciary. This prejudice boiled to the surface in Judge Chargin's words, but it also appears in the official response to his group slander. Despite his evident racism and its wide public airing, Judge Chargin was not significantly disciplined. The State Commission on Judicial Qualifications recommended censure but nevertheless described Judge Chargin as "a tolerant and compassionate judge with a background of understanding and interest in the problems of the underprivileged and ethnic minorities."[149] Judge Chargin, the commission insisted, was actually a racial liberal.

In 1960 the Mexican population in Los Angeles and the surrounding area stood at almost 630,000.[150] Los Angeles was home to the largest Mexican community anywhere in the world, save Mexico City, and East Los Angeles formed its heart. The other immigrants who had shared East Los Angeles began to leave in the 1940s and were gradually replaced by Mexican newcomers. By 1960 East Los Angeles was almost exclusively Mexican.[151] In addition, the Mexican community was again largely made up of U.S. citizens. Only 15 percent of Mexicans in the United States had been born abroad, while more than half were at least two generations removed from Mexico.[152]

Nevertheless, the political beliefs and aspirations of the Mexican American generation were fraying. For the Mexican community, mistreatment daily challenged their dream of assimilation. In some sense, the Mexican American zeitgeist's persistence from the 1930s to the 1950s, and even into the 1960s, testifies to the tenacity and courage of a people determined to make a home for themselves in this country. By the 1960s, though, a new political generation was coming of age during a time of civil rights protest and anti-war turmoil. This generation not only questioned the verities of assimilation and the American dream but also increasingly doubted the racial foundation upon which those truths depended: that Mexicans were white people.

On the eve of the Chicano movement, many but not all Mexicans viewed themselves as members of the white race, while Anglo society categorized Mexicans as officially white but often treated them as non-whites. The contending views of Mexican identity intermingled and overlapped in a general milieu pervaded by assumptions of Mexican inferiority.

In this context, the two Chicano cases—*East L.A. Thirteen* and *Biltmore Six*—seem deeply perplexing. First, if explicit prejudice against Mexicans was declining, especially in the public arena, what explains the pattern of continued discrimination typified by the Los Angeles Superior Court's exclusion of Mexicans from grand jury service? Second, given the partial but measurable successes of the Mexican community's campaign to be considered white, why did a movement arise that actively repudiated whiteness and claimed instead a non-white, Chicano identity? These two questions frame the discussion in the remainder of this book.

COMMON SENSE AND
LEGAL VIOLENCE

2

JUDGES AND INTENTIONAL RACISM

In *East L.A. Thirteen,* Acosta succeeded, though barely, in convincing the court that Mexicans constituted a distinct group. He was not able to persuade the court that this group had suffered discrimination. Judge Kathleen Parker rejected Acosta's contention that Los Angeles Superior Court judges systematically excluded Mexicans from grand juries. Importantly, the judge based her ruling on a conception of racism that stressed the role of intent. Judge Parker emphasized the lack of "any evidence of any willful or intentional desire on the part of those that are charged with the responsibility of selecting the Grand Jury to keep persons of Spanish surname, or Mexican-Americans, from the Grand Jury."[1] After finding no intentional racism, she dismissed the defendants' discrimination claim.

Despite the adverse ruling, Acosta's evidence regarding the near total absence of Mexicans from Los Angeles grand juries suggests substantial judicial discrimination against that group. What explains this legal violence against the Mexican community? In particular, how can one square this systematic discrimination with evidence that overt racism against Mexicans was declining? The answer is common sense.

THE GRAND JURY

Transplanted from England, grand juries have a long history in the United States. Unlike trial juries, which sit for one or at most a few civil or criminal trials, grand juries usually convene for an entire year and serve an independent, quasi-judicial, quasi-investigative function. A major duty of this small group of citizens is to decide whether the state may bring a person to trial on serious criminal charges.[2] Recognizing the need for a popular check on government prosecutors, the country's founders built this role for the grand jury into the federal Constitution, providing in the Fifth Amendment that "No person shall be held to answer for a capital, or otherwise infamous crime, unless upon a presentment or indictment of a Grand Jury." State grand juries play a similar role, voting on whether prosecutors may bring persons to trial. Many grand juries, including those in California, also are empowered to investigate the conduct of local government.[3]

Despite its supposed virtue as a check on arbitrary or vindictive prosecutorial power, the grand jury has two principal defects. First, it is relatively cumbersome and inefficient. Presenting potential cases to a panel of citizens is time-consuming and expensive. In Los Angeles County in 1968 alone, prosecutors brought approximately 22,000 criminal cases.[4] California law requires a single grand jury of twenty-three citizens in every county. Presenting each criminal case to the L.A. grand jury before proceeding to trial was simply impossible. Second, grand juries in fact exercise little or no independence from prosecutors. Grand jurors defer to prosecutors because they are laypersons assigned a limited role in a highly professionalized criminal justice system.[5] In practice, most grand juries, and certainly most grand juries over the years in Los Angeles County, provide no check on prosecuting officers.

The above concerns prompted many jurisdictions early on to abandon extensive reliance on grand juries. In lieu of a grand jury system, states began to bring charges against individuals via preliminary hearings. Generally, this entails bringing people suspected of a crime before a judicial officer for a hearing during which the prosecutor's office lays out the evidence against the suspect. Unlike proceedings before a grand jury, the accused can bring a lawyer and can challenge the evidence or present exculpatory material. The judicial officer then decides whether the evidence warrants binding the accused over for a full trial. In many states, this system, called "proceeding by information," supplements the grand jury system. By the late 1960s, about half the states, including California, allowed prosecutors to elect case by case whether to proceed by information or by indictment (that is, before a grand jury).[6]

Several features make proceeding by indictment attractive to prosecutors in politically charged cases. First, grand juries have the power to pursue investigations even when it is unlikely crimes have been committed; in this situation, grand juries are less constrained by the rights of the person or group under investigation than is law enforcement. In addition, witnesses called before a grand jury can be aggressively questioned under intimidating circumstances, with no right to have a lawyer present. Contempt proceedings that carry the threat of jail further pressure witnesses to speak.[7] Finally, proceeding by indictment uses the grand jury's legitimacy and prestige to generate popular support. The legitimacy and publicity attendant to grand jury indictments appeals to the prosecutor's office when it hopes to enhance its reputation or to protect itself from charges of partisanship.

For these reasons, many of the most controversial figures investigated for militant or criminal behavior during the tumultuous 1960s and 1970s were prosecuted by grand jury indictment. The Chicano defendants were in the company of indicted persons that included Sirhan Sirhan, Huey Newton, Angela Davis, Abbie Hoffman, Tom Hayden, Jerry Rubin, and Bobby Seale.[8]

THE JUDGES' FRIENDS AND NEIGHBORS

In California, counties must seat a new grand jury every year, and virtually every adult citizen is eligible to serve as a grand juror. In 1968 the prerequisites for grand jury service were relatively minimal: one had to be a U.S. citizen twenty-one years of age or older who had resided one year or more within a given county, and in addition one needed to possess "sufficient knowledge of the English language" and "ordinary intelligence" and could not be "decrepit."[9]

How were grand jurors selected from among eligible persons? The California Penal Code provided complex instructions that centered on the role of jury commissioners, who were to compile lists of eligible citizens from which Superior Court judges were to select grand jurors.[10] In fact, however, jury commissioners rarely prepared such lists and judges almost never looked at them. Instead, judges routinely nominated their friends and neighbors.

Despite the elaborate procedures spelled out in its provisions, the Penal Code authorized Superior Court judges to nominate anyone who met the minimum qualifications required of all grand jurors. "The judges," the Code provided, "may, if in their judgment the due administration of justice requires, make all or any selections from among the body of persons in the county suitable and competent to serve as grand jurors regardless of the list returned by the jury commissioner."[11] This provision encouraged judges to nominate whomever they wished. In most counties, the judges' nominations were then compiled into a list from which grand jurors were randomly selected.[12] Despite this gloss of impartiality, at base the grand juror selection system amounted to judges nominating their friends.[13]

That the Los Angeles Superior Court followed this practice became evident when Oscar Acosta called its judges to the stand in *East L.A. Thirteen*. To build his discrimination case, Acosta asked each judge to explain, name by name, his relationship to every one of his nominees. Judge after judge testified to his close social relationships with his nominees. Judge Joseph Call, on the bench since 1956, primarily nominated his tennis buddies or their wives:[14]

Q. Do you know a Dora Rombeau, R-o-m-b-e-a-u?

A. Very well.

Q. How long have you known Mrs. Rombeau?

A. Well, it would go back to approximately the very early, early 1950's . . . I know Dr. Rombeau and Mrs. Rombeau because they have been members of the Los Angeles Tennis Club since the early 50's, where I am, met them as members of the club. I see them twice a week on the courts of the Los Angeles Tennis Club, and have since 1950 . . .

Q. Do you know a Maureen Campbell? . . .

A. Oh, yes, indeed. Yes, indeed.

Q. And how long have you known her?

A. Well, let's see. I place the time through her husband, Mr. Alex Campbell of the *Los Angeles Herald,* and that would go back to the time he joined the Los Angeles Tennis Club . . . I joined there in 1932, '33, and Campbell came in about 1955, and that is when I met his wife, so I'd say from 1955.

Q. Thank you. Do you know a Mr. George Goman?

A. Very well . . .

Q. Is Mr. Goman a member of the tennis club?

A. Yes.

Q. Do you know Mrs. Leona McNeill?

A. Very well . . .

Q. Is she a member of the tennis club?

A. Well, I don't know whether she is. I know she plays there on weekends. She may have what is known as an associate membership through her husband, who is a member.[15]

Over twelve years, Judge Call nominated a total of ten people to be grand jurors. He knew eight of them through the Los Angeles Tennis Club.[16] Of the two nominees he did not know through tennis, Judge Call described one as "an outstanding citizen" whom he had known for approximately ten years when he nominated him, while the other he described as "a forthright member of the community, a housewife, if I remember correctly."[17]

Judge Call may be atypical in his nominating practices, but only to the extent that he drew from a circle more tightly circumscribed than that of most; rather, to the extent that Judge Call nominated his friends, he typified the conduct of the other judges.[18] Judge Bayard Rhone provides another example. His nominees included a friend of thirty years, a neighbor of ten, church acquaintances of fifteen and twenty-five years, a fellow Camellia Society member, a fellow Mason, and a member of his church's board of trustees.[19] Judge Rhone's social orbit was somewhat larger than Judge Call's, but it still marked the outer boundary for potential grand jurors. Exercising the responsibility to nominate grand jurors, Judges Call and Rhone nominated their neighbors and friends. From outside this circle, they drew virtually no one.

The thirty-three judges called to the stand in *East L.A. Thirteen* submitted 255 nominations in the years between 1959 and 1968, though because they nominated several persons more than once, individual nominees numbered only 230.[20] Keeping in mind that the judges described some nominees in more than one way—for example, as both friend and neighbor—the judges characterized 53 percent of their nominations as friends and described another 25 percent as members of their church, civic organization, or club. The judges also described 8 percent as neighbors, 5 percent as a friend's spouse, and 2 percent as family members. In addition, the judges testified that 15 percent were business acquaintances. Of these, the judges described 75 percent as also a friend, neighbor, or co-member of a church, civic organization, or club. The judges counted fully 82 percent of their nominees as personal acquaintances. In the remaining 18 percent of cases, the judges explained that more than a third were recommended by a friend, family relation, fellow club member, or another judge—that is, another 7 percent of the total nominations.[21]

Two points bear emphasis here. First, 89 percent or nearly 9 out of 10 nominees came from within the judges' social circles. A person in Los Angeles who did not personally know a judge, or know someone who did, had little to no chance of serving on the Los Angeles County grand jury. Second, all of the thirty-three judges testified that they effectively used the same system in selecting their nominees: they picked persons casually from among their personal acquaintances. Whether this meant nominees selected from a club, a church, the business world, or next door, each judge picked nominees the same way. To be sure, sometimes judges relied on the recommendations of fellow judges, but otherwise no judge described a different method of selecting nominees, save a lone judge who reported that he once nominated someone whose name was suggested after the judge asked for persons from underrepresented communities.[22]

OUTSIDE THE CIRCLE

While the judges picked nominees from within their social circle, much of Los Angeles County lived outside those narrow boundaries. In particular, the judges knew few Mexicans, who were thus largely excluded from grand jury service. Noting that Judge Call had drawn eight of his ten nominees from the Los Angeles Tennis Club, Acosta questioned the judge regarding the club membership of any Mexicans. The judge claimed that two Mexican tennis champions had honorary memberships, as did the captain of the Mexican Davis Cup team. "I'm sure," Judge Call told Acosta, that "honorary memberships have been given to all of those men. They are frequent visitors at the club, frequent."[23] Judge Call could not say, however, whether any other Mexicans belonged to the club, which he estimated had 700 members.

Acosta also asked Judge Call whether he personally knew any Mexicans:

Q. Do you know any Mexican-Americans, Judge? . . .

A. Well, the gentleman that is a gardener at my house is Mexican-American. I just signed his citizenship papers. I guess now he is a double-fledged citizen, if that's what you mean.

Q. Do you know any persons of Mexican descent who were born here in this country?

A. Mexican descent? If I do, I can't recall them. I probably do. Over the period of my life I have met thousands, hundreds. I have met many, many, but I can't recall it from memory. Undoubtedly, undoubtedly I know many of them. Certainly I do. Let me see. Born in this country? You are asking the question, saying born here, did you? Or is that right?

Q. Yes, sir.

A. Well, of course I do. But I can't enumerate them. It takes in such a vast field.

Q. But you do know some?

A. Undoubtedly.[24]

Judge Call did not hesitate to claim to know some Mexicans. Indeed, he initially claimed to know many, even thousands. Nevertheless, he could not actually recall the name of even one Mexican acquaintance.[25] The other judges all answered more or less the same way: they could name none, or never more than one or two Mexicans, and these one or two were frequently their gardeners or servants. When asked about Mexican acquaintances, Judge Samuel Greenfield could only name his two "domestics," Judge Harold Schweitzer offered that he knew the gardeners who worked around the courthouse, and Judge George Dockweiler responded, "The only man I know is the man who runs the gasoline station at Larchmont and First Street. He is of Mexican extraction."[26]

Of course, not only Mexicans lived beyond the judges' realm of familiarity. Rather, as one would expect, numerous social biases tainted the jury nomination process. Averill Munger here describes to a legislative committee how the judges selected him to be the foreman of the 1966 Los Angeles grand jury:

> *Munger.* When our group of 23 . . . became jurors, then the presiding judge of the Superior Court, Judge Nix, last year, and Judge Alarcon, the criminal calendar judge, presiding judge of the criminal calendar court, those two men called four or five of the male jurors, and there were only, I think, nine of us. We were outnumbered by women for the first time in the history of the grand jury. At any rate, these two men picked four or five of us who they thought might be good foremen, and we were interviewed in the judges' chambers.
>
> *Committee Chair McMillan.* They didn't think any women would make good foremen?
>
> *Munger.* Well, evidently not. Actually, when I was appointed the judge asked me if I belonged to any group that threatened change in our government, and I said, yes, I did—I belonged to the Republican Associates, and I guess with Judge Nix being a strong Republican, they made me foreman. So that's how I became foreman.[27]

As in so many places, the dryness of the transcript leaves us wondering. In what tone did Munger relate the easy exclusion of women from consideration as jury leaders? How long was the pause between Munger's "evidently not" and his "Actually" and on to the next subject? The tone and the pause might help us to understand whether the exclusion of women troubled Munger or seemed to him insignificant. But perhaps we simply can infer a light tone and a short pause. The first Supreme Court case to squarely forbid the exclusion of women from jury panels was not handed down until 1975.[28] Among judges, as apparently for Munger, women were routinely considered unfit for such responsibilities.

Note also Munger's elevation to grand jury leadership apparently by virtue of his Republican credentials. That Munger bene-

fited from gender preferences and political party affiliation illustrates the range of social biases implicated in the judges' selection
of grand jurors. Some of the characteristics that the judges relied
upon, like race and gender, drew upon what we now regard as
among the most injurious myths of difference. Others, like party
affiliation or country club membership, seem by current standards perhaps only moderately pernicious. And still others, like
class and profession, currently lie somewhere in between. Yet all
of these biases informed one another and operated to skew the
distribution of grand jurors away from one reflecting a cross-section of the community. The discrimination apparent in the
judges' selection practices favored a narrow group of people on
the higher rungs of the social hierarchy.

Table 1 offers some perspective on the extent of the exclusion
of Mexicans from L.A. grand juries in the 1960s. Mexicans constituted approximately 10 percent of the population of Los Angeles County in 1960 and roughly 18 percent in 1970.[29] In the
eleven years from 1959 to 1969, Los Angeles Superior Court
judges made 1,690 grand juror nominations, but the number of
nominated Mexicans totaled only 47. One of the four Mexican
judges on the court nominated ten of these.[30] Thus, Mexicans
constituted slightly less than 3 percent of all grand jury nominees, and if the actions of one Mexican judge are set aside, the
percentage drops to about 2 percent.

The number of Mexicans actually seated as grand jurors was
even more dismal. Between 1959 and 1969, Mexicans comprised
only 4 of 233 grand jurors—no more than 1.7 percent of all
grand jurors. If one assumes Mexicans on average constituted 14
percent of Los Angeles County's population during this period,
Mexicans were under-represented on Los Angeles grand juries by
a ratio of 8 to 1. During the 1960s, Mexicans counted for 1 of
every 7 persons in Los Angeles, but only 1 of every 36 nominees
and 1 of every 58 grand jurors. Prior to the 1960s the exclusion
of Mexicans was no doubt even greater. A study of Los Angeles
grand juries published in 1945 noted that "as far as the writer

Participation by persons of Spanish surname on Los Angeles County
Grand Juries, 1959–1969

Year	Total nominations	Number of Spanish surname nominees	Number of grand jurors	Number of Spanish surname grand jurors
1959	132	1 (0.8%)	19	0
1960	146	2 (1.4%)	19	0
1961	148	3 (2.0%)	19	0
1962	144	4 (2.8%)	19	0
1963	140	5 (3.6%)	19	0
1964	155	7 (4.5%)	23	0
1965	152	6 (3.9%)	22	2 (8.7%)
1966	162	5 (3.1%)	23	0
1967	151	4 (2.6%)	24	1 (4.2%)
1968	171	3 (1.8%)	23	1 (4.5%)
1969	189	7 (3.7%)	23	0
Total	1,690	47 (2.8%)	233	4 (1.7%)

Source: Edward Villalobos, Comment, "Grand Jury Discrimination and the
Mexican American," 5 Loyola University of Los Angeles Law Review 87, 109–110
(1972).

was able to discover no Mexicans have ever been chosen for jury
duty."[31] These numbers demonstrate discrimination; unfortu-
nately, Los Angeles County was representative of California as a
whole.

In 1970 the U.S. Commission on Civil Rights published a report entitled "Mexican Americans and the Administration of
Justice in the Southwest."[32] The report included a study by California Rural Legal Assistance, a legal aid organization, on grand
jury selection practices in the twenty California counties with the
highest Mexican populations.[33] The CRLA study confirmed the
claims of Acosta and the Chicano defendants that Los Angeles
County substantially excluded Mexicans from grand jury service, describing that county as a "leader . . . in discrimination
against minority grand jurors."[34] The study also found similar
discriminatory patterns in all of the examined counties: "Generally speaking, the judges nominate as grand jurors those whom

they or other prominent persons they know deem qualified. As a result, the racial, ethnic, social and economic composition of grand juries in California is limited by the acquaintanceship of the Superior Court judges."[35] And: "In every county studied, the percentage of minority group grand jurors was significantly less than the minority group percentage of the general population, the disparity varying from substantial in the best counties to grotesque in the worst."[36] The CRLA grand jury study indicates that the grand jury exclusion publicized by *East L.A. Thirteen* and *Biltmore Six* was not unique. Rather, nearly every Superior Court judge in California nominated friends and acquaintances to grand jury service and routinely excluded Mexicans and other minorities.

Legal discrimination occurred not only in terms of grand juries. The U.S. Commission on Civil Rights report put the CRLA study in context by making clear that routine inequality characterized the entire administration of justice. For instance, the report recorded the following problems specifically regarding police interaction with Mexican community members: frequent use of unwarranted violence; discriminatory treatment of juveniles; discriminatory enforcement of motor vehicle ordinances; excessive use of "stop and frisk" techniques; excessive use of "investigation" arrests; general discourtesy; and, particularly telling for the Chicano defendants, instances of law enforcement interference with "Mexican American organizational efforts aimed at improving the conditions of Mexican Americans in the Southwest."

Regarding bail proceedings the report criticized the following practices: the application of unduly rigid standards for release of Mexicans on their own recognizance; failure to give bail hearings until long after persons were taken into custody; and, again something the Chicano defendants experienced, the setting of excessive bail to punish rather than to guarantee defendants' appearance for trial. Moreover, with regard to employment within justice organizations, the commission reached these conclusions:

"Neither police departments, sheriffs' offices, nor State law enforcement agencies employ Mexican Americans in significant numbers"; and "Other agencies in charge of the administration of justice—courts, district attorneys' offices, and the Department of Justice—also have significantly fewer Mexican American employees than the proportion of Mexican Americans in the general population."[37]

The Chicano defendants alleged judicial discrimination against Mexicans as part of their defense. Their allegations barely scratched the surface, for anti-Mexican discrimination thoroughly infected the justice system.

INTENTIONAL RACISM

The extensive testimony Acosta elicited from the judges regarding grand jury selection apparently did not trouble the prosecutor. In responding to the defendants' discrimination claim, the prosecutor did not ask a single judge to clarify his testimony regarding his selection practices, nor did he otherwise attempt to recast the judges' testimony in any way. Rather, on cross-examination, the prosecutor asked each judge only whether he had *intended* to discriminate. The exchange between the prosecutor and Judge Call is typical:

Q. In considering or determining whom you were going to nominate, was it your purpose to deliberately exclude any member of any particular racial or ethnic group?

A. Under no condition.

Q. And in actually placing in nomination the persons whose names have been mentioned here in court, did you intend to intentionally, arbitrarily, and systematically exclude from Grand Jury service any member of any particular racial or ethnic group?

A. No way at all.

Q. Did you nominate those persons whom you did in fact nominate because you felt they were the best qualified to serve?

A. Absolutely.[38]

This brief exchange represents virtually the entire cross-examination of Judge Call. The prosecutor posed these same questions, and few if any others, to nearly every judge, and each answered in nearly the same fashion. Even the awkward but revealing circumlocution "intend to intentionally, arbitrarily, and systematically" made repeated appearances in the prosecutor's questioning of the judges.[39]

After Acosta had called thirty-three judges, the prosecutor, without presenting evidence of his own, asked the court to dismiss the Equal Protection challenge. He argued "that the defendants have not sustained their burden of proof to show that there was any *purposeful* systematic discrimination of persons of Spanish surname in selecting the jury."[40] He insisted, "There was no evidence at all of *any intent* on the part of any of the Judges or the Jury Commissioner or anyone else involved in the system of selecting the Grand Jurors in this County, to exclude any person, or to treat any person differently on account of his race or his ethnic group."[41] For the prosecutor, intent was an indispensable component of discrimination.

For his part, Acosta resisted the need to prove intentional discrimination and refrained from claiming that any such animus existed. Instead, Acosta labored to show that the practice of nominating acquaintances itself amounted to a denial of Equal Protection, regardless of whether or not the judges had intended to discriminate. Acosta explained:

> I am not arguing that the Judges wake up every morning and say, "I'm not going to look for any Mexicans today. I'm not going to submit any Mexican names today." But the whole question of discrimination is not predicated on any morality or conscious evil, we are talking about facts, we are talking about the results of a system . . . I'm not saying that the Judges are evil persons by any means whatsoever, and I'm not saying that they are even evil in the sense they don't name nominees of Spanish surname. What is pathetic, tragic, is that none of them know any of them . . . Now, since they are nominating

their friends, how in the world are they going to nominate us since they don't know us? We don't exist.[42]

Acosta urged upon the court a discrimination model that did not turn on intention, purpose, deliberation, or conscious action. Acosta readily conceded that the judges were not engaged in "conscious evil," that they did not formulate any intent to discriminate against Mexicans. In rejecting the purposeful discrimination model, however, Acosta did not default to a purely effects-based approach. He did not ask the court to look only at the results, stark as they were. Rather, Acosta urged the court to identify as discriminatory a practice of selecting grand jurors that consistently excluded Mexicans. Acosta argued that the Superior Court judges systematically (though not purposefully) excluded Mexicans when they drew only on narrow circles of friends and neighbors in submitting nominations. Acosta urged the court in *East L.A. Thirteen,* and subsequently in *Biltmore Six,* to acknowledge that a nomination process in which Mexicans did not exist amounted to discrimination under the Fourteenth Amendment.

Acosta's argument failed to persuade the courts. When the presiding judge in *East L.A. Thirteen* granted the prosecutor's motion to dismiss the Equal Protection claim, she cited the lack of any evidence showing that her colleagues possessed a "willful or intentional desire" to exclude Mexicans.[43] In *Biltmore Six,* Judge Alarcon similarly found no evidence that any judge "consciously, deliberately, [or] intentionally" discriminated against Mexicans.[44] These judges relied on, and in turn imposed, the discrimination model urged by the prosecutor, the model that required proof of intentional, purposeful discrimination in order to prevail under the Fourteenth Amendment.

Despite these holdings, in 1968 it was still a relatively open question whether one had to show a purpose to discriminate in order to establish a constitutional violation. For instance, in

Hernandez v. Texas, the Supreme Court suggested that discriminatory results alone justified constitutional intervention: "The result bespeaks discrimination," the Court ruled, "whether or not it was a conscious decision on the part of any individual jury commis sioner."[45] In other cases, though, the Court's language implied that intent was a necessary element, as in another jury case from Texas where the Court wrote that "a purpose to discriminate must be present"—though even there, the Court went on to say that discriminatory purpose "may be proven by systematic exclusion of eligible jurymen of the proscribed race," thereby implying that results could demonstrate the "intent" necessary to establish a constitutional violation.[46]

If anything, in 1968 the weight of previous judicial opinions ran counter to the decisions in the Chicano cases, with many courts finding violations of the Fourteenth Amendment on the basis of discriminatory results even without any showing of an intent to discriminate. Nevertheless, the Chicano cases anticipated the Supreme Court's eventual position, for in 1976, the Court decided *Washington v. Davis*, a case that for the first time definitively ruled that the Constitution prohibits only intentional racism.[47]

At issue in *Davis* was a decision by the Washington, D.C., police to use a civil service exam to make hiring decisions. The police force adopted the exam only after they came under pressure to desegregate. Since almost every applicant had attended segregated schools, the test excluded four times as many blacks as whites.[48] In a closely divided opinion, the Supreme Court ruled that since no intentional racism was shown, no constitutional violation had occurred. In the wake of *Washington v. Davis*, constitutional law defines racism in terms of intentional conduct. It presumes that in the absence of an intent to discriminate, race has no influence on either decision-making or behavior. Accordingly, racism is the work of individual bad actors, not systems or patterns that produce discriminatory harms, and certainly not the harms themselves.[49]

In offering an intent-centered theory of racism, the Court ha↩ not expressly identified any model of human behavior as the basis for its holdings. One reads *Washington v. Davis* or its progeny in vain for any hint that the Supreme Court has grappled with the complicated nature of racism or its behavioral engines. Nevertheless, the Court's picture of racism implies a view that social actors are guided almost exclusively by consciously formulated intentions. This behavioral model resembles rational choice theory. The correspondence between Supreme Court doctrine and rational choice theory is unfortunate, for the latter offers weak understandings of racial discrimination.

Rational choice theorists have offered two principal models to explain why actors might discriminate—the associational and the statistical. Under the associational theory, proposed in 1957 by Gary Becker, people discriminate because they have a "taste" for associating or disassociating with specific groups.[50] This model in effect asserts little more than that people discriminate because they want to, and that they act strategically to satisfy their desire.

In contrast, a statistical model in vogue recently posits that people discriminate when they can use race or some other readily apparent marker of group difference as a proxy for traits that are difficult to observe.[51] Under this model, discrimination on the basis of skin color does not have any independent utility. People do not discriminate because of, say, hostility toward a group. Rather, people discriminate on skin color grounds because, in the calculus of information gathering, discrimination is efficient. Dinesh D'Souza pushes this model, which he terms "rational discrimination": "There are many indications that black cultural pathology has contributed to a new form of discrimination: rational discrimination. High crime rates of young black males, for example, make taxi drivers more reluctant to pick them up, storekeepers more likely to follow them in stores, and employers less willing to hire them. Rational discrimination is based on accurate group generalizations that may nevertheless be unfair to particular members of a group."[52] D'Souza's account of racial discrimination, like those offered by rational choice theory generally, gives short shrift to the cultural and structural forces of entrenched racism, let alone to the continued sway of open bigotry. Instead, these models present thoughtful actors making reasoned choices.[53]

The insistence on intent as a predicate to discrimination by the Court and by conservative theorists increasingly informs contemporary debates on racism. This understanding would deny that the grand juror selection practices so amply documented in the Chicano cases amounted to racism. Nevertheless, Acosta correctly described the grand jury selection system as racially biased. Time after time each judge "normally and quite naturally selected and asked his friends."[54] Though most judges did not intend to exclude Mexicans—or, for that matter, blacks and other racial groups, the less well-off, or the otherwise socially marginal—their exclusion was inevitable. Because the judges chose from among their friends, individuals living outside this rarified circle effectively ceased to exist as potential grand jurors. These individuals, including almost the entire Mexican community, may not have been "intentionally and purposefully" excluded, but year after year they were just as surely absent from Los Angeles grand juries. We need models of race and human behavior that better explain such racism. The next chapter offers a model based on common sense.

RACE AND RACISM AS COMMON SENSE 5

Acosta's proof that the Superior Court judges excluded Mexicans from the Los Angeles grand juries tells us little about the dynamics of such exclusion. How did this racism arise? The testimony in *East L.A. Thirteen* suggests that most judges engaged in widespread discrimination without forming any intent to do so. To explain the judges' behavior, and later to help us understand why and how the Chicano activists remade Mexican racial identity, I turn to the idea that much of our behavior, including our racial beliefs and practices, depends on what we take to be common sense.

To square the judges' actions in excluding Mexicans with their testimony that they had no intention to discriminate, one might postulate that the judges simply testified falsely about their true motivations.[1] Is it plausible that thirty-three judges took the witness stand in *East L.A. Thirteen* and lied? To answer this, one must evaluate the character of the judges, as well as the likelihood that the judges had something to lie about. It seems reasonable to assume that the judges were no more venal and perhaps, because of their position, a little less so than the rest of us. With regard to whether the judges had something to lie about, in the context of the East Los Angeles cases, a few judges probably harbored conscious animus against Mexicans. Indeed, chilling evidence in that direction emerges from Judge Chargin's comments about Hitler and mad dogs. The era and general social context of the cases, though, make it unlikely that a majority of the judges intentionally embraced and acted on racial hatred. There probably was some significant element of overt racial hostility on the bench, but an account that centers primarily on intentional discrimination and outright lying would strike most people as implausible.

Recognizing that he could not show intentional discrimination, Acosta told the court in *East L.A. Thirteen,* "I am not arguing that the Judges wake up every morning and say, 'I'm not going to look for any Mexicans today. I'm not going to submit any Mexican names today.'" Acosta insisted, though, that the judges did discriminate. "The whole question of discrimination is not predicated on any morality or conscious evil," Acosta acknowledged; instead, "we are talking about facts, we are talking about the results of a system."[2] But what system? How did this system work? Why did the judges racially discriminate, if for the most part they had no intention of doing so?

Social science theory, particularly in economics and political science, often posits that humans act rationally in a goal-directed fashion—people know what they want and act in ways consciously calculated to achieve their desires. But people are also guided by nonrational influences that range from the cognitive and psychological to the ideological and cultural. In large part, these influences save us from having to examine anew every thought and act. They make things familiar, not just in the sense of helping us to recognize patterns but in the more complicated sense of imposing order. I describe such influences as common sense. At a largely unexamined level, common sense shapes how we think and what we do.[3]

I use the term common sense because it evokes the overwhelming ordinariness, pervasiveness, and legitimacy of much social knowledge. Common sense expresses the intuitive notion that certain objects and actions are simply what they are, widely known, widely recognized, not needing any explanation. We often use this term to indicate that an answer or an injunction is obvious: "Why did you slow down when you saw the police car?" "Common sense." Or, "Use your common sense, slow down when you see a squad car!" But what is obvious here? The obvious, the common sense, amounts to certain ways of behaving that have become so accepted that they do not require, and possibly are not susceptible to, explanation. Sometimes, these routines serve useful functions, such as avoiding speeding tickets. That a pattern has a discernible logic or an instrumental purpose, though, does not exclude it from functioning as common sense. It is common sense when the routine itself, rather than the underlying logic or the purpose, provides the principal impetus for the behavior. People tend to slow down when they see a police cruiser—whether they are speeding or driving below the speed limit.

Here is another way to picture the difference between rational choice and common sense theory. Imagine a traveler finishing a meal at a roadside cafe to which she believes she will never return.[4] Does she leave a tip? Rational choice theory suggests she calculates the expected utility to herself of doing so and behaves accordingly, probably leaving nothing. Common sense theory suggests something quite different: that our diner will leave a tip without giving the tipping (as opposed to the amount) any thought.

Now suppose we ask our hypothetical diner why she acted as she did. The rational choice model predicts that, having already thought things through, she will easily explain her reasoning; moreover, if given a chance to reconsider, she would not alter her behavior. In contrast, a common sense model predicts that such a question would confuse the diner, partly because she had given tipping no thought and partly because the matter seems so obvious. In addition, common sense theory suggests that, having been jarred into thinking about tipping and given a chance to reconsider, our diner might react in various ways, though probably in a manner that continued to depend on largely unconsidered understandings of appropriate behavior.

What does this model tell us about the judges' behavior? To begin with, because common sense theory stresses the nearly automatic quality of actions, it largely accepts the judges' emphatic denials of discriminatory intent. A common sense model posits that the judges did not form any intent to discriminate because, with respect to nomination practices, they formed little intent at all.

Next, common sense theory helps to explain the fact that the judges all picked their nominees the same way, casually selecting from among their acquaintances. Common sense analysis shows that standardized responses that are consistently but thoughtlessly deployed quickly develop for routine functions, especially in highly organized settings.[5] Thus, perhaps the best evidence that the judges followed common sense is the remarkable uniformity in their selection practices. It was not that some judges relied on their clerks, others on the jury commissioner or elected officials, some on newspaper advertisements soliciting applications, a few on random selection from voter or taxpayer lists, and still others on names generated by respected civic organizations or leaders.[6] If conscious decision-making drove the judges, one would expect such a wide range of practices. But judge after judge told nearly the same story about nominating his friends and acquaintances. A model of common sense behavior predicts exactly this uniformity.

Testifying in *East L.A. Thirteen*, Superior Court Judge William Levit insisted that the judges had made their nominations individually, without consulting one another: "Now, our Court Rule says that each Judge will nominate two people. We don't do it as a group, we do it individually . . . I have never discussed my nominations with any other Judge, and I don't know of any who have discussed it with me."[7] Perhaps regarding individual nominees, Judge Levit was correct. But with respect to the process, he surely erred. Contrary to his sense, the judges subscribed to a nominating system dictated by group dynamics. Judges learned from one another, sometimes directly, but also at a nonconscious level. They learned that the appropriate manner of selecting nominees involved picking from among one's acquaintances. They learned that those they personally knew described the world of potential nominees. Common sense explains why almost every judge picked grand jury nominees from a narrow circle of friends and neighbors: it was simply the way it was done, a taken-for-granted solution to a routine problem. To this extent, the selection of nominees from among a narrow class and professional range—and the resultant exclusion of Mexicans—reflected not conscious design but unconsidered activity. In effect, Acosta was correct: for discrimination to occur, the judges did not have to arrive at work in the morning intending to discriminate against Mexicans. They had only to show up.

SELECTION CRITERIA, SCRIPTS, AND ORTHODOXY

One appreciates common sense's power over grand jury nominations by examining the extent to which the judges almost totally disregarded the criteria and instructions provided them for selecting grand jurors. Several sources of guidance existed: state statute, federal and state constitutional law, and Superior Court directive.

State statute specified only minimum grand juror qualifications. In 1968 the California Code of Civil Procedure listed five prerequisites, but only two addressed the personal capacity of prospective jurors: jurors were to possess "sufficient knowledge of the English language" and were required to be "of ordinary intelligence."[8] In other words, virtually all citizens qualified to serve as grand jurors.

Several U.S. Supreme Court decisions also offered direction regarding nomination practices. In particular, the Court had held specifically that officials selecting grand jurors *must not* draw only from their acquaintances if they knew few or no minorities. "Where jury commissioners limit those from whom grand juries are selected to their own personal acquaintance, discrimination can arise from commissioners who know no negroes as well as from commissioners who know but eliminate them."[9] Along the same line, the Court in another case ruled: "The statements of the jury commissioners that they chose only whom they knew, and that they knew no eligible Negroes in an area where Negroes made up so large a proportion of the population, prove the intentional exclusion that is discrimination in violation of . . . constitutional rights."[10] The Court there went on to explicitly impose on jury selectors a "duty to familiarize themselves fairly with the qualifications of the eligible jurors of the county without regard to race and color."[11] The California Supreme Court also spoke to jury selection, declaring that "any system or method of jury selection . . . which is not designed to encompass a cross-section of the community or which seeks to favor limited social or economic classes, is not in keeping with the American tradition."[12]

Finally, the Superior Court judges received an annual administrative directive from the presiding judge. Every year for at least the six years preceding 1968, the presiding judge sent to each sitting court member a letter on selecting grand jurors that included the following instructions: "The Grand Jury should be representative of a cross section of the community. Each Judge must therefore be mindful of the need for making nominations from the various geographical locations within the County, and different racial groups, and all economic levels."[13]

The criteria and instructions for selecting grand jurors strongly suggested that the judges had an obligation to cast a wide net in making nominations. Statutory law, U.S. and California constitutional cases, and court directive told the judges year after year, implicitly and explicitly, to consider geographic, economic, and, importantly, racial diversity in making their nominations. The statute and case law may have been somewhat removed from the judges' usual awareness, but the cross-section letter arrived on their desks every year. How can the judges' actions be squared with the instructions given them?

Consider a psychology experiment concerning "the mindlessness of ostensibly thoughtful action."[14] Persons about to use a photocopying machine in a university library were approached with one of three requests: (1) "May I use the Xerox machine?" (2) "May I use the Xerox machine, because I have to make copies?" And (3) "May I use the Xerox machine, because I'm in a rush?" Requests one and two are similar in *substance*, since the "explanation" that the experimenter seeks to use the Xerox machine "to make copies" adds no new information. On the other hand, requests two and three take the same *form*: "request" plus "reason." If people respond thoughtfully, that is, to the substance of what is being asked of them, a similar compliance rate between requests one and two should emerge; if people respond to form, on the other hand, there would be a similar compliance rate for requests two and three.

The following results emerged: where the interruption was perceived as relatively minor, 60 percent of the people complied with request one, while 93 percent and 94 percent respectively complied with requests two and three.[15] People responded not to the substance of the request but to its form.

Common sense theory suggests that people often follow scripts, where scripts are standard operating procedures to which people give little or no thought.[16] To be sure, scripted responses require the use of sets of cues to readily identify types of situations. When events provide such cues, though, scripted responses follow, sometimes in derogation of relevant, readily available information. The experiment above makes a cooperation script apparent. People using university libraries will cooperate with others on minor matters so long as the request takes a relevant form; if the appropriate form is used, lack of meaning within the form may be irrelevant.

As for the grand jury selection process, it may well be that, accustomed to letters taking the form of instructions regarding administrative duties, the judges disregarded the substance of such letters, albeit without formulating an intent to ignore them. The judges' testimony supports this hypothesis. Acosta asked virtually every judge whether he recalled the cross-section letter. Judge

Call responded: "Well, I don't specifically recall it, but I would say I undoubtedly did receive it."[17] Judge John Frazer echoed the point: "Well, I presume that I received it . . . This is more than a year ago, but if it was sent out to all the Judges, I no doubt did receive it . . . I don't recall specifically all the letters that I received. We have a mimeographed process in this Court, and I think I probably receive on an average of two, if not three, letters a day from Court, letters on different subjects. I just don't remember each letter, but I would say that I probably received that one."[18] The judges received many letters, perhaps too many to allow the careful consideration of every one. If a particular letter took a recognizable form, that alone probably conveyed sufficient information for the judges to conclude that they already knew its content.

Many judges disregarded the court's instructions to nominate persons from among all racial groups because, at least cognitively, the judges simply never "saw" the letter. Judges like Call and Frazer almost certainly testified honestly that they did not recall the letter that instructed them to pursue a nomination process starkly at odds with actual practices. It is unlikely that they consciously registered the letter's content, decided to disregard it, and lied on the stand about their recollection. More likely, they routinely ignored the directive, just as they routinely nominated their acquaintances.

But most judges did recall receiving the cross-section letter.[19] Did these judges decide simply to discard it? No, on the contrary, they remembered the letter because they supposed that it *confirmed* the very practices they pursued. When familiar elements trigger scripts, such scripts often encourage actors to misconstrue what they perceive. At the same time, the whole script, with all of its component parts, becomes further entrenched.[20] Thus, the judges who saw the cross-section letter registered a reference to grand jury nomination practices that, in turn, authorized the pick-your-friend script. Without even reading the letter, they knew what it said: continue in your current practices.

In September 1965, Police Chief William Parker testified before the Senate regarding the origins of the Watts riot. Parker blamed "communists in the ghetto." *(Herald Examiner Collection/Los Angeles Public Library)*

Lincoln High School students walk out to protest school conditions, March 1968. One student holds a sign proclaiming "Chicano Power." *(Raul Ruiz)*

On June 2, 1968, several thousand protesters marched around the block housing Parker Center, the downtown Los Angeles police headquarters, to protest the arrests in *East L.A. Thirteen. (Herald Examiner Collection/Los Angeles Public Library)*

Police watch the protesters march around Parker Center on June 2, 1968. Several signs accuse the police of racism. *(Herald Examiner Collection/Los Angeles Public Library)*

Sal Castro, out on bail after being arrested in *East L.A. Thirteen*, speaks to students at Lincoln High School regarding the inferior education provided to the Mexican community. *(Herald Examiner Collection/Los Angeles Public Library)*

Protesters march outside of Lincoln High School on September 16, 1968. *East L.A. Thirteen* attorney Oscar Acosta carries a sign reading "Sal is For You. Are You For Him?" *(Herald Examiner Collection/ Los Angeles Public Library)*

Brown Beret leader and *East L.A. Thirteen* defendant David Sánchez, in a 1968 photo. *(Herald Examiner Collection/Los Angeles Public Library)*

Recruitment add for the Brown Berets, published in the East Los Angeles activist newspaper *La Raza* in February 1968. *(Raul Ruiz/La Raza Archives)*

La Raza editor and *East L.A. Thirteen* defendant Eliezer Risco, in a 1968 photo. *(Herald Examiner Collection/Los Angeles Public Library)*

Front page of *La Raza* covering the raids and arrests in *East L.A. Thirteen*, including the police sweep of the *La Raza* offices and the incarceration of editor Eliezer Risco. June 1968. *(Raul Ruiz/La Raza Archives)*

The Chicano 13 vs. the Grand Jury

A political cartoon from the pages of *La Raza*, December 1968. Entitled "The Blind Pig," the cartoon depicts the police as a pig with empty eye sockets, clutching a tattered, blood-spattered flag that proclaims "law and order." The cockroach represents alternatively the Chicano community or the East L.A. Thirteen, whose names encircle its feet. Activists sometimes referred to themselves as cockroaches to lampoon the Anglo view of Mexicans as numerous, brown, despicable, and subhuman. *(Raul Ruiz/La Raza Archives)*

Oscar Acosta in a photo for *Rolling Stone* magazine. *(© 2002 Annie Leibovitz)*

Oscar Acosta the lawyer. *(Raul Ruiz)*

Oscar Acosta in the courtroom during the 1970 trial of Rodolfo "Corky" Gonzales. *Los Angeles Times* correspondent Rubén Salazar wrote that "Acosta [is] easily recognized in court by his loud ties and flowered attaché case with a Chicano Power sticker." *(Raul Ruiz)*

Oscar Acosta and Corky Gonzales outside the courthouse in 1970. *(Raul Ruiz)*

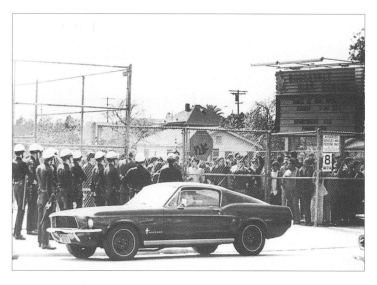

Police respond to renewed protest as students gather behind the high fence surrounding Roosevelt High School, 1970. *(Raul Ruiz)*

Police outside Roosevelt High School, 1970. The signs read, "Call Off the Pigs" and "Schools, Not Jails." *(Raul Ruiz)*

Youngsters from a housing project in East L.A. protest police brutality.
(Raul Ruiz)

Los Angeles Times reporter Rubén
Salazar in Mexico City in a photo
taken in 1967 or 1968, several
years before he was killed by police
during the riot following the August
1970 Chicano Moratorium march.
*(Lisa Salazar Johnson and Mario
T. García)*

Thousands of protesters peacefully march through East L.A. during the first Chicano Moratorium rally against the Vietnam War, held on August 29, 1970. *(Raul Ruiz)*

Police move through a neighborhood in East L.A. firing tear gas after police violence in breaking up the Chicano Moratorium rally sparked a riot. *(Raul Ruiz)*

A Brown Beret member and others watch over a casualty of the violence that followed the second Chicano Moratorium rally in January 1971. A police officer stands over the scene. *(Raul Ruiz)*

Though it is hard to believe that the judges could have understood the cross-section letter to support their system of picking
friends, this is exactly what Judge William Levit argued:

> Q. Do you recognize the rule of law that says that the Grand Jury
> must be representative of a cross-section of the community?
> A. I have no quarrel with that. I would assume that with a hundred
> and thirty-four Judges, selected as they are and each one given the
> right to nominate up to two people, that this would be what I
> would consider a cross-section of the community, broadly de-
> fined.[21]

Judge Richard Fildew gave a similar response even when
Acosta asked him pointedly about racial representation:

> A. I just presume that . . . as the Superior Court should and does, I'm
> sure, represent a cross section of the community from the ethnic
> background we have, Japanese, well, we had a Japanese, we just
> lost him . . . we have people of Mexican background, and then we
> have a few Mexicans that, when they got to the Superior Court,
> became Spanish, and—you know what I'm talking about—and we
> have Negroes, and so forth on this Court, that they were all nomi-
> nating, we were all nominating, and you would get a cross sec-
> tion.[22]

According to many judges, selecting a cross-section of the
community is exactly what they did. These judges understood
the thrust of the presiding judge's letter to commend rather than
to condemn the standard practice of picking one's friends. For
many judges, nominating one's acquaintances became so natural
and appropriate a practice that they understood the presiding
judge's admonition to do otherwise as an injunction to continue
to do the same. For the judges, nominating one's friends operated
as a powerful script—for them, it was simply common sense.

The pick-your-friends script was not only routine but ortho-
dox. The script took on a normative quality, such that it ap-

peared to be natural and legitimate to select one's acquaintances but disconcerting and disrespectful to challenge that practice. This sense of transgression came across when Judge Emmett Doherty responded with hostility to Acosta's question whether he recalled the cross-section language:

> Q. Do you recall the words in the letter . . . relating to representatives of a cross section of the community?
> A. I never received any orders.
> Q. Do you recall the letter?
> A. I was never bound by anything more than my own discretion.[23]

Given Acosta's questions, Judge Doherty's responses make no sense—except as an expression of the judge's conviction that his discretion to select grand jurors should be beyond question.

Common sense functions so powerfully that deviations can appear to be transgressions against a moral or natural order.[24] For the judges put on the stand in *East L.A. Thirteen*, the suggestion that they do otherwise than nominate their friends seemed to have that quality. Nominating grand jurors entailed selecting one's friends—and doing so became routine, legitimate, even rational.[25] The presiding judge's challenge to this process could not be heard, or was heard but misconstrued, or simply repudiated.

Meanwhile, for Acosta, the harder he pushed, the more agitated the judges became. Acosta ultimately challenged not just a particular practice but the judges' identity as possessors of the discretionary power to name their acquaintances as grand jurors—in the end, he challenged reality, which is nothing if not common sense.

RACE AS COMMON SENSE

In selecting grand jurors, the judges drew upon scripts of appropriate professional behavior that developed within the court as a bureaucratic body. But they also relied on general background knowledge, especially with respect to race.

In Los Angeles in 1968, just as here and now, race existed partly as common sense. Racial ideas can be disaggregated in terms of characteristics, categories, and properties. Characteristics refer to the stereotypes that attach to races, such as stock conceptions of Mexicans as lazy, dirty, crime-prone, and inferior, as well as beliefs that whites are rational, just, intelligent, and superior.[26] Ideas regarding group categories include the understandings that specify which groups count as races. The presumed existence of certain racial groups—for instance, whites and Mexicans—constitutes an essential component of racial knowledge, as does the set of ideas regarding which factors—for example ancestry and appearance—define group membership. Finally, ideas about racial properties encompass a culture's understanding of what race is—for instance, assertions that race reflects fundamental biological divisions among humans and contributes to group abilities or shapes a people's destiny. On all of these levels, but more decidedly so with respect to categories and properties, racial ideas operate as common sense.

All racial ideas can be explicitly debated and contested. But they very rarely are. Instead, ideas regarding racial characteristics, categories, and properties usually remain in the background, a body of knowledge so widely shared and so frequently depended upon that most people treat racial beliefs as timeless truths. It is not just their ubiquity, though, that makes racial ideas seem like common sense. In addition, U.S. racial ideology asserts that race is a part of nature, a feature of the physical world that exists outside of culture and beyond control. Race's property as a supposed natural fact combines with the prevalence of racial ideas and practices to ensure that most people take race for granted.

The Los Angeles Superior Court judges incorporated racial common sense in their daily actions. Racial common sense's influence over the judges' actions explains why effectively they nominated their racial peers. The judges' penchant for nominating acquaintances amounted in effect to tapping persons they saw as similar to themselves, and almost invariably this involved picking white people. Acosta offered the following composite of the typical Los Angeles grand juror, but he may as well have been describing the judges:

> From the testimony of the thirty-three judges subpoenaed to testify [in *East L.A. Thirteen*], at times vague if not downright hostile, a reasonable composite of the 1959–1969 "grand juror" was constructed: (1) He is comparatively advanced in years. (2) He is wealthy, of independent financial means. (3) He is, or was, a business owner, executive, or professional—or married to one. (4) He is a close personal friend, occasionally once removed, of a Superior Court Judge. (5) He is White . . . In a word, as characterized by an appellate Judge: WASP.[27]

Although Acosta set out to caricature grand jury nominees, he depicted the judges. Every Superior Court judge shared most of the listed characteristics, and many possessed them all: mature in age, wealthy, professional, male, and white. Charged with the duty to select grand jurors, the judges picked people like themselves.

A racial common sense of white superiority and Mexican inferiority informed the Los Angeles Superior Court judges' nominating practices. A large literature now centers on the cultural significance of white identity. This cultural meaning extends to the cognitive level, where a positive conception of whiteness functions as a default position.[28] Thus, in striking up friendships and in nominating grand jurors the judges drew on assumptions of white social worth and respectability. Some, even many, may have done so consciously. There can be little doubt that a considered preference for white peers informed the social ambitions of many judges. At the same time, other members of the bench may have actively sought out acquaintances across racial lines, taking to heart the civil rights era's integrationist spirit.

But regardless of any conscious decision, every judge on the Superior Court drew on stereotypes of white superiority.[29] The common knowledge regarding race made the superiority of whites "obvious," in the sense that it was simply taken for granted. For social elites such as the judges, their own whiteness (and all but a small handful of the 134 Los Angeles Superior Court judges were white) had facilitated their upward mobility. In turn, it was a matter of course that their personal acquaintances would be similar to them—that is, similarly elite and similarly white. The judges as well as most of society assumed that whiteness formed an essential component of elite identity.

Background beliefs regarding Mexicans also played a role. Irrespective of their level of consciously held prejudice, the Superior Court judges harbored notions of Mexican inferiority. No judge conversant in the culture of California at the time could fail to have been influenced by regnant ideas concerning Mexican character. Stereotypes of Mexican degeneracy—the Mexican as dark, dirty, lazy, cowardly, and criminal—continued to thrive in the late 1960s. Think of the Arrid deodorant commercial with the foul-smelling bandido, or Judge Chargin's explosive expression of anti-Mexican views. The common sense regarding Mexican identity could not be avoided or ignored, though the Chicano movement shows it could be battled. For the majority of judges, it was simply natural that they did not know any Mexicans; quite simply, Mexicans were not the sort of people the judges associated with as social equals. Background presumptions of white worth and Mexican worthlessness powerfully skewed the judges' nomination patterns.

Most judges probably believed that they were not prejudiced against Mexicans, in part because they knew none. But the lack of Mexican acquaintances and the judges' considerable distance from the Mexican community in East Los Angeles—geographically and socially—itself encouraged reliance on racial common sense. To be sure, structural segregation played a crucial role in explaining why the judges had few Mexican friends, as almost no

Mexicans moved through the judges' rarefied neighborhoods and business networks and the judges themselves infrequently or never entered the Mexican Eastside.

Nevertheless, this segregation also had important ramifications for how the judges viewed Mexicans. The judges who did not know Mexicans at all, or only as gardeners and servants, in fact thereby knew Mexicans solely in terms of the common sense of race. Those judges who had no Mexican acquaintances had nothing but common sense to inform their impression of Mexican identity. And for those judges who were acquainted with only Mexican gardeners and servants, the specific identity of the individuals they knew most likely confirmed many of the menial traits associated with the group as a whole.[30] In deciding whom to nominate, the judges looked to their friends. But in choosing their friends, the judges almost uniformly rejected Mexicans.

COMMON SENSE CHANNELS AND THE BEST QUALIFIED

The judges followed a script in nominating their friends, giving their actions little or no thought and accepting them instead as routine and legitimate. Being put in the witness box by Acosta, however, jarred the judges into thinking consciously about their standard operating procedures. No script told the judges how to respond on the stand to Acosta's aggressive questioning, and the setting surely induced considerable conscious, purposeful, strategic thinking on the part of the judges. But the judges were not thereby free from common sense.

Even when scripted or nearly automatic behavior is not appropriate, taken-for-granted ideas proscribe boundaries to thoughts and action. Common sense establishes channels—decision-making frameworks that allow some latitude while still constraining the range of possible alternatives.[31] The background knowledge that provides the nearly indispensable and largely unconsidered basis for rational thought also establishes channels within which such thought most often occurs. In daily life, we continually make decisions, yet these decisions are al-most never based on a complete reevaluation of a situation's ev-ery facet. Instead, we use mental short-cuts to choose from pre-set alternatives. These short-cuts and alternatives often function as common sense.[32]

Scripts and channels compliment each other. Scripted behav-ior describes a first-order phenomenon, in the sense that scripts are spontaneously triggered and involve little or no conscious thought. Channeled behavior implies a second-order phenome-non wherein thoughtfulness occurs but remains constrained. Channels explain how common sense continues to influence be-havior even when individuals self-consciously reject the scripts on which they typically rely. A theory of channeled behavior sug-gests that people rely to some extent on common sense even when they make every effort to ensure that their behavior is solely the product of reasoned thought.

The Chicano cases focused attention on the judges' pattern of nominating their friends to the grand jury, interrupting the judges' easy reliance on a nomination script. Put under a mi-croscope in *East L.A. Thirteen*, the judges defended their prac-tices by insisting that they had intended to nominate only the most qualified persons. Recall that the district attorney asked Judge Call not only about any intent to discriminate but also: "Did you nominate those persons whom you did in fact nomi-nate because you felt they were the best qualified to serve?"[33] Judge Call answered, "Absolutely," summarizing his selection criteria by explaining, "It's a question if they have got the brains or capacity to be on the Grand Jury, is the whole thing in a nut-shell. Very neatly stated."[34] Judge Call's testimony typifies that of the other judges.

Compare how various judges defended their nomination prac-tices: "It wouldn't make any difference who came before me if they are *qualified* as a nominee, but I don't want to nominate people I don't know." "I think it is the duty of each Judge to pick a nominee who he feels is *qualified* for the position, regardless of what race, nationality, or religion he may be." "My primary motivation was to get the most *qualified* people, regardless of race, color, creed, or religion, or national origin." "I think that if they are *qualified* Mexican-Americans, they should be selected." "I would say that getting *qualified* people of various races is good." "Had I known . . . of anyone of a minority group who might have been *qualified* . . . I would have gone out of my way to have appointed him." "It wouldn't make any difference what their ethnic background would be if I felt they were *qualified* to serve as Grand Jurors." "The only attempt I made, as I have indicated, was to select people whom I felt were *qualified* to serve, not on any basis of race, or religion, or nationality, anything like that." "I went out to get the available people who I thought were the *best qualified* to serve as Grand Jurors."[35]

A desire to legitimate their actions motivated the judges to describe their practices as directed toward securing the best-qualified grand jurors. But the likelihood that the judges considered their answers carefully and tailored them to the setting does not mean that the judges lied outright. Rather, the judges probably believed that securing qualified jurors in fact constituted their actual motivation. The legitimacy accorded their claim no doubt stems from our culture's celebration of merit. The claim's *plausibility*, however, especially to the judges themselves, must lie in the judges' conviction that those they nominated actually were the best qualified.[36]

How could the judges have thought that their friends, their tennis buddies, their neighbors and co-Camellia Club members were the best-qualified people to serve as grand jurors? The judges' continued reliance on common sense, in particular racial common sense, accounts for the judges' uniform claim to be nominating the best qualified even as they nominated their white friends.

The discourse of qualifications in the court testimony carried with it a strong racial subtext: qualified persons were white; non-whites were unqualified. This becomes clear in Acosta's questioning of Judge Richard Fildew regarding whether minorities should sit on grand jury panels:

> Q. Do you believe that the Grand Jury should be represented by the different racial and ethnic groups?
> A. If the people are qualified, definitely; if they are not qualified, no.
> Q. I'm talking about the ultimate result, the end result.
> A. I answered you; I said if they are qualified. If the end result is you are getting unqualified people on there, my answer would be definitely no.[37]

Frustrated by Judge Fildew's focus on the "qualified" issue, Acosta attempted to set that question aside:

> Q. I am assuming that the Grand Jury is eventually composed of qualified people. Now, my question is: Do you believe that the ultimate result of any Grand Jury should be that it be composed generally of a cross section of the community?
> A. It would be fine if it could, and I will agree with that, that it would be very nice if it could, but if you are going to impair the quality and get on people just because they are of certain races, then I am not in favor of that.[38]

Acosta grew increasingly irritated with Judge Fildew's implication that placing minorities on the grand jury would amount to seating unqualified jurors, but the judge persisted:

> Q. What do you mean by "impair the quality" by certain people? I don't—
> A. Well, if you are going to get somebody who isn't qualified just because he is an American Indian or an Eskimo, because you have to have an Eskimo on the Grand Jury, but this fellow isn't qualified, I

am against that. I don't think the Grand Jury should be composed of people like that.[39]

Judge Fildew consistently interpreted the suggestion that he should try to include a cross-section of the community as a threat to the quality of the persons on the grand jury.

Racial common sense in the nominate-your-friends script operated only insofar as racial ideas shaped the judges' social orbits. In the context of defending their practices, in contrast, the judges drew on racial common sense much more directly, relying on background stereotypes of white superiority and Mexican inferiority to provide an unexamined foundation to their claim that they had nominated the most qualified persons.

Had the judges in fact set out to recruit those best suited for grand jury service, they could have established a rational process geared to that end. Such an approach might have involved carefully delineating the various tasks grand juries faced, using those tasks to articulate the sorts of skills and knowledge a grand juror required, and then devising some means of evaluating and ranking potential nominees in terms of the relevant criteria. But the judges did none of this.

Instead, the judges drew generally on racial common sense concerning the competence, virtue, and social respectability of different groups. The judges most likely developed an unexamined image of a prototypical grand juror, and then matched potential nominees against this prototype.[40] Racial ideas about various groups would have heavily influenced how the judges envisioned the "typical" grand juror. In addition, this vision would have incorporated the judges' evaluations of past grand jurors' most salient features, where such persons were overwhelmingly white. The racial identity of past grand jurors, itself a function of prior discrimination, bolstered the unexamined certainty that whites were well-suited to become grand jurors, and that other races were not. Beliefs regarding racial group characteristics combined with patterns established by past discrimination to provide the judges with a composite picture of a typical grand juror that prominently featured a white face. By this equation, racial minorities were outside the qualified pool. More than that, the push to include minorities on grand juries violated the judges' sense of what was natural, and so seemed unfair and improper, even discriminatory. Here is the final significance of Judge Fildew's relentless insistence on linking the question whether minorities should sit on grand juries to the dangers of impaneling unqualified jurors. This judge simply could not understand minority representation on the grand jury except as a threat to merit; he typified those Los Angeles Superior Court judges for whom "qualified" described themselves and their friends, not minorities. Through racial common sense, the judges' nominations of their white friends emerged as the race-neutral and legitimate seating of qualified grand jurors. In contrast, the cross-section requirement appeared to illegitimately demand the race-conscious inclusion of unqualified minorities. Many judges perceived racial discrimination not in the almost exclusive nomination of their white acquaintances but in the demand for minority representation.

COMMON SENSE RACISM

The presiding judges in *East L.A. Thirteen* and *Biltmore Six* held that an intent to discriminate was a predicate for racist behavior. This understanding now reigns under U.S. Supreme Court doctrine. But it is wrong: especially today, racism is largely common sense.[41]

Common sense is so integral to racism in the contemporary United States that I suggest a new definition: racism is action arising out of racial common sense and enforcing racial hierarchy. I specifically include the requirement that racism enforce hierarchy in order to preserve "racism" as a term that describes actions that perpetuate racial status inequality.[42] The intentional use of race to counteract racial inequality, for instance through affirmative action, is not racism. In the United States, racial hierarchy is rooted in white supremacy. As a result, racism occurs whether one injures minorities or favors whites.[43]

By this definition, the Los Angeles Superior Court judges' actions qualify as racism. Their reliance on background racial ideas led directly to behavior that privileged whites and excluded Mexicans from grand jury service. It matters on the level of moral culpability that the judges did not intend to discriminate. But on the level of racial harm, the judges' intentions are irrelevant. By relying uncritically on racial common sense in a way that supported white supremacy, the judges engaged in racism.

Of course, not all racism is unintentional. Many people purposefully discriminate, as surely some of the Los Angeles Superior Court judges did.[44] To engage in purposeful racism, though, is not to shed but to embrace common sense understandings of race. Those judges who consciously discriminated against Mexicans did so not in spite of but because of unconsidered notions of racial difference.[45]

The difference between purposeful and common sense racism does not lie in whether background ideas of race play a prominent role, for racial common sense undergirds all forms of racism. Nor does the distinction lie in the presence or absence of consciously considered action. Recall that even when people act purposefully, common sense continues to channel their decision-making. Instead, purposeful racism is "common sense racism plus." Common sense racism is action arising out of racial common sense that furthers racial hierarchy. Purposeful racism is that, *plus* the conscious decision to do racial harm. In addition to reliance on background ideas of race, purposeful racism involves a *knowing decision* to increase racial inequality.

Understanding racism as common sense has three important implications. First, racism is ubiquitous. Racial common sense is just that, a widely shared, taken-for-granted set of ideas within the culture. Just about everyone relies on such ideas, and just about everyone practices racism. When racial common sense informs how you think about others and the world around you (and it often does), and when you rely on these background ideas in ways that support racial inequality (and this frequently happens), you have engaged in racism. The racism evident in the Los Angeles Superior Court judges' actions typifies the racism prevalent throughout the criminal justice system and, indeed, across law and society generally.

Second, the common sense quality of racism ensures that good intentions do not guarantee against racist conduct. Recall that the prosecutor directly queried the judges on whether they had intended to discriminate, and all of them denied it. Almost all of the judges believed their negative answer, even as they continued to rely on background racial beliefs in determining who would sit on the grand jury. Script analysis shows how the judges thoughtlessly discriminated by blindly following a uniform selection practice centered on picking friends. But channel analysis makes clear the judges' remarkable commitment to the same practice even *after* they assured themselves that they did not intend to discriminate. *Assurances of self-reflection and innocent intent, even when genuine, do not eliminate the possibility of racism.* Common sense racism occurs even under exacting self-examination and with the purest of intentions.

Finally, conceptualizing racism as common sense suggests that racism is highly intractable.[46] Racial scripts and channels pervade our society, and these background patterns and understandings are not easily defeated. For individuals to overcome common sense racism, they must recognize bias in their thinking, correctly estimate its extent, and exercise sufficient control over their mental processes to actually allow correction.[47] Far higher hurdles confront efforts to remake racial common sense on a group- or culture-wide basis. Calling into question what otherwise seems normal and right jeopardizes one's social standing. Because race operates as common sense, challenging racial inequality becomes tantamount to attacking orthodoxy—rather than being heard and debated, the challenger is more likely to be dismissed and possibly judged insane. The claim that "this is wrong" engenders the retort that "you're crazy." In addition, organizing large groups and mobilizing people to oppose widely-shared opinions raises collective action problems. Fighting for social change entails large personal risks but generates benefits for all. Many people will sit back, while those who stand will come into conflict with one another over issues of strategy, leadership, and goals.

These roadblocks pale, however, when set alongside the problem of motivation. To the extent that racial ideas and practices support a stratified society, the current distribution of power and prestige depends on racial common sense. All but those at the very bottom continually rediscover that they have some stake in keeping things the way they are, even if in other ways they realize that the status quo harms them. Racial activists must be willing to risk whatever privilege their racial standing gives them. Beyond that, though, proponents of racial change must overcome the determined opposition of those who benefit in some way from racial hierarchy. These beneficiaries will include many people within the very groups the militants seek to help. And then, of course, racial insurgents must enlist significant numbers of whites to work against their own racial advantage. Without white participation, racial change does not occur in the United States.

Despite these daunting hurdles, people and communities have long struggled and advanced in efforts to combat racism. Historically, such efforts have involved broad campaigns against the inequalities created by racial practices, as well as concerted efforts to discourage purposeful racism. But they have also included attempts to reformulate basic understandings of race. All of these efforts alter racial common sense. From this point of view, the Chicano movement can be understood as a sustained effort to combat the common sense of race.[48]

UNCONSCIOUS AND INSTITUTIONAL RACISM

The contention that racism is common sense appears similar to the argument describing racism as largely unconscious, in the Freudian sense. This argument typically posits that whites experience a conflict between internalized racist beliefs and more socially acceptable ideas of racial egalitarianism, and that the desire to avoid feelings of guilt associated with racial animus leads the conscious mind to suppress such animus without fully defeating it.[49] Psychoanalytic theories also underlie the aversive racism thesis, which posits that whites experience anxiety and discomfort (rather than overt hostility) in the presence of minorities because of the tension between social norms they consciously hold and unacknowledged racial biases.[50]

In contrast to these theories, I do not attribute common sense racism to individual psychology. An emphasis on psychodynamics in the study of racism produces a somewhat strained methodology, wherein strong claims about *individual* psychological responses rub uneasily against the careful examination of *group* practices. I posit that group interaction, not conflicts within individuals, generate racial common sense. To be sure, this taken-for-granted knowledge in turn influences individual behavior. But it remains the ideas and practices within specific cultural settings that determine common sense and thus lay the groundwork for common sense racism.

Common sense and Freudian processes do not exclude one another—one might engage in both unconscious and common sense racism. These processes, however, remain distinct. Racial common sense informs action not through the relatively hot processes of egotistical turmoil and repression but through a cooler dynamic of cognitive distortion. Individuals are not struggling to reconcile conflicting values and thoughts but are operating as socialized group members according to an accepted manner of thinking and acting. When people treat racial ideas as a legitimate, expected part of the natural order, common sense racism often results.

While there is some distance between claims of common sense and unconscious racism, common sense racism could also go by the name "institutional racism," a label I have used before.[51] Stokely Carmichael and Charles Hamilton introduced the phrase in 1967, the year before the East Los Angeles student protests erupted, to explain harms inflicted on minorities that cannot be traced to the actions of individual racists:[52]

> Racism is both overt and covert. It takes two, closely related forms: individual whites acting against individual blacks, and acts by the total white community against the black community. We call these individual racism and institutional racism . . . When white terrorists bomb a black church and kill five black children, that is an act of individual racism, widely deplored by most segments of society. But when in that same city—Birmingham, Alabama—five hundred black babies die each year because of the lack of proper food, shelter and medical facilities . . . that is a function of institutional racism.[53]

References to institutional racism gained popularity in the 1970s and 1980s as a means of highlighting the way that racial inequality continued and by some measures deepened even though overt acts of individual racial hostility were abating.[54] Institutional racism is a term still frequently invoked by many.[55] Nevertheless, a theory of institutional racism has been elusive, with the term functioning more often as a label for a problem than as a theory of social behavior. For some, institutional racism amounts to intentional racism in institutions—that is, purposeful discrimination in formally organized settings.[56] For others, it refers to widespread race-neutral practices that impose harmful effects on minority communities, irrespective of the attitudes of individual decision makers.[57] While the first model focuses on purposeful action, the second denies the relevance of individual behavior altogether.

Common sense racism analysis hews between these extremes,

focusing on behavior yet positing that such behavior is rooted not primarily in intentions but in accepted grammars of meaning and action. Common sense racism suggests that in their daily lives most individuals act to entrench racial hierarchy, though by relying on background racial understandings rather than discriminating purposefully. Institutional racism is a more widely known term, and Oscar Acosta himself used this idea in summarizing his defense strategy: "I contended that all Grand Juries are racist since all grand jurors have to be recommended by Superior Court judges and that the whole thing reeks of 'subconscious, institutional racism.'"[58] In referring to common sense racism, I try to introduce a term grounded in theory that will also resonate strongly in the popular sphere. Common sense racism expresses the idea that racial discrimination is standard and accepted, even among those who consciously intend not to discriminate. Nevertheless, of far greater importance than the label is the underlying claim: racism is routine.

LAW ENFORCEMENT AND

LEGAL VIOLENCE

The defendants in the Chicano cases complained bitterly about the courts discriminating against Mexicans. Yet on a day-to-day basis the Mexican community interacted much more regularly with law enforcement agencies. In East Los Angeles, these included primarily the Los Angeles police and sheriff's departments. With both agencies, brutality against East Los Angeles's residents was routine.

In 1968 the Los Angeles Police Department (LAPD) was arguably the most professional and most respected police force in the country. The untrained and dishonest officers of the 1930s who earned L.A. the reputation for having a corrupt and incompetent police force had been replaced by a disciplined cadre of obedient, physically fit, and neatly dressed police.[1] Behind this transformation stood William Parker, the Los Angeles Chief of Police from 1950 to 1966. Parker, a national leader in the police professionalization movement, transformed the LAPD into a model big city police force.[2] The television series *Dragnet* promoted the new LAPD officers as coldly efficient crime fighters, "civil to all, polite to none."[3] Parker himself possessed a national reputation in law enforcement exceeded only by that of FBI Director J. Edgar Hoover.[4]

Core reforms pursued by Parker included the institution of civil service standards in promotions and dismissals, as well as increased political autonomy for the police force. In addition, however, police professionalization involved two innovations that together pitted the LAPD against minority communities: the development of a "statistical" approach to force deployment, and a "crime-prevention" orientation.

Chief Parker explained both innovations in 1957 when he published his ideas on policing under the title *Parker on Police.*[5] The statistical and crime-prevention approaches figured prominently in the chief's philosophy regarding police deployment in minority communities:

> Every department worth its salt deploys field forces on the basis of crime experience. Deployment is often heaviest in so-called minority sections of the city. The reason is statistical—it is a fact that certain racial groups, at the present time, commit a disproportionate share of the total crime. Let me make one point clear in that regard—a competent police administrator is fully aware of the multiple conditions which create this problem. There is no inherent physical or mental weakness in any racial stock which tends it toward crime. But, and this is a "but" which must be borne constantly in mind— police field deployment is not social agency activity. In deploying to suppress crime, we are not interested in why a certain group tends toward crime, we are interested in maintaining order.[6]

Statistical policing used arrest numbers and other indicators of criminal activity to assign law enforcement personnel. Crime prevention deployed police power primarily in anticipation of, rather than in response to, criminal conduct.

Both the statistical and the crime-prevention model had antecedents in the LAPD's engagement with minority communities through 1950. From 1924 to 1949, the LAPD compiled statistics on arrests tabulated by race, counting Mexicans as "red."[7] These statistics assisted the LAPD in identifying minority communities as special threats to law and order. From the 1920s onward, the department began to link race and crime, and race gradually gained in significance as an explanation for criminal conduct.[8]

Crime statistics tied to race seemingly confirmed a criminal propensity among minorities generally, and reinforced stereotypes regarding Mexican criminality specifically.[9] Recall the 1942 Ayres Report, issued by the sheriff's department after the *Sleepy Lagoon* indictments. That report tracked the LAPD's conception of Mexicans as both Indians and criminals: "The Mexican Indian is mostly Indian—and that is the element which migrated to the United States in such large numbers and looks upon leniency by authorities as an evidence of weakness or fear, or else considers that he was able to outsmart the authorities . . . Again, let us repeat, the hoodlum element as a whole must be indicted as a whole. The time to rehabilitate them is both before and after the crime has been committed."[10]

The sheriff's reference to cracking down on the hoodlum element not just after but also *before* a crime had been committed corresponds to the second important evolution in the LAPD's practices. After the Depression, a rapprochement between unionized labor and business interests in Los Angeles effectively eliminated the LAPD's earlier role as a bulwark against labor organizing in that city.[11] The LAPD's reduced role raised the specter of reduced funding, so in response the department articulated a new mission for itself: it would conduct a war on crime.[12] The LAPD increasingly presented itself as a force that would not merely respond to crime, but one that would actively suppress criminal elements before they committed illegal acts.

Chief Parker harnessed together these two changes in policing. Insofar as crime statistics purportedly identified minorities as criminals, and the police promised to suppress criminals before they committed crimes, Parker's police professionalization became a public promise to forcefully control minority communities. For William Parker and the LAPD, racial suppression emerged as the department's mission, albeit suppression defended mainly in the clinical and sterile language of crime facts and arrest statistics. Parker often insisted that aggressively policing minority communities reflected not racism but reality: "Discrimination is not a factor . . . If persons of Mexican, Negro, or Anglo-Saxon ancestry, for some reason, contribute heavily to other forms of crime, police deployment must take that into account. From an ethnological point of view, Negro, Mexican and Anglo-Saxon are unscientific breakdowns; they are fiction. From a police point of view, they are a useful fiction and should be used as long as they remain useful."[13] Parker instituted a modern police model that was technical and purportedly antiracist and yet supremely race-conscious. The LAPD saw its job as policing minorities.

POLICING THE WILD TRIBES

The LAPD was rife with both conscious and common sense racism.[14] Purposeful racism almost certainly operated among the LAPD officers to a greater degree than among the Los Angeles Superior Court judges during the same period. Joseph Woods, a generally laudatory student of Los Angeles police reform, called the LAPD under Chief Parker "a bastion of white supremacy." "Departmental regulations forbade racial discrimination, but the notion of white supremacy, rooted deep in the working class society that spawned most policemen, seemed to flourish in the corrupting situations that the gun, badge, and uniform encouraged."[15] Woods described a "well known incident" in which "the day room of a police station featured a picture of Eleanor Roosevelt with the words 'nigger lover' scrawled on its face. Blacks removed the photo, but a similar one, bearing the same epithet, soon replaced it."[16]

Racism flourished no doubt partly because Chief Parker himself was an overt bigot. Parker routinely sought to parlay white fears of minorities into support for the police department. He usually did so using coded language, for instance by constantly proclaiming that the LAPD was the "thin blue line" between "civilization" and "chaos."[17] But at other times, Parker made his racial meaning abundantly clear. In 1965 Parker warned a television reporter "that by 1970, 45 percent of the metropolitan area

138 RACISM ON TRIAL

of Los Angeles will be Negro. If you want any protection for your home and family, you're going to have to get in and support a strong police department. If you don't do that, come 1970, God help you!"[18]

Parker also expressed racist views about Mexicans. In 1960, in testimony regarding police-minority relations delivered before a panel from the U.S. Commission on Civil Rights, Chief Parker offered this revealing appraisal: "The Latin population that came here in great strength were here before us, and presented a great problem because I worked over on the East Side when men had to work in pairs . . . and it's because of some of these people being not too far removed from the wild tribes of the district of the inner mountains of Mexico. I don't think you can throw the genes out of the question when you discuss behavior patterns of people."[19] Echoing the remarks of the Ayres Report eighteen years earlier, Parker insisted that genes—or, in still more graphic language, descent "from the wild tribes . . . of the inner mountains of Mexico"—determined Mexican character.

Parker's occasional lapse into language that openly invoked demeaning racial stereotypes contrasts with the dispassionate discourse Parker usually favored to justify LAPD practices. In response to public criticism of his testimony, Parker returned to statistics to defend himself. Protesting that "It's 'get Parker' time," Parker asserted that his critics sought to divert attention from Mexican crime rates by attacking the police: "In plain fact," he contended, Mexicans committed five times more offenses per capita than whites. Parker offered "cultural conflict" as a possible explanation, then decided that he could not explain crime among Mexicans; after all, he was not a "sociologist."[20] Along similar lines, Parker also routinely alleged that complaints about police brutality from the NAACP and ACLU were designed to divert attention from the high crime rate among blacks.[21]

Parker used crime statistics to defend as purportedly race-neutral both his views regarding minorities and the LAPD's aggressive policing of minority communities. Arrest statistics ostensibly established Mexican and black criminality and in turn justified police practices and attitudes. But Parker had the causal relationship backwards. The statistics did not produce accurate group generalizations or justify intense police pressure. Rather, racial stereotypes combined with abusive police practices to produce high arrest and incarceration rates.

MEXICAN CRIME STATISTICS

In a 1972 study Armando Morales compared arrest statistics and major crime rates for two Los Angeles regions, East Los Angeles and the West San Fernando Valley area.[22] Morales relied on LAPD jurisdictional boundaries and reports but also incorporated statistics from the sheriff's station that policed East Los Angeles's unincorporated areas. The East Los Angeles and West Valley regions defined by police boundaries had similar populations of 260,000 residents each, although the East Los Angeles zone was half as large. Within that region, persons with Spanish surnames accounted for between 50 and 60 percent of the population, while in the West Valley jurisdiction whites comprised 95 percent of the population.[23]

What, then, of the respective crime rates? Both regions had almost exactly the same ratio of major crimes to population, 4.9 percent in East Los Angeles and 4.8 percent in the West Valley region.[24] That is, when measured in terms of major crimes, there was very little difference in the crime rates between the white and Mexican areas of Los Angeles.

While the overall ratio of major crimes did not differ, the police presence in the respective communities did: 375 law enforcement officers operated in East Los Angeles, compared with 151 in the West Valley region. Law enforcement officers numbered 1.5 per 1,000 East Los Angeles residents, compared with 0.6 officers per 1,000 West Valley residents; in the geographically more compressed Eastside, roughly four times as many police officers patrolled each square mile.[25] These numbers suggest a dramatically different level of policing in East Los Angeles.

The increased police presence on the Eastside manifested itself in far higher arrest rates for minor infractions. In the East Los Angeles area in 1968, LAPD officers and sheriffs made 6,676 arrests for drunkenness or drunk driving, roughly 26 arrests for every 1,000 persons. In addition, the California Highway Patrol (CHP) made another 3,000 such arrests, raising the ratio to about 37 arrests per 1,000 persons. In the West Valley area, by comparison, the LAPD made arrests on the same charges at a ratio of 6 per 1,000 persons (figures for CHP arrests were not available for this region). Excluding the CHP arrests, the arrest rate for alcohol-related offenses was 430 percent greater in East Los Angeles than in the West Valley; with the CHP numbers, persons in East L.A. were over six times more likely to be arrested on a drunk or drunk driving charge. These alcohol arrests made up *over 50 percent* of all arrests in East Los Angeles.

Did these arrest numbers reflect different rates of alcohol abuse? No. The California Department of Public Health found an identical level of alcoholism in both regions. The disparity in alcohol-related arrests must be explained on some ground other than differing patterns of alcohol abuse.[26]

The explanation is more likely racial prejudice. High arrest levels of Mexicans for liquor-related offenses continued a pattern established early in the twentieth century. In 1923 a police report noted that 48 percent of all Mexican arrests involved either alcohol or vagrancy. The report opined that "our Mexican population who are caught in the meshes of the law are very largely in trouble because of weakness of will and lack of initiative."[27] In 1928 liquor and vagrancy charges accounted for over 70 percent of all LAPD arrests of Mexicans. After that year vagrancy charges dropped off but liquor charges picked up the slack; in 1936 alcohol offenses alone accounted for 76 percent of the

LAPD arrests of Mexicans.[28] As mentioned, in 1968 they still counted for half the arrests in East Los Angeles.

Alcohol-related arrests both reflected and supported pervasive stereotypes of Mexican degeneracy among law enforcement personnel. This is not to say that alcohol abuse did not trouble the Mexican community, for it did—though, again, not at a level any different from that in the Anglo community. Rather, police discretion, exercised in a context of racial prejudice, produced high rates of arrest for minor offenses among Mexicans as compared with whites.[29] Officers arrested Mexicans for conduct they overlooked in the white community, especially among the middle and upper classes.

Purposeful racism partly explains this pattern. Some law enforcement officers consciously set out to harass Mexicans because of a race-based antipathy to that group. But these statistics also resulted from, and further buttressed, common sense knowledge regarding Mexicans. Police vigorously pursued liquor violations in the Mexican community because they took for granted that drunkenness and crime went hand-in-hand with Mexican identity. In turn, these statistics became the hard numbers that proved the "fact" of Mexican criminality. Chief Parker's arrest figures, cited to justify aggressive police deployment in minority communities, reflected not the reality of criminality that Parker suggested but the predictable consequence of racial prejudice.

ROUTINE VIOLENCE

In communities like East Los Angeles, racial prejudice produced more than increased arrests; it also fueled high levels of police violence. In a legislative hearing on police–community relations held in East Los Angeles in 1972, Preston Guillery, a former deputy posted to the East Los Angeles sheriff's station in the late 1960s, testified regarding normal police practices. Guillery affirmed that arbitrary stops were the order of the day: "It's quite normal for suspects, in East Los Angeles, to be arbitrarily

stopped and searched without justification, merely because
they're in East Los Angeles—which, at the time I was there, was
felt by officers to be more or less of an occupied area."[30] He also
testified that physical beatings routinely accompanied arrests:

> One of my first experiences as a trainee was making arrests in East
> Los Angeles one evening. I believe it was a narcotics arrest. After the
> actual arrest had been made and we began driving toward the East
> LA Station to book our suspect, the suspect made some comment to
> my partner which my partner took offense to—he was a senior of-
> ficer with about, I believe, 15 years in the department, I was sitting in
> the back directly behind my partner, and the suspect was on my right.
> The officer pulled off onto a side street, in the dark, parked the car,
> and began beating the suspect about the head and face with his sap
> for having opened his mouth. He then reached back and grabbed the
> suspect so he could have a better hold on him and continued to beat
> him with his sap. Another patrol car pulled alongside, and the officer
> inquired as to what was going on. My partner responded that he was
> advising the suspect about his conduct. The officer smiled, and he
> and his partner drove off. Because in East LA this isn't the sort of
> thing that causes an officer to stop and look twice. It's accepted pro-
> cedure . . . People in East Los Angeles who are arrested expect, as
> part of their arrest procedure, that they may be beaten. Their uncles,
> their brothers, their friends that they know who have been arrested
> have quite often been subjected to beatings . . . It isn't only in the
> black and white cars that beatings sometimes take place. They take
> place in the station, with full knowledge of the watch sergeant, and
> sometimes often the watch commander.[31]

After beating someone, Guillery reported, a standard procedure ensued: "In the sheriff's academy, officers are told that if
you ever hit a suspect, or have to strike a person, that person
shall be arrested for assaulting a police officer. Yet, it is usually
the suspect that winds up getting medical attention, after he's
beaten to the ground by the officer. But, whenever you touch a
suspect, or hit him in any way, you must arrest him for assault,
assault on a police officer."[32] Rudy Acuña, a historian of East Los

Angeles, corroborates Guillery's dismal report on sheriff's department practices: "For most people, especially those outside Los Angeles, the sheriff's deputies are probably less known for their brutality than the LAPD—but they deserve a similar reputation."[33]

The ACLU of Southern California published a study in 1969 regarding the police violence suffered by East Los Angeles residents.[34] In 1966, responding to widespread police malpractice, the ACLU set up an office in East Los Angeles as well as one in Watts to assist police brutality victims in pursuing claims against law enforcement agencies.[35] Between August 1966 and July 1968 the East Los Angeles office identified 205 cases "in which there was a substantial belief that police malpractice occurred."[36] Among these, 108 cases involved the LAPD and 76 involved the sheriff's office.[37] There were 153 claims of extreme physical abuse, defined as "two or more blows by a police officer on an unresisting civilian."[38]

The ACLU reported the charges, if any, brought by the police against the victims. Among the 205 victims in East Los Angeles, 162 were charged with an offense. But most charges were for crimes committed against the police: 59 charges for assault on an officer, 29 for interfering with a police officer, and 28 for resisting arrest.[39] Guillery's testimony suggests that most of these charges were false, designed only to protect the officers. For crimes not committed against the police, 33 were alcohol-related, followed by 25 charges of disturbing the peace, and 14 citations for vehicle code infractions.[40] Law enforcement officers brought only 5 charges for narcotics possession and 15 charges for other felonies against the 205 victims of police brutality.[41] There were only 20 serious charges against the more than 200 persons who had credible claims of having suffered police brutality. The ACLU concluded that the "largest number of crimes allegedly committed took place only after police arrived on the scene. In most cases, those arrested find themselves booked for no substantive crime (burglary, robbery, etc.) but only for 'crimes' against the police."[42] Those beaten by the LAPD and the sheriff's deputies had not committed hard-core criminal acts; rather, they were East Los Angeles residents randomly caught out on the streets.

For many, the beatings and the subsequent prosecution for crimes against the police made them into the criminals the police apparently already thought them to be. Among those actually tried on criminal charges for whom the case disposition was known, 12 were found not guilty, but 48 were convicted. Assault on an officer, the most common charge against those beaten by the police, was a felony that carried a ten-year penalty.[43] People beaten by the police often found themselves on trial with almost everything at stake: their reputation, their family life, their job, their freedom. For victims of police brutality, the actual assault was often just the beginning of a long ordeal that devastated their lives.[44]

The ACLU also compiled statistics on the number of officers involved in each episode of brutality, as well as the number of witnesses. These numbers drove the ACLU to conclude that police violence was overwhelmingly routine. The report conservatively estimated that "approximately 10 percent of sworn law enforcement personnel have been identified as actively engaging in some form of police malpractice," though "the percentage may well be higher." In addition, "in the greatest number of cases, there were witnesses."[45] More than three-quarters of the 205 cases of probable misconduct in East Los Angeles occurred in front of others. The vast majority of victims corroborated their account through the testimony of between one and four persons who saw the violence. The high proportion of officers involved in brutality and the consistent presence of witnesses led the ACLU to conclude: "Malpractice is not, apparently, a furtive thing confined to the station house . . . The cases gathered at the centers indicate that police malpractice in one or another form is a routine part of police work . . . Police malpractice may occur at any time, and in any place, and apparently without the officers feeling any great fear of punishment despite the large number of police and civilian witnesses."[46] Excessive violence against Mexicans was part of the work-a-day world of law enforcement in East Los Angeles, an accepted and expected part of the job.

POLICE DISSERVICE

The police not only frequently engaged in abuse, but also commonly refused to provide typical police services. To begin with, the police refused to punish officers who engaged in brutality. The ACLU reported that despite its intervention and advocacy on behalf of victims, only 90 cases were resolved after two years, only 6 of these resulted in dispositions favoring the complainant, though "in no case was the punishment made known to the victim."[47] Compare the police department's zeal in punishing infractions of internal department policy. In 1965 the LAPD's disciplinary body upheld 5.6 percent of the 231 citizen complaints alleging excessive use of force, but 81 percent of the internally generated complaints involving neglect of duty.[48] The respective punishments also reflected this disregard for citizen's complaints but concern for internal discipline. In 1968 two officers who "discharged service revolvers at a suspect" without sufficient cause were given "reprimands," but an officer found sleeping while on jail duty was suspended for four days.[49] The police enforced internal discipline but brushed aside crimes committed by the police against civilians.

Perhaps more detrimental to the community, the police also refused to provide essential services in East Los Angeles, the sort provided as a matter of course in Anglo communities. Former deputy Guillery testified about the harrowing disregard for human life and well-being this disservice reflected:

Other stations I worked, and in Malibu, when a citizen called in with a call that was of an emergency nature, that being a drug overdose, an attempted suicide, a serious injury involving a child, a drowning child, these stations would dispatch the radio unit (the black and white patrol unit) on what is called "Code 3," red light and siren.

East Los Angeles would not send a patrol unit with red light and siren . . . [In] East Los Angeles it was not uncommon for the desk man
to send a radio car on normal response before sending the ambulance
or the requested emergency equipment to verify there actually was a
need for that equipment. In East Los Angeles a citizen's word that a
piece of emergency equipment is needed is not always sufficient to
justify the dispatching of that equipment.[50]

Stop and imagine the frustration and anger you would feel if
the police responded to your call for help on behalf of a seriously
injured child by sending a patrol car, in no particular hurry, to
confirm whether an emergency existed. East Los Angeles residents lived daily with just this frustration and anger, on top of
the fear and intense resentment borne of perennially being the
potential victims of police violence.

In 1970 the U.S. Commission on Civil Rights published its report on the administration of justice in the Southwest. It corroborated the existence of "widespread patterns of police misconduct against Mexican Americans," including "excessive police
violence."[51] It also found that Mexicans felt alienated from and
oppressed by the law. "The attitude of Mexican Americans toward the institutions responsible for the administration of justice—the police, the courts, and related agencies—is distrustful,
fearful, and hostile. Police departments, courts, and the law itself
are viewed as Anglo institutions in which Mexican Americans
have no stake and from which they do not expect fair treatment."[52] At the onset of the Chicano movement, a routine of
brutality and neglect characterized police conduct in East Los
Angeles and in turn engendered deep community resentment.

POLICING SUBVERSIVES

When the Mexican community in East Los Angeles began politically mobilizing in late 1967 and early 1968, activists focused
initially on education, but they also expressed concern over police malpractice. Law enforcement agencies reacted to this political mobilization with the characteristic aggressiveness reserved

for minority communities. In addition, though, Los Angeles police drew on past experiences in suppressing "radicals" during the McCarthy era, and they also learned from the national law enforcement reaction to minority activism.[53] As models of apparently appropriate police conduct, these interactions added a new common sense regarding East Los Angeles: not only were minorities criminals but minority activists were ideological enemies.

LAPD Chief Parker believed that minority mobilization resulted from communist infiltration, a conclusion he initially applied to Los Angeles's African American community. Before the Watts riot in 1965, Parker argued that minority communities in L.A. were basically passive and apathetic, if not actually content with their social position. He steadfastly maintained that "race violence could not and would not occur in Los Angeles because of good relations between the police and the black community." According to Parker, "the old established Negro community" knew they were well-treated and understood that "Los Angeles is not Birmingham."[54]

Despite these assurances, in 1965 riots tore Watts apart. Touched off by a botched arrest for a minor traffic violation, this uprising lasted seven days, burned large sections of Los Angeles, killed 34 people, and destroyed $40 million in property. The LAPD, the sheriff's department, the California National Guard, and the U.S. Army used massive force and made 4,000 arrests to reassert control.[55] The riot's shattering events did not, however, lead Parker to reassess his belief that blacks were basically satisfied. In the riot's wake, Parker dismissed suggestions that the conflagration reflected longstanding grievances against the police or fundamental political discontent. Instead, the chief thought he spotted "communists in the ghetto"—he accused the Communist Party of stirring unrest in black areas and neutralizing the supposedly complacent leadership there.[56]

Significantly, in the wake of the riot, white esteem for Parker and the LAPD solidified. According to Joseph Woods, a police reform scholar, "Whites, especially conservatives, gave the chief broad support. The *Times* and the *Examiner,* the mayor and the city council, the county board of supervisors and many writers of letters to newspaper editors praised the chief and the department . . . The post-Watts period found Chief Parker at the height of his influence. He had the white majority behind him and he knew it." [57]

In 1966, at the pinnacle of his career and with unprecedented influence over the LAPD and Los Angeles generally, Chief Parker died. He was succeeded in turn by Tom Reddin, Edward Davis, and eventually Daryl Gates, the police chief during the 1992 riots that resulted from the acquittal of the officers tried for beating Rodney King. All three successors have been described as "Parker clones." [58] Certainly, they each apparently accepted Parker's belief that protest in minority communities stemmed not from local grievances but from world communism.

In 1967, at a national meeting of police chiefs hosted by the FBI, Chief Reddin declared that the "Negro movement . . . is just as subversive as the past Communist movement," adding that to prevent urban unrest the police should go for "overkill—kill the butterfly with a sledge hammer." [59] As police chief in 1970, Ed Davis warned that Chicano groups, including the Brown Berets, were "avowedly Communist-Marxist"; that Mexican youths were being manipulated by "swimming pool Communists" and "Bolsheviks"; and that communist revolutionaries were infiltrating "Negroes, Mexicans, homosexuals—any dissident group." [60] In 1971 Davis criticized a rare federal effort to prosecute police officers for recklessly killing two Mexicans in what the police called a case of mistaken identity. The chief charged that the prosecution amounted to "harassment of police by federal authorities which encourages people like the Chicano Moratorium Committee, Brown Berets, the Black Panther Party, and any Marxist organization. Why, it encourages them to perform." [61] Then Assistant Chief Gates joined in this chorus presenting minority activists as Bolshevik agents, claiming in a 1970 Chamber of Commerce address that minority protest movements aspired to "a revolution against the free enterprise system."[62]

The common sense that linked minority protest to communism prompted an immediate, powerful law enforcement response to politicized groups in East Los Angeles after the high school student walkouts. Coincidentally, on the day before the blowout, J. Edgar Hoover had circulated a memo to top law enforcement officers throughout the country urging them to target minority nationalist movements.[63] In the walkouts' wake, Hoover took a personal interest in Mexican activism, ordering a "penetrative" and "aggressive" investigation of Mexican groups:

> There has been a recent rise in the formation of various Mexican-American organizations mostly throughout the Southwestern part of the United States. While they all originate with the purpose of bettering the educational, economic, and general stature of the Mexican-Americans . . . experience has shown that these organizations do become more militant and aggressive as time goes on. Certain . . . organizations are coming under communist influence and are holding classes in Marxist-Leninist ideology. Others . . . are arming themselves and holding classes in weaponry. Others have tried to align themselves or cooperated in activities of the Black Panther Party . . . Your investigation . . . should be penetrative and receive aggressive attention.[64]

Heeding this advice, both the LAPD and sheriff's department in 1968 placed undercover agents among the Chicano activists.[65]

Law enforcement plants in Mexican organizations did much more than gather information; they acted as provocateurs, disrupting the organizations and providing excuses for raids and arrests.[66] Consider the actions of Eustacio "Frank" Martínez, an agent of the Alcohol, Tobacco, and Firearms Division of the U.S. Department of the Treasury. Recruited from Texas, where he had infiltrated the local Brown Berets organization, Martínez arrived in Los Angeles in October 1970 and rose to leadership in the

Chicano Moratorium Committee, an organization opposed to the war in Vietnam.[67] Martínez fomented dissension between the anti-war group and the Brown Berets that eventually caused a bitter rift between the two organizations. He also provoked police attacks, on one occasion walking the sidewalk in front of the Moratorium Committee office brandishing a shotgun and on another attacking police officers during a demonstration. The shotgun incident sparked a police raid with drawn weapons and swinging clubs that led to numerous arrests and put three people in the hospital.[68] The January 1971 anti-war demonstration staged under Martínez's leadership ended in a riot in which police killed one person and injured scores of others; the riot finally destroyed the Moratorium organization.[69] When Police Chief Davis blamed violence in the Chicano movement on infiltration by a "small, hard core group of subversives," he was talking about a supposed communist vanguard, but his comments more accurately described the activities of undercover law enforcement personnel.[70]

Militant organizations were not the only targets of an ideologically inspired police hostility. Just about anyone conceivably associated with a left political position was also targeted, as testimony from sheriff's deputy Guillery makes clear: "Any car bearing a bumper sticker indicating 'Boycott Grapes,' 'Boycott Lettuce,' that sort of thing, [was] stopped . . . Because it indicated the person was probably interested in the grape strike, Cesar Chavez. People that had bumper stickers that indicated any kind of liberal philosophy . . . which the officer could read something into it, or if the bumper sticker said, 'Support the Panther's Breakfast Program,' like that, that's where it is."[71] Guillery noted as well that any car carrying an interracial couple was "automatically stopped."[72] Law enforcement personnel treated East L.A.'s Mexican residents with casual violence. But they responded especially aggressively toward that community's politicized members, whether they belonged to an organization, wore their politics openly, or violated racial taboos.

The link in law enforcement's mind between militant politics and racial taboos resulted from the sense that challenges to racial hierarchy amounted to ideological heresy. This connection was particularly manifest for the police with respect to criticism of the police themselves. A police report on two activist newspapers demonstrates that the police equated anti-police protests with anti-white politics. In 1969 the LAPD issued an "intelligence summary" which concluded that *La Raza* and the Brown Berets' *La Causa* "do nothing but preach and foment hate of minorities toward whites and in particular, law enforcement. It would be beneficial if some of these publications could be forced to stop publication or at least, control the biased and unfounded reports they print."[73] In addition to calling for the censorship of these papers, the LAPD report equated hate toward whites with hate toward the police. In the police view, hostility toward the police equaled antipathy toward whites, and protests against racism indicated the subversive politics of communism.

In responding to political activism among Mexicans in East Los Angeles, law enforcement agencies drew on a common sense connection between race and crime, and also between racial militancy and ideological heresy. Apparently, law enforcement officers understood themselves to be guarding democracy, even as they acted as agents of racial domination.[74] The legal violence that afflicted East Los Angeles included a significant component of police brutality prompted, after 1968, by both racial prejudice and ideological hostility.

POLICE MALPRACTICE AND CHICANO IDENTITY

In 1972, as part of a larger study of police–community relations in East Los Angeles, Armando Morales surveyed community residents regarding their perceptions of law enforcement. Morales disaggregated his results in terms of "self-ascribed ethnic identity."[75] Among respondents, 43 described themselves as Mexican American and 21 as Chicano.[76] The table on page 152 summarizes some of Morales's findings, focusing on the percentage of

Percentage of respondents believing that law enforcement engages in
specific forms of malpractice, East Los Angeles 1972

| | Self-ascribed ethnic identity | |
	Mexican American	Chicano
Do you believe the following happen to residents of East Los Angeles?	Yes	Yes
Insulting language	72%	90%
Illegal roust and frisk	85	95
Illegal stop and search of cars	89	95
Unnecessary force in arrest	60	100
Unnecessary force in custody	71	100
Average	75	96
Have the following happened to you?		
Insulting language	43	76
Illegal roust and frisk	28	71
Illegal stop and search of cars	39	81
Unnecessary force in arrest	16	71
Unnecessary force in custody	19	40
Average	29	68

Source: Armando Morales, "A Study of Mexican American Perceptions of
Law Enforcement Policies and Practices in East Los Angeles," table 12, 327
(Ph.D. diss., University of Southern California, 1972).

respondents who believed that law enforcement personnel engaged in specific forms of misconduct.

These data reveal that those who considered themselves Chicanos were almost one-third more likely to perceive police malpractice, compared with those who saw themselves as Mexican
Americans. Among Chicanos, proportionally 25 percent more
believed the police used insulting language; 12 percent more and
7 percent more thought that law enforcement engaged in illegal
rousts and illegal searches of cars; 67 percent more perceived excessive force in arrests; and 43 percent more suspected unnecessary violence against persons in custody.

Morales accounted for this difference by arguing that persons identifying themselves as Chicano were more likely to be politicized and so more likely to criticize police practices. This conclusion draws an arrow from politicization to perceptions of abusive police practices; that is, people become politicized first, and perceive police abuse second.[77] More likely, the relationship ran in both directions: participation in the Chicano movement prompted negative views of the police, while perceptions of police malpractice precipitated involvement in Chicano politics.

This dynamic relationship seems even more important regarding personal experiences with police abuse. Chicanos were more than four times as likely to say they had experienced excessive force in arrests and more than twice as likely to claim that they had been the victim of an illegal roust and frisk, car stop, or use of unnecessary force while in custody. These numbers partly reflect the influence of political orientation on how people perceive social events. The numbers also partly result from the way in which new beliefs often cause people to reinterpret the past. It is also evident, though, that personally experiencing police abuse increased the likelihood that one would come to see oneself as Chicano.

At work here is not simply a two-dimensional relationship involving political action and police criticism. Morales's data capture a more complex relationship that also involves racial identity. Differences in the perception of police malpractice between Chicanos and Mexican Americans resulted not simply from their distinct politics but reflected—and contributed to—different racial identities. Mexican politicization in East Los Angeles during the late 1960s took place in specifically racial terms. Thus, perceiving or experiencing police violence made people more likely to think that they were brown, and considering oneself to be brown made individuals more likely to perceive police practices as oppressive. Race and law constituted each other, in the sense that law influenced how people understood their racial identity, and race shaped how they conceived of law. The legal construction of Chicano identity is an important theme in Part Three.

Before getting to that part, though, we should note a more fundamental point proven by Morales's research: police malpractice was a fact of life in East Los Angeles. One can trace this violence through the testimony of a former sheriff's deputy, or with the statistics and conclusions of the ACLU and U.S. Commission on Civil Rights reports. But one can also measure the extent of police brutality through the perceptions of East Los Angeles residents. Somewhere between 75 percent and 96 percent of East Los Angeles residents thought that the police regularly committed malpractice. Police brutality was routine in East L.A., and its residents knew it.

THE CHICANO RACE

3

THE CHICANO MOVEMENT
AND EAST L.A. THIRTEEN

Oscar Acosta and the defendants presented themselves in the courtroom as challenging a discriminatory system. But outside the courtroom the activists used a stronger vocabulary, describing the judges as bigots and racists and depicting the trials as efforts to suppress the Chicano people.[1] How did the Chicano defendants come to see themselves as victims of racism? Why did they begin to consider themselves brown? What role did legal violence play in shifting their identity? This chapter turns to these questions, suggesting that the answer is again common sense.

The Chicano movement in Los Angeles has various roots. At the most general level, U.S. society's fixation with race and the resultant racial construction of Mexicans provide indispensable elements. Had Mexicans not been treated as an inferior race, they would not have turned to a politics based on non-white identity. But external factors alone do not explain the Chicano movement's rise. Internally, increasing frustration with the limited success of Mexicans' efforts to assimilate created fertile space for a new approach to Mexican identity. After trying for more than thirty years to achieve equality through traditional political routes, new groups emerged in the Mexican community in the early 1960s that clamored for fair treatment on terms different from those set by the politics of the Mexican American generation. Three of these groups in particular inspired Chicano militancy in East Los Angeles.

First, César Chávez organized Mexican farm laborers to strike against agribusiness in California's Central Valley beginning in fall 1965. The farmworkers successfully organized a union on a non-racial and nonviolent basis, becoming the largest and most prominent Mexican movement in U.S. history. Though Chávez opposed a primarily nationality-based approach to organizing, he nevertheless encouraged pride in Mexican identity. The farmworkers rallied around symbols such as the *Virgen de Guadalupe,* an image of the Virgin Mary dear to Mexicans, and their efforts demonstrated to many that even the most powerless Mexicans could organize and stand up against the most powerful Anglos.[2]

Chávez's efforts directly and indirectly inspired a wave of activism in Los Angeles.[3] Chávez spoke and traveled widely, appearing several times at L.A. rallies to garner support for the farmworkers and to encourage a more widespread political mobilization.[4] Two of Chávez's organizers moved to Los Angeles to work on *La Raza,* the leading movement newspaper in L.A.[5] Even Acosta felt Chávez's influence: a visit with Chávez during his fast in April 1968 helped Acosta decide to dedicate himself to the fulltime defense of Chicano activists.[6]

The land grant movement in New Mexico led by Reies López Tijerina provided a second model of Mexican activism. In contrast to the pacifism espoused by Chávez, López Tijerina demonstrated the potential for violent, armed opposition. He began to organize people around the issue of land titles in rural New Mexico in the early 1960s, arguing that the federal government had acquired the land held as national forest by fraud from Mexicans—or Hispanos, as they called themselves in New Mexico.[7] Under the banner of *La Alianza Federal de Mercedes,* the Federal Land Grant Alliance, López Tijerina's early strategies involved claims that the Treaty of Guadalupe Hidalgo ending the U.S.-

Mexico war guaranteed Mexican property rights, as well as appeals to the Mexican government for assistance, and political pressure on elected and judicial officials. By 1966, however, these tactics segued into mass demonstrations, including the occupation of national forest land.

In one dramatic action, in October 1966 López Tijerina and the Alianza occupied portions of the Kit Carson National Forest, declaring the land an independent republic. When park rangers sought to intervene, the *aliancistas* took two officers hostage and tried them in a mock court for trespassing; they convicted them and sentenced them to jail before suspending the sentences and releasing the startled rangers.[8] The next year, on June 5, 1967, López Tijerina and armed Alianza members stormed the county courthouse in Tierra Amarilla, New Mexico, to make a citizen's arrest of a district attorney they considered abusive. A gun battle ensued, a jailer and a state police officer were wounded, and twenty hostages were held for about an hour.[9] The actions of López Tijerina and the Alianza represented a resurgence of armed opposition to Anglo domination after almost a hundred years of quiescence.[10] Their deeds provided Mexicans across the Southwest with a model of violent Mexican militancy; and many East Los Angeles activists, including Brown Beret officer Carlos Montes, traveled to New Mexico to witness the Alianza in action.[11]

Finally, the East Los Angeles Chicano movement was also inspired by the actions of a Denver, Colorado, organizer, Rodolfo "Corky" Gonzales. Gonzales initially followed the political route prescribed by the Mexican American generation.[12] By 1965, however, after stints as a precinct captain for the Democratic Party and as director of Denver's War on Poverty, Gonzales began to favor increased activism.[13] In 1966 he founded the Crusade for Justice, an organization that spoke not to rural farmworkers or disenfranchised landholders but to disenchanted urban Mexican youth. Whereas Chávez stressed labor and López

Tijerina focused on land, Gonzales placed Mexican identity at the center of his organizing.

Gonzales was the first prominent activist to reclaim the name Chicano, previously often used pejoratively by Mexicans and Anglos alike to refer to lower-class or darker-skinned Mexicans.[14] In 1967 Gonzales wrote a poem entitled "I Am Joaquín/ *Yo Soy Joaquín*" that captured for many young Mexicans the cultural schisms that fractured their identity, evoking not only those divisions rooted in the mixture of Spanish and Indian ancestry and culture but also those engendered by the tensions between American and Mexican national identities.[15]

"I Am Joaquín" did not offer a racial conception of Chicano identity of the sort that soon developed in East Los Angeles. Instead, it depicted a racially and culturally fragmented self, as in the following passage: "I am Joaquín. I am lost in a world of confusion, caught up in the whirl of Anglo-Society . . . The Victor, and Vanquished, I have killed, and have been killed . . . Mejicano, Español, Latino, Hispano, Chicano, Or whatever I call myself, I look the same, I feel the same . . . I am Aztec prince and Christian Christ. I shall endure."[16] Gonzales' poem highlighted the self-doubts and confusions at the heart of Mexican identity, thereby striking a powerful chord with Mexicans coming of age during the tumultuous 1960s. *La Raza's* first issue in September 1967 published "I Am Joaquín" on a two-page spread, and copies of the poem circulated throughout the Southwest.[17] Gonzales himself spoke often in Los Angeles, appearing at least three times in 1967, further inspiring Chicano activism there.[18]

The farmworkers, the Alianza, and the Crusade all contributed directly to Chicano activism's development in East Los Angeles. When students first marched in protest outside of Garfield High School in March 1968, their chants included not just salutes to Mexican revolutionaries such as Pancho Villa and Emiliano Zapata but also shouts of *¡Qué Viva!* to the names César Chávez, Reies López Tijerina, and Corky Gonzales.[19]

THE CHICANO MOVEMENT AND BLACK POWER

While Mexican activism in the Southwest strongly influenced the advent of Chicano militancy in East Los Angeles, the movement there was also inspired by other groups and events of the 1960s. Internationally, the Cuban revolution, student protests and violent government repression in Mexico, the war in Vietnam, and the global emergence of anticolonial struggles all contributed to Chicano activism.[20] On the national scene, increasing protest and campus radicalism, including the Free Speech movement and student strikes at the University of California, Berkeley, also inspired a new politics among young Mexicans.[21] More than any of these, though, the African American campaign for social equality stands out as one of the most powerful forces leading to political mobilization in East Los Angeles.

In arguing that the black struggle beginning in the 1950s inspired other popular movements in the 1960s and 1970s, social movement scholars frequently identify civil rights as the preeminent modality of black protest.[22] Certainly forces within the black struggle—for instance, the NAACP, the Southern Christian Leadership Conference, and leaders such as Martin Luther King Jr.—stressed the rhetoric of rights over the language of race. But especially in the 1960s, segments of the black movement started mobilizing around pride in a non-white racial identity, and this facet of the African American struggle profoundly shaped activism in East Los Angeles. There, racial identity played a much more significant role than talk about rights. For Chicanos, the most directly influential component of the African American fight was not the southern organizing of the 1950s but the Black Power movement of the mid to late 1960s.

Even before the first high school walkouts in East Los Angeles in 1968, local Mexican youth had met with Black Power activists. High school students in East L.A. formed a group called Young Citizens for Community Action in 1966. The next year, YCCA opened *La Piranya,* a coffee house and cultural center that hosted community events and social gatherings but also political activists. The various speakers who talked with East Los Angeles's nascent protesters included Black Power militants H. Rap Brown and Ron Karenga as well as Stokely Carmichael, one of those who coined the phrase "Black Power."[23] In addition to meetings with Black Power advocates, a few Mexicans cut their political teeth in black organizations.[24] Oscar Acosta apprenticed in the black struggle, spending four years working with the civil rights movement in San Francisco while attending law school.[25] Brown Beret officers Carlos Montes and Ralph Ramírez were participating in Martin Luther King Jr.'s Poor People's March on the nation's capitol when the police came to arrest them on the *East L.A. Thirteen* charges.[26] Black protest and Black Power in particular directly influenced the Chicano movement's rise in East Los Angeles.[27]

But Chicano activists did not simply adopt black protest strategies whole-cloth. Rather, East Los Angeles residents observed the black movement from the distinct social position Mexicans occupied in the Southwest. In part, this meant that East Los Angeles activists learned black protest lessons as filtered through the efforts of Chávez, López Tijerina, and Gonzales. Chávez gave Martin Luther King Jr.'s nonviolence a central role in the farmworkers' movement; the 1965 Delano Plan that outlined the union's aspirations adopted King's steadfast optimism and embraced the African American credo "We shall overcome."[28] López Tijerina signed a treaty with Black Panthers proclaiming that "the two peoples agree, to take the same position as to the crimes and sins of the Government of the United States of America," and that "Brown and Black should be together."[29] Gonzales acknowledged, "I learned from the Black movement. Look at Watts. The day after the riots the government was dumping millions of dollars to help the people . . . I've been taught that five loose fingers by themselves are nothing. Bring them together and you have a fist."[30]

On another level, the residents of East Los Angeles had to

grapple with the black struggle's relevance to them as members of a community that had long claimed a white identity. In the early 1960s, *Los Angeles Times* reporter Rubén Salazar noted that "several of the more conservative Mexican-American leaders strongly oppose any 'mixing' of Mexican American and Negro grievances," and that "many Mexican-Americans say that they have had a long, painful and lonely battle for acceptance and that a coalition with Negroes now would set them back."[31] As late as 1966, mainstream Mexican American civil rights organizations positioned themselves in opposition to blacks. Shortly after the Watts riot, the Mexican American generation's leading organizations, including LULAC and the American GI Forum, sent President Lyndon Johnson a resolution pointedly contrasting their assimilationist orientation with black militancy. These groups argued that their constituency deserved special consideration in antipoverty programs and civil rights initiatives because, unlike blacks, Mexican Americans eschewed civil disobedience and violent confrontation in favor of loyalty to the democratic system.[32]

As with 1960s protest politics generally, age played an important role in the willingness of Mexicans to identify with black insurgency. To be sure, in the 1960s some Mexican Americans abandoned their prior orientation. This was clearly the case with Corky Gonzales, as his embrace of black militancy demonstrates. Nevertheless, the majority of Chicano protesters came of political age in the movement, in the sense that the movement served as their first introduction to political activity. Mexicans who matured in the 1960s frequently struggled against the general orientation of the community but not, as their seniors did, against values that they had previously relied on as the basis for political involvement. Far more so than their parents, Mexican youth in Los Angeles and across the Southwest were willing to identify with the black fight for equality.

Rubén Salazar noted this intergenerational aspect: "Faced with an identity crisis, many young Mexican Americans—ex-

cited by black militancy—decided that they had been misled by
their elders into apathetic confusion . . . The ambivalence felt
vaguely and in silence for so long seemed to crystallize in the
light of the black revolution. There was talk now of brown
power."[33] Acosta too observed a generational element in the
community's reactions to the high school walkouts as well as to
his allegations of judicial discrimination in *East L.A. Thirteen:*
"The older, passive/fatalistic Mexican had become threatened by
this sudden public attention now given to his race by the walkouts. His ancient fear of identification with the peon—translated
'black' in '68—supported his need for anonymity . . . And now
this Grand Jury challenge accusing Superior Court judges of bigotry."[34]

The fear of identification with blacks that Acosta identified
contributed to conflict between young people and their parents.
Older Mexican Americans, wedded to the ideals of white identity
and assimilation, often shunned any association, actual or meta-
phorical, with blacks. Younger people were more willing to learn
from blacks, and this generation became the vanguard of the
Chicano movement. This is not to say that youthfulness determined movement participation, or that Chicano activists were
adolescents playing at protest. The Chicano movement involved
every age group, and even the young participants often had families of their own.[35] But to participate in the Chicano movement
required rejecting Mexican American political and racial values,
something more readily done by those who came of age in the
1960s. Whereas Mexican Americans shied from associating
themselves with African Americans, the Chicano activists in
1968 and early 1969 more willingly embraced not only blacks
but, as we shall see, blackness.

PROTEST, LEGAL REPRESSION, AND RACE

The Black Power movement's explicit celebration of non-white
identity directly influenced activism in East Los Angeles. By
shaping the common sense of race, however, the African Ameri-

can struggle had an even more pronounced effect on the rise of Chicano racial consciousness. Twenty years and more of black activism established strong conceptual links among community protest, legal repression, and race. These common sense connections influenced participants in the Chicano movement to construct a non-white Mexican identity.

By 1968, when the first major protests erupted in East Los Angeles, the African American struggle had held the attention of the nation for decades. The nightly news brought protest marches, sit-ins, and freedom rides, swinging police clubs, snarling dogs, and spraying fire hoses into the homes of the Southwest. Place names like Selma, Montgomery, Birmingham, and Jackson evoked images of marches and police lines, demonstrations and mass arrests, protests and repression. Events in Detroit, Newark, and Watts also entered the public imagination, juxtaposing enraged faces, clamorous voices, milling mobs, and burning buildings with riot police, national guardsmen, sirens, and tear gas, all against a background of desperate urban poverty and extreme segregation. America's image became one of rioting minorities, flame-engulfed cities, and massive police intervention. In April 1968, a month after the East Los Angeles walkouts, Martin Luther King Jr. was assassinated in Memphis, Tennessee. And in June, days after the *East L.A. Thirteen* indictments and arrests, Robert Kennedy, who had supported the walkouts and who had walked arm-in-arm with César Chávez, was shot to death in Los Angeles. As Chicanos in East Los Angeles mobilized around conditions in the schools and later around the arrests of community leaders in the spring and summer of 1968, they did so in the midst of social upheaval and violence.

The fight for black equality established seemingly natural connections among community protest, legal repression, and racial identity. The protesters were not the working poor or a religious minority but blacks in general. The violence that met them was not wielded by society at large but by white police forces and by enraged white mobs. Though it was obvious, the very quality of being obvious reinforced the common sense significance of a core fact: the African American struggle was at root a racial fight. The black movement involved a racial minority demanding social equality and political rights, and in turn being met by violent repression at the hands of a white majority and the police force it controlled. Black Power put racial identity into play explicitly, but African American activism as a whole made race an implicit, key feature of social protest.

The cognitive power of this new linkage between protest, repression, and race comes through vividly in the pages of *La Raza*. Published regularly between September 1967 and February 1970, the newspaper counted on its editorial staff two *East L.A. Thirteen* defendants. The police in fact raided the paper's offices when making arrests in that case.[36] Underground newspapers such as *La Raza* disseminated not only news but also new ways of thinking. The activist press self-consciously set out to provide the Mexican community with alternative ways to understand their position in society.[37] Such papers thus constitute a unique record of social rebellion, and *La Raza* is perhaps the best contemporary window through which to view the changing ideas animating the Chicano movement in East Los Angeles.[38]

La Raza articles repeatedly emphasized the connections among protest, law, and race, as in a September 1968 article entitled "Barrio and Ghetto Communities Protest Police Violence":

> A potentially explosive situation has been created by the police department in East Los Angeles. The police have conceived a conspiracy against the Mexican people who are making just demands for social progress. In May, thirteen of our brothers were arrested and indicted, a newspaper was suppressed, and student leaders were jailed. Daily incidents involve the beating of teen-agers, constant citizen harassment on commercial streets, arrogant interfering with family social functions, and, of course, the daily insults meted out to Black and Brown people in their contacts with officers.[39]

All three elements are here. First, the paragraph describes Mexicans as making "just demands for social progress." Second, it decries legal repression in the forms of harassment, beatings, arrest, indictment, and jailing. Finally, it links these together with race, not only identifying Mexicans as "Brown people" but implicitly equating their identity with that of "Blacks." Developing this implicit equality, the article continues: "We, Brown and Black, stand here together . . . hermanos unidos! We, Brown and Black, make this statement together, mano-a-mano, because we are one. Although you have attempted to separate us by geography, a barrio here, and ghetto there, we are in fact united by history . . . Our oppressions are one. Our dreams are one. Our demands are one. We suffer as one, we react as one, we struggle as one!"[40]

It is hard to imagine a fuller equation of Mexican and black identity. *La Raza* here asserted that Mexican identity, when measured in terms of history, geography, oppressions, and dreams, was functionally black. More importantly for our analysis, such commonality emerged in the context of community demands for social change amid repressive police violence. For Chicanos, the links between protest, repression, and race evolved into a common sense that put minority racial identity forward to explain legal repression following community protest. Drawing on this common sense, East Los Angeles residents increasingly saw police brutality in response to political activism as evidence that they were non-white. These connections operated so powerfully that some Mexican activists initially came to consider themselves effectively as black.

UNDERSTANDING EAST L.A. THIRTEEN

From the very beginning, the triangular relationship linking race to protest and legal repression informed the developing understanding of *East L.A. Thirteen*. Despite thousands of students walking out in March and the continuing negotiations between community leaders and the school board, East Los Angeles in May 1968 was relatively quiet. The indictments and arrests brought this peace to a crashing end. The day after the arrests, 200 protesters gathered. On the day after that, Sunday, June 2, more than 2,000 people came together to protest the arrests—not in front of the Board of Education, the site of earlier, smaller demonstrations, but in front of the Los Angeles Central Police Station.[41] At noon that Sunday, protesters picketed the station, defying the gathered police with chants of "Set Our Brothers Free" and "Chicano Power."[42] The school activists were there, of course. But now so too were many folks who had not been involved in March. Oscar Acosta credited the arrests, much more than the school walkouts themselves, for mobilizing the East Los Angeles community: "The issue was no longer discriminatory education. Now it was abusive and excessive prosecutorial power by an unrepresentative government."[43]

The indictments and arrests galvanized the community.[44] But more than simply mobilizing Mexicans, legal violence contributed to the rise of a non-white Chicano identity.[45] At the outset, Acosta and the defendants charged that the prosecutions reflected local politics. The arrests fell on the weekend preceding California primary elections. Defendant and *La Raza* editor Eliezer Risco charged in a news conference a few days after the arrests that District Attorney Evelle Younger, up for reelection, targeted the Mexican community in order to appear to be a "savior in a moment of danger." Risco further alleged that the police had a similar interest, insofar as a police bond measure was on the early June ballot.[46] Seeming to support that charge, thousands of leaflets opposing the bond measure had disappeared from the *La Raza* and Brown Beret offices during the police raids that occurred simultaneously with the arrests.[47]

But the charge that local politics played a role did not detract from the defendants' almost immediate conviction that the police sweeps, multiple charges, and high bail were designed to crush their effort to empower the community. Upon their arrest, five of the East L.A. Thirteen began a hunger strike. Joe Razo, one of the strikers, wrote a letter from prison explaining their decision: "They have separated us and put the five of us: Risco, Razo, Cruz Olmeda, Moctezuma Esparza, and David Sanchez into one cell. We are entering our 3rd day on the HUNGER STRIKE. Make no doubt about it, WE ARE POLITICAL PRISONERS and we are paying for our political viewpoints. We are prepared to spend the rest of our days in jail to further the Chicano cause."[48]

According to Razo, the arrest and prosecution of the Thirteen resulted from their political viewpoints—that is, their demands for improved schools in East Los Angeles and social equality for the Mexican community. This claim explicitly invoked two of the three elements linked together by the African American struggle: protest and legal repression. The third element, racial identity, followed: it was as "Chicanos," and not as "Mexican Americans" or simply as "persons," that the state targeted the defendants. The picket signs carried by protesters outside the courthouse on June 2 succinctly voiced this racial element: "Let My People Go," they read, and "Withdraw Racist Cops."[49]

La Raza's first issue to report on the arrests came out on June 7, a week after the police raids. By this time, the conclusion had solidified that the indictments amounted to legal repression of minority demands for reform. On the front page, under the title "Noticia a la Jefe Placa" ("Notice to the Chief Cop"), *La Raza* proclaimed in bold letters: "Sunday, June 2, 1968, la Raza Nueva served notice on RED RED REDDIN, la Jefe Placa, that La Raza can no longer be intimidated . . . WE WILL BE HEARD FROM THE PRISON OF OUR BARRIOS AND OUR CELLS. Protest is poverty inspired, is frustration inspired . . . There is no hope in your 'laws' in your 'courts.' OUR ONLY HOPE IS IN OUR OWN PEOPLE!! QUE VIVA LA RAZA NUEVA!"[50]

An us-them rhetoric dominates this excerpt, placing "la raza nueva," "our own people," "our barrios," and "la raza" in opposition to "your 'laws,'" "your 'courts,'" and "la Jefe Placa."

This rhetoric reflects how events in early June shifted community attention away from education and toward police–community relations. More importantly, it demonstrates the developing sense among Mexicans that something fundamental divided "us" from "them," and highlights the terms of that divide: Mexicans were a people, a new race, *una raza nueva*, standing against an unjust police force. Finally, the excerpt shows that political activism provided the fulcrum in this opposition: it was poverty-inspired protest that produced police repression. The African American movement clearly provided the terms—community protest, police repression, and race—by which the Mexican community struggled to understand the arrests and indictments in *East L.A. Thirteen*.

The repeated use of the term *la raza* suggests that this label offered a transitional vocabulary. La Raza's ambiguous meaning allowed its use both before and after a non-white conception of Mexican identity fully developed. Initially, la raza almost certainly connoted not race in the biological sense used in the United States but rather the notion of peoplehood with which Latin American usage imbued the term. As a term of self-description suggesting a close-knit group, la raza had a long history in Los Angeles's Mexican community, dating back to its use by residents of the central Los Angeles barrio at the end of the nineteenth century.[51] Nevertheless, Mexicans using that phrase in East Los Angeles in the late 1960s were not deaf to its resonance when translated into English as "race." Increasingly, the U.S. sense of race informed the activist community's invocation of la raza as they moved toward a non-white conception of themselves.

If there was a critical moment when la raza began to translate more readily into "the race" rather than the "the people," it seems to occur in East Los Angeles in conjunction with the arrests of the Thirteen. Two articles appeared in *La Raza's* first issue after the weekend raids that suggest that this new meaning had achieved dominance. Both articles involved Luís Valdez, then widely known in his position as the director of *El Teatro Campesino,* the theater group associated with Chávez's farmworkers' movement. Valdez was the first prominent movement leader to emphasize Mexican non-whiteness, and his insistence that race should be the principal organizing focus among Mexicans led to an eventual rift with Chávez.[52]

In the first key article, Valdez argued for understanding the educational crisis afflicting Mexicans in racial terms. "The American educational system," Valdez protested,

> has demanded that we assimilate, acculturate, melt into the American pot and disappear. In other words, it has asked us to commit suicide as people by becoming agabachados [whitened] as soon as possible. It has tried to speed things up by reassuring us that we, as Chicanos, are Caucasians—even if we are dark as zapote—and members in good standing of the white race. It has convinced many Chicanos that they are "brown Anglos," and that their roots in America are as shallow as any gringo's—including the over-glorified descendants of the Mayflower. It has tried to make our Raza ashamed of its very blood by suppressing, distorting, and destroying our powerful, beautiful history.[53]

Valdez linked raza to race in a U.S. sense, invoking the powerful metaphor of blood while stridently distinguishing Chicanos from Caucasians, itself a purportedly biologically-based racial category. Valdez also provided a race-informed critique of public schools and urged Mexicans to see educational problems as a racial conflict between themselves as an oppressed race and whites as an oppressing one, again seeming to deploy race in ways more typical of the United States.

It seems likely that Valdez's race-based educational critique would have engendered some sympathy, irrespective of other events in East Los Angeles. Yet the police reprisals against the East L.A. Thirteen gave added bite to Valdez's analysis. Reflecting this context, the second article relevant to the changing meaning of la raza reported on demonstrations outside the Central Police Station, where Valdez had joined the crowd. In excited language, the newspaper recounted that Valdez led protesters in singing about Chicano blood: "The words of one song 'The Mejicano doesn't want, cannot . . . The Mejicano doesn't want to be a gringo and will never be one . . . Because in his veins runs the blood of Aztecas . . . Mayas . . . Zapata . . . and the heroic Pancho Villa' sent bursts of pride pounding through the hearts of Chicanos and sowed the seeds of fear in the establishment."[54]

In the rally protesting the *East L.A. Thirteen* arrests, Valdez's invocation of blood to explain the irreducible difference between Mexicans and Anglos struck a chord with the editors and with the community. Valdez presented Mexicans as inheritors of Emiliano Zapata and Pancho Villa's revolutionary spirit and valor, and as a people who shared an identity because they descended from Aztecs and Mayans. The crowd, shouting in protest outside a police station, enthusiastically seized upon this message of racial pride and innate racial difference. When articles in *La Raza* linked together community protest, police repression, and identity as una raza to explain *East L.A. Thirteen,* they used the common sense connections established by black protest. This common sense, in turn, helped transform la raza from a generic reference to peoplehood into a specific reference to blood and descent—that is, into the concept of race regnant in the United States.

EXPECTING LEGAL VIOLENCE

Oscar Acosta too relied on common sense to understand *East L.A. Thirteen.*[55] For Acosta, though, the common sense connections among identity, protest, and repression did more than accentuate the importance of race. These background links led Acosta to expect legal violence.

In September 1968, Acosta cautioned *La Raza* readers that they should not expect the defendants to prevail at the trial court level in *East L.A. Thirteen.* "Since this is a political case from beginning to end, we can't necessarily expect [the judge] to rule favorably on the matter. After all," Acosta warned, "she too is a part of the system."[56] Some defendants shared Acosta's pessimism. Joe Razo in his jailhouse letter insisted that the militants were willing to spend their lives in jail to further the Chicano cause.[57] Razo's words convey not just bravado but also fear about the defendants' futures. Such pessimism followed in part from memories of the community's past encounters with the police and the courts. More importantly, though, as the defendants came to understand their prosecution in common sense terms, they increasingly came to expect repression from the courts. They were minority protesters; it seemed obvious that legal violence would follow.

For the Chicano militants, events confirmed this expectation relatively quickly. In October 1968 Francisco Martínez was convicted on charges arising from the walkouts. Not one of the Thirteen, Martínez was tried in municipal court on a misdemeanor count of disturbing the peace. According to Mexican prosecutor Ricardo Torres, "Martinez was taken into custody when he refused to stop leading a small group of students in loud chants after school had begun for the day."[58] Acosta defended Martínez before Judge John Arguelles, one of the few Mexican municipal court judges; a jury of eight Mexicans and four Anglos heard the case.[59] Acosta contended that the First Amendment insulated Martínez from conviction for carrying a picket sign and walking the sidewalk while shouting "Viva la Raza!" In addition, Acosta put Chicano activists on the stand to explain their philosophy and to read movement poetry.[60] Torres described the poetry as "poison," and Judge Arguelles ruled that the First Amendment did not apply because the "many 'Negro sit-in' cases" no longer accurately reflected the "mood" of the country.[61] The jury convicted Martínez after deliberating less than two hours.[62]

After the conviction, Acosta published an article in *La Raza* explaining the *Martínez* case's significance. Acosta voiced profound doubt about the possibility of securing justice in the courts for Chicanos and wondered aloud whether revolution might not make more sense than responsible protest.

> If both juries, prosecutors and judges, all Mexican-Americans, will no longer allow citizens to engage in nonviolent protest as the constitution and the Supreme Court have said they could, should these men jeopardize themselves any longer? Should the time and money and frustrations be spent on such orthodox protests any longer? Especially if they are no longer effective? . . . Is it not time to go underground? Is it not time to put aside our poetry, our music and romance until after the revolution?[63]

Because legitimate protest led only to arrest and conviction, Acosta reasoned, perhaps public demonstrations should be forsaken in favor of revolution.[64] Like Razo's fear that he would spend his life in jail, this conclusion seems extreme, especially in the wake of a single misdemeanor conviction. But Acosta and the defendants understood the prosecution of Chicano activists in the common sense terms that connected race, protest, and repression. Perceiving in Chicano activism the elements of race and protest, the militants expected Martínez's conviction, and the conviction in turn seemingly confirmed that they faced further legal repression.

PROVING THEIR OWN EXISTENCE: DEFENSE STRATEGY

Convinced that he could not expect to win cases on their merits, Acosta came to believe after Martínez's conviction that trials should be used not so much to free the accused but to educate the masses and advance the movement. After reporting Martínez's conviction to *La Raza* readers, Acosta insisted: "The only purpose to be served by a prolonged and extensive jury trial for a political case is to educate and organize around the trial itself."[65]

Acosta readily transferred this lesson to *East L.A. Thirteen*. His article on Martínez's trial appeared side by side with another entitled "The East Los 13 Are Ready." Writing about himself in the third person, Acosta made clear that his strategy would not focus principally on proving the defendants' innocence: "Chief Counsel for the 13, Chicano Lawyer Acosta, will attempt to prove that the hand-picked, blue ribbon Grand Jury violates the constitutional guarantees of equal protection. 'Not only do they discriminate against Chicanos,' Acosta said, 'but in fact they are discriminating against all poor and young and minority persons. The law says they must pick indiscriminately from a cross-section of the community, but in fact they pick their friends . . . Every Superior Court Judge who has nominated anyone over the past ten years will be subpoenaed to testify why it is he never once, in ten years took a Mexican to dinner, let alone nominated one to serve his fellow citizens as a Grand Juror."[66] Acosta hoped to use *East L.A. Thirteen* to show, in his more succinct explanation offered a month earlier, "that the Judges themselves are the bigots."[67] The common sense of the situation contributed not just to the way Acosta framed his general analysis but also to how he orchestrated the defense in *East L.A. Thirteen*.

There is a certain irony in all this, however, for while Acosta seemed convinced that being brown made legal violence certain, it was legal repression that contributed to Acosta's belief that he was brown. Acosta and the defendants drew upon connections among protest, repression, and race in concluding that because Mexicans were non-white, they suffered legal mistreatment. But another conclusion also seems apt: because Mexicans suffered legal discrimination, they came to see themselves as brown. Acosta and the defendants perceived the relationship as running in only one direction, from minority status to legal violence. It is also the case, though, that such violence contributed to the development among Mexicans of a sense that they were non-white. Mexicans did not possess a fixed racial identity that law enforcement officials and Chicano activists recognized and reacted to; rather, the actions of the police and the protesters also helped to fashion Mexican racial identity.

The influence of the common sense racial protest model on defense strategy provides fresh insight into the decision to argue the Fourteenth Amendment in *East L.A. Thirteen*. In order to advance the grand jury discrimination defense, Acosta had to show as a threshold matter that the defendants were members of a distinct class of persons. In this context, rather than standing as an onerous hurdle, the need to prove Mexican identity served as a principal attraction. Increasingly convinced by the legal action against them that they were racial minorities, Acosta and the defendants sought to proselytize in the courtroom not only regarding judicial racism but also concerning Mexican racial identity itself.[68]

Acosta later described the significance of the trial as follows:

> [The East L.A. Thirteen] retained expert witnesses and used cardboard boxes filled with documentary and statistical evidence to legally establish their identity as a people separate and distinct from the majority . . . An expert urban sociologist lectured to a singularly silent court and counsel that the defendants did *indeed* belong to a separate and distinct group of persons despite their governmental classification as Caucasians and their legal recognition as citizens . . . [The activists] emotionally and intellectually knew the potential implications of the testimony . . . The staccatoed, computerized, analytical statistics "justified" their very existence; what had been but an inchoate propaganda of their own now became a rational truth to serve them not only in their confrontations with the Anglo establishment but more importantly in their painful attempts at the proselytizing of a Mexican community which condemned the walkouts with their patent nationalism and which winced at the racial rancor in their verbosity.[69]

For Acosta, the expert testimony's importance lay outside of, rather than within, the courtroom. It provided powerful ammunition for the militants in their efforts to convince Mexicans that they were non-white—that they were "a separate and distinct group of persons despite their governmental classification as Caucasians." In addition, though, Acosta suggested that the experts' documents and statistics played a role in educating the defendants themselves. The experts transformed the defendants' "inchoate propaganda" into "rational truth." Though the defendants professed a brown identity to explain their arrests and indictment, they were not yet fully convinced of their new identity—to this extent, the trial served as an opportunity for the Mexican militants to prove not just to the courts and the community *but to themselves* that they were a non-white race.

Acosta and the *East L.A. Thirteen* defendants drew on common sense connections among protest, race, and legal violence in coming to see themselves as brown. They also drew on this linkage when they formed expectations—and subsequently perceptions—of judicial mistreatment. These common sense connections, accentuated by the black struggle for equality, provided Mexicans in East Los Angeles with a framework of ideas and relationships for understanding not just their social situation but themselves. For the defendants, *East L.A. Thirteen* became a forum for proving that they were a minority race. More than the testimony of the experts, however, the prosecution itself served for many as the most compelling evidence that they were not white.

FROM YOUNG CITIZENS

TO BROWN BERETS

By 1970 the Brown Berets had over sixty chapters across the Southwest and as far away as Chicago. Emphasizing pride "in our race and the color of our skin," the Berets fashioned themselves as the "shock troops" of the Chicano movement, protesting perceived injustices through militant street action and loudly proclaiming their willingness to fight for Mexicans "by all means necessary."[1] As far as law enforcement was concerned, the Berets were Chicano public enemy number one. Prosecutors indicted the leadership; FBI agents tracked their members; city, county, and federal officers infiltrated the organization; and the Berets starred in congressional reports on un-American activities in California.

But the Brown Berets had not started out as a radical minority group. Instead, their origins lay in the Young Citizens for Community Action (YCCA), a group of public-spirited Mexican high school students who got together in 1966 to participate in local elections and to provide community service. According to an original member, "We were basically a very civic-minded little group of do-gooders."[2] What transformed these Mexican American do-gooders into Chicano shock troops? The short answer is police brutality. *East L.A. Thirteen* demonstrates judicial discrimination's contribution to the Chicano movement. The

Brown Berets' evolution exemplifies the role of law enforcement violence more generally.

The high school students who first formed the YCCA did so according to the integrationist terms set by the Mexican American generation. In April 1966 the Los Angeles County Commission on Human Relations sponsored a three-day conference for Mexican youth leaders to "examine emotions, feelings, values, identity and the label 'Mexican American.'"[3] For many of the young participants, this conference provided the first formal opportunity to discuss substantive issues concerning their community in East Los Angeles.[4] Several who attended, among them Vickie Castro, Jorge Licon, John Ortiz, Rachel Ochoa, Moctezuma Esparza, Ralph Ramírez, and David Sánchez, continued these discussions on their own, and in May 1966 they formed the YCCA.[5]

Under the leadership of Vickie Castro, then a Roosevelt High School senior, the YCCA conducted a survey of student needs, met with school officials, and decided to support state college professor Julian Nava in his subsequently successful bid for a position on the school board.[6] YCCA members also served on the Mayor's Youth Advisory Council in Los Angeles.[7] In 1966 the Mayor personally presented David Sánchez a gavel to welcome him as chair of that group, describing him as an "exemplary young man" and an "outstanding high school student."[8]

The YCCA initially met in the basement of an Episcopal church in Lincoln Heights, an East Los Angeles neighborhood. The pastor, Father John Luce, introduced the group's members to older activists from the Community Service Organization and the United Farm Workers, including César Chávez, and this contact further inspired the YCCA to emphasize Mexican identity as a key part of their own organizing.[9] By the summer of 1967 the YCCA had replaced "citizens" with "Chicanos" in their group's name, calling themselves Young Chicanos for Community Action.[10] At the end of the summer, several students moved on from the YCCA to attend college. Vickie Castro left her leadership position when she matriculated at California State University, Los Angeles, where she became active in United Mexican American Students.[11] Following Castro's departure, David Sánchez led the YCCA.[12]

In the fall of 1967, with the help of Father Luce and a grant from the Volunteers in Service to America program, the YCCA opened a coffeehouse called La Piranya.[13] Located on Olympic Boulevard in the heart of East Los Angeles, La Piranya served as a general meeting house and social hangout for Mexican youth. The center hosted various functions, including a program called Educational Happenings designed to increase college enrollment.[14] It also brought to East Los Angeles a range of speakers, including not only local elected officials but also César Chávez, Reies López Tijerina, Corky Gonzales, Stokely Carmichael, and H. Rap Brown. A YCCA member recalled La Piranya's heyday: "It was just like a hangout where anybody could hang around, be they Chicano hippies, gang members, musicians—they jammed there, like there would be one night where musicians used to come and jam, another night maybe a car club or gang wanted to have a meeting there . . . And it worked out pretty well."[15]

On November 24, 1967, an incident of police brutality occurred in East Los Angeles that led YCCA members to picket the police. Responding to a call regarding a disturbance of the peace, sheriff's deputies beat a man into unconsciousness and assaulted his wife and daughter, slapping, kicking, and throwing them to the ground before arresting them.[16] During the assault, the officers called the victims "Mexican animals"; after the attack, the deputies charged them with assaulting peace officers.[17] On December 20, the trial day for several of those arrested, YCCA members joined other protesters outside the East Los Angeles sheriff's station and the East Los Angeles municipal courthouse.[18] *La Raza* reported that "the picketing, itself, was beautiful but more important as one looked on the faces of these young Chicanos, one

could see anger; anger not only because of this particular incident but also because of the countless others in the past which
have caused the Chicanos so much grief and injustice."[19]

Reacting to the protests, the sheriff's department and the
LAPD focused on the YCCA. Law enforcement agencies began
systematically harassing group members as well as intimidating
and arresting patrons of La Piranya. Speaking later about the tar-
geting of the coffeehouse, *La Raza* editor Eliezer Risco recalled:

> The sheriff decided [the coffeehouse] was a bad place, because the
> kids drew a picket line in front of the sheriff's station where there had
> been a case of police brutality. So they [the police] went at it—every
> night, every night, every night. They would shine their lights into the
> coffeehouse, they would come in and pick up people for selling coffee
> without a license; the band that was playing there for nothing would
> be given a ticket for entertaining without a license, and anybody un-
> der eighteen would be picked up and held for six hours before they
> would release them, and [they would] tell the parents not to allow
> the kids to go there because they were Communists, they were dope
> pushers, they were addicts.[20]

The harassment helped to shift the YCCA's identity, driving
away some members while further politicizing others.[21] Around
the same time, a new military-style garb appeared among some
partisans.[22] Encouraged by David Sánchez, by January 1968 YCCA
members frequently wore brown berets and field jackets, accou-
trements that were intended to suggest an allegiance with radical
groups such as the Black Panthers and the Puerto Rican Young
Lords.[23] Whatever imagery the activists hoped to convey, though,
was soon bound up in how the police perceived and reacted to
them.

Describing violence and intimidation by sheriff's deputies, *La
Raza* made police harassment of La Piranya its headline story on
January 15, 1968.[24] For the first time, *La Raza* referred to YCCA
members as Brown Berets:

Last Friday night as four members of the Brown Berets were leaving the Piranya, they were stopped by a Sheriff's Deputy who called on his radio for [backup] . . . The patrol officers rushed around the corner with their hands on their guns and their riot sticks drawn. They illegally searched the youth's car. They took the keys from the driver and opened the trunk even though the Brown Berets warned them that this was a violation of their constitutional rights. The cops said f—k the constitution and they spent twenty minutes searching the whole car. When one of the Brown Berets attempted to take a picture of the highway patrolmen, one of them said, "Take a picture of me, Mexican, so I can shove that f—king camera up your a—."[25]

David Sánchez was among those arrested on minor charges during the campaign to intimidate La Piranya patrons. He recounted his experience and how it helped form the Berets: "I was jumped by the fuzz. They had me at the jail for some minor kid thing and I didn't want to get booked. I said I hadn't done anything and I didn't want to sign. One cop got me in a judo hold and another came up behind me from the back and knocked me flat. When I woke up they were booking me. So I began to change my mind about things. I began to see something was wrong with America. Things were no longer Stars and Stripes. We formed the Brown Berets, and one of our main jobs is to keep an eye on the cops."[26]

Brown Beret Gilbert Cruz Olmeda also recalled the origins of the group in terms of police violence: "[At first,] we didn't call ourselves the Brown Berets. Who started calling us the Brown Berets were the East L.A. Sheriffs . . . and we got pissed off. We would hear it because every time they had us up against a wall we'd hear all the radio messages from the patrol cars, 'Brown Berets here,' and 'Brown Berets over here,' and so then it stuck. So, then we just stayed with it."[27] In the end, perhaps Eliezer Risco explained most succinctly the process that transformed the Mexican American YCCA into the Chicano Brown Berets: "Who organized them? The police organized them."[28]

EARLY BROWN BERET IDEOLOGY

In early 1968, what it meant to be a Brown Beret was far from clear. David Sánchez's arrest in February 1968 at another protest against police helped to shape an answer. While incarcerated at the Wayside Maximum Security facility, Sánchez wrote a three-page manifesto entitled "The Birth of a New Symbol."[29] In it, Sánchez described the Brown Berets as prophets, symbols of hope, and instruments of change, and gave them the responsibility to proselytize within the Mexican community in order promote a new Chicano identity.[30] "It is the job of every Brown Beret to preach the new words. You cannot have a community that is aware, until you have people preaching awareness."[31] Under the heading "Every Mexican-American Is a Potential Chicano," Sánchez ordered Brown Berets to "talk to every potential Chicano who crosses your path. Because every Chicano that you miss is a potential enemy."[32]

In addition, Sánchez insisted that to lead the community required a disciplined cadre: group leaders must be obeyed, and self-discipline in the form of neat dress and upright conduct must be maintained at all times.[33] Success required "an organization that is efficient, disciplined, and organized,"[34] Sánchez wrote, insisting that "because your people, the land, and the enemy are watching you, you must look good, act right and move with the precision of a clock."[35] Sánchez also warned activists against becoming "hung up on theory and ideology." "Intellectuals aren't able to communicate with the dude on the street," Sánchez cautioned, "because their thinking has been alienated from the community."[36]

"The Birth of a New Symbol" anticipated certain organizational hallmarks that eventuated among the Brown Berets. The emphasis on discipline, for example, evolved into an ersatz military hierarchy. Brown Beret leaders adopted exaggerated titles and members formed and performed as military drill teams.[37]

The manifesto also foreshadowed the anti-intellectual and eventually anti-middle-class inclination of the Berets, whose membership changed from an organization of clean-cut students into a group of tough street kids, former gang members, and previously incarcerated youths.[38] If groups like United Mexican American Students represented college activists, the Brown Berets eventually helped to politicize and speak for more marginalized elements, the young toughs on East L.A.'s mean streets.[39]

Nevertheless, "The Birth of a New Symbol" said surprisingly little regarding the nature of the new "Chicano" identity activists should preach, and it failed to suggest which issues the community should organize around. Instead, it emphasized the evils of Anglo racism. "For over 120 years, the Chicano has suffered at the hands of the Anglo Establishment. The Chicano is discriminated against in every phase of his life," Sánchez insisted. He warned: "Do not talk to the enemy, for he is either a dog or a devil. A dog may look nice and let you pet him, but you will never know when he'll bite you. A devil is sly and slick, he will drag you to hell without you knowing it."[40]

The bitterness of a young man feted by the Los Angeles mayor only two years before comes through in Sánchez's condemnation of Anglo trickery. In addition, in analyzing the Chicano's political and social situation, "The Birth of a New Symbol" advanced a model, however crude, of overwhelming Anglo racism. Race was emerging as a means to comprehend the Mexican experience. The fact that Sánchez developed this model while in jail suggests that legal repression helped to convince him and other young Mexicans that a basic racial analysis best explained their situation.

THE BROWN BERETS AND THE BLOWOUTS

Until the East Los Angeles high school walkouts in March 1968, the Brown Berets probably had no more than a handful of members.[41] David Sánchez led the organization with the title of prime minister, while other officers included Chairman Gilbert Cruz

Olmeda, Minister of Information Carlos Montes, and Minister of Discipline Ralph Ramírez. Although women had played an important role in the YCCA, they were not a part of the Berets until April 1968, when Sánchez's sister Arlene along with her friends Grace and Hilda Reyes became members. Gloria Arellanes also joined during this period, eventually serving as the minister of finance and communication.[42] Arellanes was the only woman to serve in a formal leadership capacity, though women would do much of the institutional work that allowed the Brown Berets to flourish.

During the first months of 1968, police harassment of the Berets increased. Under police pressure, La Piranya closed on March 3, 1968, just two days after the first students walked out of East Los Angeles schools.[43] Despite the police crackdown, during the strikes the Berets helped make picket signs and traveled to various schools, organizing demonstrators and cajoling students to join the protests. According to police testimony, Brown Berets were standing outside Garfield High School on March 5 at noon when two fire trucks arrived in response to a bomb threat.[44] The school principal decided against any search of the building and the fire engines soon left, but not before the commotion had drawn students to the front of the school. From their position on the sidewalk, the Berets began yelling to the students to walk out, which they began to do in groups of about a dozen or more. Within two hours, thirty sheriff's deputies and fourteen highway patrolmen had arrived on the scene.[45] The Brown Berets began directing the students to sit down in the street, and about forty students did so.[46] Sheriff's deputy Dan Castrellon testified that while dispersing the students, "I observed [Berets] to be yelling, 'Sit down, don't move.' And specifically, they were yelling a phrase, 'Don't be a cherry, sit down.'"[47]

The Brown Berets' prominent involvement in the student walkouts increased the group's visibility in East Los Angeles. In addition, they did not shy from self-promotion. The Berets sought to recruit new members by bragging of their role in the walkouts in *Chicano Student News,* an activist paper aimed at high school students:

> When the cops moved in, it was the Berets that received the short end of the stick, it was the Berets that were dragged behind bars. The Brown Berets became a target for the Placa, and anyone wearing one was [a] suspect to be picked up. It is the Brown Berets who are presently behind bars or have warrants out for their arrests.
>
> You know, *ese,* when you lay it on the line, there are people who mouth about taking care of business, and there are people who take care of business. The Brown Berets take care of business and leave the "politicking" and mouthing to others.
>
> The Brown Berets are strictly a defense organization but reserve the right and duty to defend themselves, Chicanos and La Raza wherever and by whatever means necessary.[48]

Below this article, a drawing caricatured Uncle Sam. Under a caption that proclaimed "La Raza Needs You," the cartoon depicted an activist, draped with crossed bandoleers, wearing a beret and holding a rifle in his left hand. With his right index finger, the figure pointed at the viewer, admonishing "Join the Brown Berets Now."[49]

By helping to lead the walkouts, the Berets not only attracted new attention and new members from the community, they also garnered intensified law enforcement scrutiny. The prosecutor's office saw the Brown Berets as the principal agitators behind the student protests, which accounts for the fact that five of the thirteen persons indicted for involvement in the blowouts were Brown Berets: officers Sánchez, Cruz Olmeda, Ramírez, and Montes, as well as Fred López.[50]

EAST L.A. THIRTEEN AND THE FIRST BROWN BERET PROGRAM

For the Berets, the arrests and indictments in *East L.A. Thirteen* consolidated a shift in politics. *La Raza's* June 7 issue reported on the police sweeps, the charges against the Thirteen, and the

tumultuous public response. In that same issue, the Brown Berets
published the first extended statement defining their mission.
The statement began:

> For over 120 years the Mexican-American has suffered at the hands
> of the Anglo establishment. He is discriminated against in schooling,
> housing, employment, and in every other phase of life. Because of
> this situation the Mexican-American has become the lowest achiever
> of any minority group in the entire Southwest.
>
> Because these injustices have existed and the Anglo Establishment
> shows no signs of changing them, because the cries of individuals
> have gone unheard and fallen upon deaf ears, a group of young Chi-
> canos have come together under the name of the Brown Berets to
> demand an immediate end to the injustices committed against the
> Mexican-American.[51]

Converting their critique of Anglo discrimination into demands for changes in the treatment of Mexicans, the Berets set
out a ten-point program. In addition to advocating reforms including bilingual education, an end to urban renewal programs,
and a right to vote irrespective of English-language ability, the
program contained four central demands directly related to legal
violence:

- We demand that all Mexican-Americans be tried by juries consisting
  of only Mexican-Americans;
- We demand a Civilian Police Review Board, made up of people who
  live in our community, to screen all police officers, before they are assigned to our community;
- We demand that all police officers in Mexican-American communities
  must live in the community and speak [Spanish];
- We demand the right to keep and bear arms to defend our communities against racist police, as guaranteed under the Second
  Amendment of the United States Constitution.[52]

In addition to these points, the Berets also adopted a new
motto, one that played on the LAPD's slogan, "To protect and to
serve." The Berets distilled their mission into the following:

- To Serve—To give vocal as well as physical support to those people and causes which help the people of the Mexican-American communities;
- To Observe—To keep a watchful eye on all federal, state, city and private agencies which deal with the Mexican-American, especially law enforcement agencies;
- To Protect—To protect, guarantee, and secure the rights of the Mexican-American by all means necessary.[53]

In this rhetorical reversal, the Berets lampooned the LAPD's motto by promising to watch over and control the police.

Finally and most importantly, the June 1968 statement pronounced a distinct racial identity for Chicanos. In the immediate wake of the high school walkouts and the *East L.A. Thirteen* arrests, and in the context of defining a political program that spotlighted police brutality, the Berets publicly proclaimed: "The Brown Beret was chosen because it is a symbol of the love and pride we have in our race and in the color of our skin."[54] Here for the first time, one sees in the pages of *La Raza* an unequivocal statement of Mexican racial difference: Mexicans were a brown race marked by brown skin.

The common sense connections among protest, repression, and race that helped to establish *East L.A. Thirteen's* significance for Acosta and the defendants played that same role for the Brown Berets. The indictment of the Beret leadership helped to propel them toward a more militant stance focused on police brutality and emphasizing non-white identity. After *East L.A. Thirteen* the Berets concluded that legal violence was the issue and that Mexicans were brown. The tight relationship between these two conclusions demonstrates the role played by common sense in the Berets' developing ideology.

That the Berets drew upon background understandings engendered by the black struggle is further suggested by their emulation of the Black Panthers. Like the Panthers, the Berets adopted a militant stance, a hierarchy with elaborate titles, a ten-point program, and a penchant for quoting Malcolm X's maxim

"By all means necessary."[55] To be sure, the Brown Berets differed significantly from the Panthers in that the Berets were younger, less organized, relatively unsophisticated ideologically, poorly funded, and without strong ties to the middle class or to white liberals.[56] Nevertheless, the Berets' use of Panther rhetoric and practices confirms the black struggle's important influence on the Mexican community's emerging conception of itself as a racial minority.

When *East L.A. Thirteen* began, the Brown Berets had just a few members. Over the next couple of years, the organization grew to include over sixty chapters as far away as the Midwest.[57] Perhaps because of the increasing legal violence imposed upon them, young Mexicans joined the Brown Berets in large numbers. Those who joined had come to believe that they belonged to a brown race and needed to confront legal violence in order to achieve a better life for their community.

A SPIRAL OF VIOLENCE

The YCCA's early focus on police brutality precipitated a radicalizing dynamic. The police, operating according to their own common sense regarding political mobilization in minority communities, responded as though the demonstrators threatened democracy. This aggressive response played into the tripartite connections among protest, repression, and race, strengthening the belief among Mexicans that they were non-white. The same connections convinced many young Mexicans that, as minorities facing injustice, they must protest. Escalating unrest led to increased repression and to additional demonstrations, in a bitter spiral of community militancy and legal violence. Ultimately this dynamic produced police killings, riots, calls by Brown Berets for a bullet in the heart of every police officer, and a fatalistic view among militants that Brown Power could be achieved only by destroying the white race.

Between May 1969 and April 1971 the Brown Berets produced their own paper, *La Causa*, which recorded this spiraling conflict in hostile rhetoric.[58] By mid 1969 the Brown Berets had suffered eighteen months of police abuse, including the firebombing of their headquarters on North Soto Street that destroyed one room and damaged the rest of the office.[59] The first two issues of La Causa, in May and July 1969, chronicled continuing police harassment.

In the May issue, La Causa's editorial staff—David Sánchez, Cristo Cebada, Grace Reyes, Hilda Reyes, Gloria Arrellanes, and Jesus Ceballos—railed against a police informer: "Through Brown Beret Intelligence, we discovered Robert Avila dressed in the black uniform of a marano (pig), packing his 38 caliber white solution piece . . . thus, as a spy for the L.A.P.D., he became ineffective and was ordered back to his job as an ordinary pig."[60]

In the July issue, Hilda Reyes described being jerked from a car and accosted at gunpoint by police when she arrived at Brown Beret headquarters:

> We were on our way home when all of a sudden rifles were cocked and pointed at our heads, we were grabbed and thrown out of the car . . . One of our brothers asked, "Could I see a search warrant or any kind of identification?" The pig replied, "This is enough" and pointed the rifle to his head . . . We were enraged, but in our position what could we do? We blew their minds and began to sing some chicano songs . . . "No more white pigs, no more white pigs, over me and before I'd be a slave I'll be buried in my grave and go home to Aztlan and be free" . . . The pigs don't have anything else to do but to harass and kill our people, La Raza.[61]

By the summer of 1969 the Brown Berets consistently referred to law enforcement personnel as pigs or maranos, a Spanish equivalent carrying an especially strong connotation of filthiness. In addition, notions of race regularly informed the Berets' denigration of the police. The May editorial described the officer's gun as a "white solution piece"; Reyes referred to "white pigs" and claimed that the police "harass and kill our people, La

Raza." From the start, in discussing police harassment *La Causa* expressed antipathy toward law enforcement in the terminology of race.

Police abuse became a routine feature of Brown Beret membership. In September 1969 Lorraine Escalante reported a courthouse police assault on her and Carlos Montes, the Berets' minister of information and a defendant in both *East L.A. Thirteen* and *Biltmore Six:*

> On August 19 a few of us went to court [as spectators in a trial of a Brown Beret member]. While we were in court [L.A.P.D.] Sgt. Armas saw Carlos Montes leave the court room; he then jumped out of his chair and followed Carlos to the phone booth. We all then got up and followed because Carlos was in trouble. Armas claimed that Carlos had a concealed weapon in his brief case which later on was found to be untrue. Armas . . . broke into the phone booth and then handcuffed Carlos. There was much confusion in the hall with the pigs pushing and hitting everyone in sight . . . I went . . . to go back to the courtroom when two pigs said I was under arrest, I asked what for when all of a sudden four pigs were beating on me. I was handcuffed then taken to a small room where they also handcuffed me to the chair. Carlos was also in the room and was being harassed and slugged by Officer Early. I was then told to shut up or I was going to have a sanitary napkin across my mouth. I was then searched in front of at least ten pigs . . . Carlos was taken to a cell where then I was left with Officer Early. He locked the door and proceeded to harass me telling me that his friends when they arrest girls they first go and seduce them . . . I was charged with assault on an officer, interfering, resisting arrest. This is typical of the harassment we go through everyday.[62]

Escalante's story, as well as that of Hilda Reyes, gives us some sense of the abuse the police routinely inflicted on Brown Berets. In addition, their experiences show that the police did not spare Brown Beret women. Not surprisingly, this police harassment differed in some ways from that imposed on the men. In addition to insults, false arrests, and physical assaults, Beret women also faced sexual taunting and humiliation.

As Escalante relates, during this period Carlos Montes attracted considerable police attention. He was put under extended LAPD surveillance, issued multiple spurious traffic tickets, physically beaten, and at least twice threatened with death, including once when a police officer told him, "I'm either going to kill you or see that you spend the rest of your life behind bars."[63] He also spent several months in jail, unable to raise the bail imposed after he was arrested on the *Biltmore Six* charges.[64] The police also frequently harassed David Sánchez, arresting him numerous times on a variety of charges. In addition to being picked up in the Chicano cases and for protesting in front of a police station in early 1968, the police busted Sánchez in May 1970 for allegedly throwing a molotov cocktail at the Hollenbeck Police Station; in September 1970 for armed robbery after supposedly finding him as a passenger in a car carrying a loaded M-1 carbine rifle; and again in March 1971, this time on federal charges of evading the draft.[65] All Brown Berets, but especially the leaders, suffered constant police harassment. For Montes, the violence and the risk of long prison sentences in the Chicano cases proved too much. He fled Los Angeles, going underground in January 1970.[66]

During this time, violence and conflict continued to escalate in East Los Angeles. In 1970 and 1971 firebombings swept the Eastside, burning stores, damaging high schools, and threatening police stations. A shadowy group called the Chicano Liberation Front often claimed responsibility.[67] Meanwhile, school protests also continued. In March 1970 more than one hundred students were arrested in protests at Roosevelt High School, and over the following six months the school suffered at least two arson attacks and one bombing.[68] In May 1970 classroom walkouts and sit-ins at Roosevelt and Lincoln High Schools resulted in additional arrests on charges ranging from failure to disperse to assault on a police officer.[69]

THE CHICANO MORATORIUM RIOT

As tensions increased on the streets of East Los Angeles during 1969 and 1970, opposition to the Vietnam War also accelerated. The Brown Berets, like other Chicano groups, opposed U.S. involvement in a war fought disproportionately by working-class people of color.[70] In February 1970, chanting "Viva La Raza, Afuera de Vietnam," Brown Berets joined 6,000 protesters in a march along Whittier Boulevard, one of the main avenues through East Los Angeles. Afterwards, demonstrators gathered for a rally where Oscar Acosta among others condemned the war.[71] This demonstration was the first in a series of marches organized by an anti-war group called the Chicano Moratorium Committee.[72]

The largest Mexican rally against the war, often simply referred to as the Chicano Moratorium, began in East Los Angeles on August 29, 1970, and ended with rioting and bloodshed.[73] The march itself concluded peacefully, with 20,000 demonstrators of all ages, including many families with children, gathered in Laguna Park to listen to speakers. Just before 3:00 P.M. and about a block from the park, however, a small store named the Green Mill filled with customers. Two sheriff's vehicles soon arrived with red lights flashing, as if responding to a burglary in progress. Hostility erupted between the crowd and the deputies, who promptly called for reinforcements. During the commotion that ensued, a group of protesters attacked a deputy, wrestled his gun from him, and fired two shots in his direction. Eight or ten more patrol cruisers and a busload of deputies soon arrived. The officers decided to clear people from the park and claimed to have used loudspeakers to order the assembly to disperse, but observers at the park said that they heard no such orders. The deputies formed a line and began moving into the crowd, firing tear gas and swinging their nightsticks. While most people retreated, some began to battle the police, throwing rocks and bottles and flinging the tear gas canisters back toward the advancing officers.

At 3:25 P.M. the police received the first reports of looting. The violence in the park spread into the streets of East Los Angeles, and Whittier Boulevard in particular suffered damage from the rampage of angry residents and police. What started initially as a police riot developed quickly into a general conflagration that engulfed East Los Angeles. In addition to beating and gassing marchers in Laguna Park, the police killed three persons. Angel Gilberto Díaz, thirty, died of multiple gunshot wounds received when he allegedly attempted to drive his car through a barricade set up by the sheriff's department.[74] And a fifteen-year-old Brown Beret activist named Lynn Ward bled to death after an exploding tear gas canister hurled him through a plate-glass window.[75]

But the death that caused the greatest outcry was that of *Los Angeles Times* reporter Rubén Salazar, a prominent member of the Mexican community.[76] At around 5:30 P.M., having just toured the riot area on foot, Salazar and three companions were seated in the Silver Dollar Saloon, a nearby bar. One of Salazar's friends pushed through the hanging curtains that served as a door to the street, to look around. Four deputies ordered him back inside at gunpoint. Returning to the bar, he urged his companions to leave by the back entrance. Before they could exit, however, the officers fired four tear-gas missiles into the bar. The missiles were ten-inch long, high-velocity projectiles designed to pierce barricades and were capable of penetrating inch-thick pine boards at one hundred yards. The deputies fired from a distance of fifteen feet through the curtain hanging in the open doorway. The first missile hit Salazar in the head, killing him instantly.[77]

Salazar's death stunned the community. Thousands paid their respects as his body lay in state, and flags were lowered to half-mast at Los Angeles County buildings until after his funeral.[78] A coroner's inquest into Salazar's death was covered live on a rotating basis by all of the major television stations in Los Angeles.[79] The sheriff's deputies changed their stories several times, but the nature of the inquest prohibited questions from anyone but the hearing officer, who proved solicitous to the deputies. Nevertheless, Oscar Acosta repeatedly interrupted to challenge the proceedings as a whitewash, unfair, and racially biased.[80] When the hearing officer accepted without question testimony by the deputy who fired the fatal shot that he had been aiming at the bar's ceiling, Acosta jumped to his feet and shouted: "He was aiming at Ruben Salazar, that's what he was aiming at! This is an obscenity . . . We are sick of it. This room is polluted with perjury and you know it!" Acosta then stormed out, followed by about twenty-five activists.[81]

In the inquest, jurors could reach one of two verdicts: either that Salazar died at the hands of another or that he died by accident. After sixteen days of hearings, the jurors split four to three in favor of death by another.[82] The four jurors explained publicly that their verdict "was meant to reflect strong criticism of the Los Angeles County Sheriff's Department." While not suggesting that the deputies had planned to assassinate Salazar, the four jurors nevertheless concluded that "those deputies expected they had a good chance of killing somebody."[83] But a week after the inquest verdict—during which time two of the three jurors who voted for "death by accident" said that they had made a mistake—District Attorney Evelle Younger concluded that negligence on the part of the deputies, "if any," did not rise to the level required under involuntary manslaughter, and so refused to bring any charges.[84] Sheriff Peter Pitchess insisted that "there was absolutely no misconduct on the part of the deputies involved."[85] The coroner's inquest, like the walkout cases, spurred many in the community to reevaluate their relationship with law enforcement.

MARTYRS AND CALLS TO KILL POLICE

For the Brown Berets, the most significant death in the late August riots was not that of Salazar but that of fifteen-year-old Lynn Ward.[86] In its December 1970 issue, *La Causa* covered Ward's death as well as the Moratorium riots generally. *La Causa* eulogized Ward by recounting his bravery earlier on the

day of his death when he took "people out of Laguna Park as the
battle raged on with its swinging clubs and tear and nausea
gas."[87] But even more than Ward's service, La Causa celebrated
his opposition to the police. "Ward died standing on his feet
fighting for Justice for his Raza, the victim of a pig's exploding
tear gas canister. He did not take the oppression of the pigs on his
knees as many have in the past."[88] La Causa concluded: "To all
the youth of Aztlan, let Lynn's example show you the way to help
your Raza."[89] Ward's death became a symbol of police violence,
his life a testament to resistance, and Ward himself a Brown Beret martyr.

Side by side with Ward's eulogy, La Causa also lamented the
recent death of another Brown Beret, Danny Rodríguez. The paper showed photos of Rodríguez's coffin draped with a Mexican
flag and surrounded by Berets. The issue's last page featured pictures of Ward and Rodríguez on either side of the Berets' symbol,
crossed rifles over a crucifix, while bold letters proclaimed them
"Soldados de La Raza."[90] If they were soldiers, though, the enemy had to be the police. While the last page of the issue featured
them as soldados, the first page showed a sheriff's car burning
during the August riot, over which La Causa printed Mexican
revolutionary Emiliano Zapata's injunction to "seek justice . . .
with a rifle in your fist."[91]

In reporting on the Moratorium riot and its casualties, La
Causa preached a new level of hatred toward the police, for the
first time extending this antipathy to whites generally. The growing hostility toward the police permeated La Causa's graphics
and text. A cartoon showed a Brown Beret partisan aiming a rifle
at a police officer, who stood with a target stenciled on his chest.
The caption says, "To protect and to serve . . . who says Chicanos can't shoot straight."[92] A separate drawing depicted an AK-
47 assault rifle, with the slogan "Viva la Raza!!!! Kill the Perro
[dog]!"[93]

Next to this, an article entitled "Justicia o Revolucion" excoriated the police and judges: "Does law and order mean peace

and quiet to chicano people? No! The whiteman's *law* means the same law that murders chicanos on the street and let's their pig murderers go unpunished . . . yes the law that locks up chicanos in jails like animals (Judge Chargin, 'Maybe Hitler was right, the animals in society should be put in cages')." The article then all but invited Chicanos to kill white police: "They say Rubén Salazar was a great man, he had made it in society, yet he was shot dead in the Barrio streets like a common dirty greaser . . . The Brown Berets are asking the Chicano people to stop fighting, stabbing, and killing each other . . . and start fighting, shooting and killing this piggish racist society."[94] *La Causa* no longer simply called the police names. Now, its graphics and articles promoted the idea of murdering law enforcement officers.

Hostility toward the police also expanded into a general hatred of all whites. A December 1970 article entitled "Destroy the White Mind" asked: "Was it all white men that kept us down or was it only some of the white men? This was a hard question to answer, because many white people were helping us, such as Fred Ross who trained Cesar Chavez. But still it was hard to keep our hate down for the white man."[95]

Even as the Brown Berets' rhetoric grew more strident, the Chicano Moratorium Committee was planning a second major anti-war protest. The committee purposefully held the rally in Belvedere Park next door to the East Los Angeles sheriff's station, to protest "the suspicious deaths of Chicano prisoners" there, "and because of the way they attacked the people on [August] 29th," according to one organizer.[96] By the time the rally occurred on January 31, 1971, the Committee had been infiltrated by a provocateur working for the U.S. Treasury's Alcohol, Tobacco, and Firearm Division. Federal agent Frank Martínez later admitted inciting a riot after the rally by "shouting and throwing things at the East Los Angeles Sheriff Station and talking about doing in police."[97] The riot ended with one person killed by a police shotgun blast, more than twenty others wounded by police bullets, seventy-eight sheriff's cars damaged, eleven deputies injured, and Whittier Boulevard once again in flames.[98] The number of Chicano victims rivaled the four dead and nine wounded at the Kent State massacre four months earlier that had shocked the country. Very little national attention focused on the carnage in East Los Angeles.[99]

La Causa reported in February 1971 on the second Moratorium riot, and again mourned Chicano martyrs and condemned the police as well as whites, but with a yet more vitriolic tone. Under the heading "Police Genocide," the paper listed twenty-three Chicano dead, including not just those killed in the preceding riots but all those whom the paper alleged the police had killed over the previous fifteen years.[100] La Causa then offered a new pledge of allegiance: "I pledge allegiance to my raza, of the oppressed land of Aztlan, and to the pigs where ere they art hiding, one bullet in thy heart, *por libertad y justicia por todos los chicanos.*"[101]

La Causa also ran an article offering legal advice on when police could be killed in self-defense, concluding: "The community . . . has this right, indeed a duty to protect the lives of individual members. Remember—Shoot To Kill."[102] Next to this article a drawing showed a Brown Beret couple: the woman wore crossed bandoleers and the man carried a rifle. They stood over the body of a dead pig, the man resting a booted foot on its head as if just having shot it, while across the pig's body was scrawled "Police genocide. Continuous killing. Physical and mental denial of human rights and civil rights. Oppressor of Chicanos."[103] Another article warned, "The only way in which all our problems will be resolved is through the entire destruction of the white race."[104]

THE SECOND BROWN BERET PROGRAM

In the December 1970 issue of *La Causa,* among the articles reporting on the first Moratorium riots and after a photo spread of Whittier Boulevard burning, the Brown Berets issued a new, thirteen-point program.[105] In their ten-point program, despite a strident tone, the Berets had called for incremental changes largely consonant with Mexican American politics.[106] In contrast, the thirteen-point program mixed Marxism with demands for Chicano self-governance and a Chicano homeland.[107] The Brown Berets' new language brooked no compromise with Anglo society but instead inveighed against a "U.S. capitalist ruling and exploiting class" and "barbaric capitalist invaders," while declaring "solidarity with all revolutionary people who are engaged in the struggle for self-determination and freedom."[108]

In moving to a Marxist analysis and demands for Chicano sovereignty, the Brown Berets did not abandon but rather supplemented their racial analysis. Their new ideology did not replace race with class; rather, it applied a class-based analysis to Chicanos as a racial group: "The Chicano people are an example of the aggression of the racist brutal rule of U.S. imperialism. First our land was taken from us and then our people forced to work for this corrupt system at its own racist, exploiting conditions to keep for centuries a people and its culture oppressed."[109] The Berets' racial analysis permeated their political program, even after they leavened it with a Marxist irredentism.

In the political program the Berets laid out in December 1970, race continued as the touchstone, and police relations persisted as the most pressing concern. The thirteen-point program included a host of demands, but by far the weight of the program addressed Chicano-law relations. One point stated: "We want all Chicanos being held in jail released [because] no Chicano has ever had a fair trial in the racist U.S. judicial system." Another demanded "a judicial system relevant to Chicanos and therefore administered by Chicanos . . . Any sentences imposed on La Raza should come from La Raza." And a third called for "the immediate end to the occupation of our community by the fascist police." "We realize," the Berets explained, "that the police occupy our communities just as the U.S. imperialist armies occupy foreign countries. Only by organizing and arming ourselves can we ever hope to stop police brutality and genocide in our communities."[110]

Some scholars have criticized the Brown Berets' radical ideology for throwing more heat than light.[111] Certainly, the group's exaggerated rhetoric failed to produce a trenchant analysis of the situation confronting Mexicans in the United States. Nevertheless, the Berets' success should not be measured by their ideology but rather by the new identity they helped to create and disseminate. The Berets developed a racial analysis that pictured Mexicans as a brown people victimized by pervasive racism, and identified the legal system as a prime culprit. This assessment still rings true for many in the Mexican community today.

Given the common sense of the times, it is entirely understandable why the Berets so rapidly and fully embraced a brown racial identity and a radical commitment to the belief that the police represented an entrenched, oppressive white enemy. While juvenile bravado and other conceits sometimes influenced them, the Berets' recourse to inflammatory rhetoric and destructive action reflects not so much a lack of political sophistication as the influence of common sense. As they challenged the forces that oppressed their community, the Berets drew on a model of racial struggle linking protest, police violence, and race. Common sense's influence on the Chicano movement's trajectory can be measured in condensed form in the evolution, actions, and rhetoric of the Brown Berets.

GENDER AND MILITANCY

While racial common sense shaped the Brown Berets' evolution, so too did other taken-for-granted ideas, including the common sense of gender. Gender relations in the Mexican community in Los Angeles strongly influenced gender divisions in the Brown Berets. More than that, though, gender identity contributed to an emphasis on militancy within the Berets.

Many Berets envisioned the militant's role in masculine terms and saw the provision of services as women's purview; these ideas dictated the division of labor within the Berets. Men spoke at rallies and led the demonstrations, while women ran the

Brown Berets' free medical clinic and breakfast program and did the tedious work necessary to publish *La Causa*.[112] Very few of the many women in the Berets occupied leadership positions.[113] As one disgruntled Beret woman from East L.A. recalled: "They [the men] wanted to make all the decisions and we always got the shit jobs. At fund raisers the girls did all the cooking and always got stuck with all the cleaning, and the guys would just be there hanging around . . . The girls put the newspaper together, but had no say about what went into it. The guys made all the big decisions."[114]

Women did frequently participate in militant actions, for instance marching and demonstrating in Beret uniform, and in September 1969 seven Brown Beret women staged a hunger strike to protest conditions in the L.A. county jails.[115] Nevertheless, the Beret culture largely relegated women to the role of supporting the "real" protest work done by men. In a potent symbol of women's inferior status in the East Los Angeles Berets, for a while women were required to meet at different times and locations than the men.[116]

In addition to dictating status relations within the Berets, gender also influenced the style of Beret protest politics. Many Beret men believed that, as men, they were required to defend Mexican women. Brown Berets thus often presented themselves as opposing sexual predation by outsiders. In exposing the work of undercover police officer Fernando Sumaya, *La Causa* alleged that he "was not so much a hero 'in the line of duty,' but a married man who committed adultery, and a seducer of innocent young girls . . . There is no telling how many unwed mothers he left behind."[117]

Beret men also often believed that their masculinity required them to engage in militant actions, and in turn supposed that militancy confirmed their manhood. Beret men valued and sought to enhance the group's confrontational reputation as "shock troops" because it burnished their own masculinity. Indeed, chief among the male activists' most sought-after possessions was a "rep," or reputation, for the masculine attributes of being tough and fearing no one, especially not "the man." The Berets' inflated emphasis on militant protest manifested itself most dramatically in internal fighting over the value of the free clinic, which, David Sánchez argued, distracted members from the more important work of planning and participating in demonstrations. This infighting eventually led to a mass exodus by women from the Los Angeles Brown Berets, greatly weakening that organization.[118]

Notions of masculinity contributed to the Berets' preoccupation with street demonstrations and violent rhetoric. At the same time, gender norms also influenced the conduct of the police, leading the overwhelmingly male officer corps to construe challenges to their authority as invitations to violence.[119] The LAPD even used appeals to masculinity to recruit Mexicans. A billboard in East Los Angeles read "Macho! Join the LAPD." Graffiti across the billboard responded "Kill the Pigs."[120] Hypermasculine politics helped to destroy the Brown Berets by exposing members to escalating violence on the part of law enforcement and by driving out key activists such as the women.

THE BROWN BERETS' DISSOLUTION

After the second Chicano Moratorium in January 1971 ended in violence, public sentiment turned strongly against the idea of further demonstrations. Prominent Mexican community members, including leaders of LULAC and other civil rights organizations, called for an end to large demonstrations in East Los Angeles, warning "the Chicano community against being drawn into violence that produces nothing."[121] The *Los Angeles Times* also counseled against further rallies, suggesting that the Chicano Moratorium Committee did not speak for most Mexicans, that the demonstrations distracted attention from the community's "legitimate grievances," and that more protests would "damage the proud name 'Mexican-American.'"[122]

The Brown Berets published the last regular issue of *La Causa*

in April 1971, three months after the second riot. This issue
listed sixty-six active Brown Beret chapters, reprinted the thirteen-point program, and advised on what to do if arrested.[123]
The next *La Causa,* undated, reported that Brown Berets under
David Sánchez's leadership had departed Los Angeles in a
"Reconquest Caravan" that would travel throughout the Southwest between October 1971 and August 1972.[124] Promoted as a
mission to spread the message of Chicano Power, surely the caravan's attractions included providing Brown Berets a temporary
exit from the turmoil in Los Angeles.

In late August 1972 the Berets returned to Los Angeles and
staged their last major protest, invading Catalina Island, which
lies just off the coast, to draw attention to the "deplorable conditions for people of Mexican descent living in the U.S."[125] After
camping for three weeks above Avalon Harbor, the Berets abandoned their protest and went home.[126] On October 21, 1972, the
Brown Berets National Headquarters Central Committee fired
David Sánchez after he allegedly killed another member, committed rape, and stole money from the organization.[127] Sánchez
responded by calling a press conference to announce that he
was disbanding the Brown Berets. Reporting on Sánchez's per-
formance at the press conference, the *Los Angeles Times* wrote:
"He answered most questions with rambling discourses filled
with the dialectic of the militant Chicano. Newsmen were unable
to get specific details of why the organization was being dis-
solved."[128]

By late 1972 some quiet had returned to East Los Angeles.
But what peace prevailed did not stem from general improvements. The community had retreated to a state of shocked
exhaustion and "subdued bitterness."[129] According to the *Times,*
every Mexican community leader "insisted that the basic problems which created the conditions for rioting—unemployment,
lack of political representation, poor housing, lack of adequate educational opportunities and sometimes strained police-
community relations—are all still festering."[130] The community

leaders specifically rejected the claim that police relations had improved. "Most community activists . . . say that any peace in East Los Angeles is more a reflection of the community's caution and wariness than of any improvement in relations with the police."[131]

The Brown Berets and the Chicano movement between 1968 and 1972 aggressively protested police mistreatment of Mexicans in Los Angeles. Yet during those years, police abuse intensified. In just one year, between spring 1971 and spring 1972, six Mexican youths died—their deaths labeled suicides—inside the East Los Angeles sheriff's station.[132] The police continue to deploy massive force in East Los Angeles to this day, and community residents still fear the police. The Brown Berets reworked Mexican identity, but they did not come close to ending legal violence in East L.A.

Mexican students walked out of East Los Angeles high schools in March 1968 brandishing signs that proclaimed "Chicano Power!" Yet the meaning of "Chicano" only fully emerged over the next few years. Police repression did much to shape this developing meaning, but the Chicano movement also worked constantly, creatively, and self-consciously to fashion a new racial identity. The militants sought to counteract the stereotypical image of Mexicans established over a century before as dark, dirty, lazy, cowardly and criminal, and to build a positive identity in which all Mexicans could take pride. Put differently, Chicanos sought to change the common sense regarding Mexican identity. In doing so, though, the insurgents too relied on racial common sense.

Racial ideas can be disaggregated along three lines: characteristics, the traits associated with different groups; categories, the groups that count as races; and properties, the supposed attributes of race, including cultural conceptions regarding race's power to determine individual and group identity. These component notions of race can be explicitly debated, but even when some racial ideas are forthrightly challenged, the remainder almost always continue to function as background knowledge.

Mexican Americans had attempted to counteract negative views regarding themselves by asserting that they were white persons with Spanish surnames. In effect, this generation sought to claim the positive characteristics associated with white identity by asserting that Mexicans belonged in the white category. At the same time, Mexican Americans understood race to have relatively little power to determine identity. Mexican Americans drew on a progressive racial ideology that had been gaining ground in the United States since the 1920s. Associated with an emphasis on ethnicity, this ideology argued that race was only skin deep—that is, that race altered only physical features, and that race specifically did not determine individual and group identity. On all three levels, the Chicano militants took decidedly different approaches.

NOT WHITE

Frustrated by the persistent negative treatment of Mexicans despite the claim to be white, and inspired by the Black Power movement, Mexican activists in East Los Angeles almost immediately began to think of themselves as not white. Chicano militants rejected two sorts of whiteness: that within their own community and that of Anglos.

Chicanos broke with Mexican Americans over whether Mexicans were white, often causing family rifts. A former activist recalled, "When I was in high school I thought I was a real radical. I guess I thought of myself as Chicana and I used to cause a lot of fights at home. I used to call myself a Mexican and my dad would say 'you're Mexican American,' and I'd say, 'no I'm not, I'm not white!'"[1] A Mexican American scholar observed this same fracture in 1971, lamenting: "There are cases in which children who insist on calling themselves Chicanos have had to leave home because their parents consider this a self-denigrating term which in years past was used to refer to the lower caste Mexicans. The insistence in defining the Mexican-American on racial terms with an undue emphasis on his Indian heritage courts the prejudice and discrimination that for centuries has been part of Anglo-American culture."[2]

This battle within families shaded into one between political generations. Dr. Hector P. García, the founder of the American GI Forum, chastised references to Brown Power. "That sounds as if we were a different race," García said. "We're not. We're white. We should be Americans."[3] Chicano activists often responded by charging false consciousness and self-hate. One activist retorted that the "whole Spanish American thing, it's pretty much of an apologia for being what one is . . . This is a form of self-hate . . . It's the big lie, man; the apologetic."[4]

More than simply disagreeing regarding Mexican racial identity, Chicanos used racial language as a shorthand to criticize certain political viewpoints and social orientations. Activists began to accuse other Mexicans of trying to be white. David Sánchez berated a Mexican undercover police officer in these terms: "His mind has been messed with—the poor guy is trying to be a white Anglo."[5] Sánchez did not mean that the officer was attempting to become a member of the white race but that he had adopted a politics inimical to the Mexican community. In a related complaint, activists frequently described some community members as being "whitened," using terms such as *agringado* or *agabachado*. These insults made *gringo* and *gabacho* into adjectives, where especially gabacho carried a pejorative connotation. According to Chicanos, "whitened" Mexicans identified with and aspired to the status of whites. They were also those who, because of physical features, wealth, profession, education, or business position, possessed characteristics associated with whites.[6] For Chicanos, those who were agringado or agabachado were alienated from an authentic Mexican identity.

The emphasis on not being white ultimately included a change among Chicanos regarding how to value and understand the physical features of individual Mexicans. Taking their cue from status systems in both Mexico and the United States, Mexicans had long invested European features with heightened value. But the advent of the Chicano movement changed community perceptions. As one activist reported, "The lighter-skinned Mexican is no longer the favored son; quite the contrary, the darker Indian type is now idealized as are other characteristics and customs which derive from our Indian heritage."[7] When Chicanos moved to considering themselves non-white, they colored their prototypical Mexican with brown features and espoused dark looks as an ideal.

According to Chicanos, and many Mexicans today, Mexicans were racially brown by nature, and contrary beliefs, politics, or attitudes could render one inauthentic but not actually white. Chicanos considered the idea that Mexicans were white patently false, just as the belief that Mexicans were brown seemed obviously true. It was in this sense that Chicanos thought Mexican Americans suffered from "false consciousness": ostensibly, Mexican Americans had convinced themselves of a fact—Mexican whiteness—that simply was not true. Worse, according to Chicanos, political and social aspirations to be white betrayed both the Mexican American individual and the community as a whole by supporting white supremacy.

Bitterness and hostility marked many debates between Chicanos and Mexican Americans regarding identity. The high emotions may seem out of place given that both groups sought to improve the situation of Mexicans and to respond to Anglo racism. But anger and outrage make perfect sense when one remembers that at stake was nothing less than common sense. Chicanos and Mexican Americans alike thought that their opponents, be they family members, community leaders, or activists, were contesting an obvious truth. Though both groups debated Mexican racial identity, all concerned considered Mexican identity to be beyond debate: it was indisputable to Mexican Americans that they were white, and similarly incontrovertible to Chicanos that they were not.[8]

ANTI-WHITE

Chicanos rejected whiteness in order to give themselves space in which to define a positive Mexican identity. But before they figured out what was good about what they were, they focused on what was bad about what they were not. As the Chicano movement progressed, activists increasingly depicted Anglos as the hated enemies of Chicanos, and Anglo culture as a threat to Chicano survival.

One East Los Angeles militant explained his hate for whites this way: "All white men have the bill that has been done to any minority, therefore you can say, 'The *gabacho* has done this to us.' And when a person, when a kid gets killed on the streets of East L.A. by a policeman and he is killed unjustly, that man is nothing but a dirty *gabacho*. You want to say it, you feel hate and naturally all hate stretches out to any white person, even sometimes the white people that are with you."[9] The rage expressed by this activist stemmed on one level from the injustices suffered by Mexicans. On another level, though, by defining his anger in race-based terms, this activist's anti-white politics accentuated the common identity of Mexicans. It created an us-them dynamic in which race defined both "them" and "us."

Chicano rhetoric often used hate against whites to unify and motivate the Mexican community. José Angel Gutiérrez, leader of the Texas-based Mexican American Youth Organization and one of the founders of La Raza Unida Party, used this approach. Three scholars, including Gutiérrez himself, later summarized his tactics: "Gutierrez urged Chicanos to unite against that devil, whom he referred to as bigoted, un-American, racist, animalistic, foreigner, thief, exploiter, barbarian, white supremacist, clever (in a negative sense), and full of hatred."[10] To be sure, not all Chicanos expressed hatred toward whites or attempted to use such hatred to encourage Mexican solidarity. Nevertheless, many East Los Angeles activists, in particular Brown Berets, used anti-white rhetoric to help unify Mexicans.

Chicanos defined themselves not only against Anglos as enemies but against what they negatively perceived as white culture. Whiteness for Chicanos became synonymous with a dominant culture that they caricatured as unremittingly shallow, materialistic, and base. Armando Rendón's 1971 "Chicano Manifesto" expressed this disgust: "The North American culture is not worth copying: it is destructive of personal dignity; it is callous, vindictive, arrogant, militaristic, self-deceiving, and greedy; it is a gold-plated ball-point pen . . . a Mustang and old-folks' homes . . . an $80 billion defense budget and a $75 a month welfare; it is a cultural cesspool and a social and spiritual vacuum for the Chicano."[11] *La Raza* shared Rendón's sense that Anglo culture boiled down to grubbing materialism: "As we, La Raza, detach ourselves from the superficiality of materialism, we realize how blindly we led ourselves through dark alleys that stripped us of our humanity. 'La Causa' is not seeking an abundance of money, two-car garages, and gluttonous appetites, but it seeks those essential elements necessary for bodily function and self-respect."[12]

By attributing the dominant culture's negative aspects to whites as a race, Chicanos laid the groundwork for accepting, and eventually promoting, the idea that race determined culture. At the beginning of the Chicano movement, Corky Gonzales in his 1967 poem "I Am Joaquín" depicted Mexicans as acculturated, even if he posited that such acculturation led to existential confusion. "I look at myself and see part of myself who rejects my father and mother, and dissolves into the melting pot," Gonzales wrote.[13] But as the Chicano movement progressed, activists increasingly rejected the notion that they shared in "white" culture. Anglo cultural influences came to be seen not as contributing to a new, distinctive Mexican culture in the United States but as tainting the otherwise pure culture of Chicanos. Of course, this posed a problem: what was Chicano culture?

TRIANGULATING BROWN FROM BLACK AND RED

If Mexicans were not white, what were they? Influenced specifically by the Black Power movement and generally by the common sense of race, protest, and repression, Chicanos initially drew strong parallels between brown and black identities—indeed, in some accounts, brown and black were supposedly "one": in the fall of 1968 *La Raza* had insisted, "Our oppressions are one. Our dreams are one. Our demands are one. We suffer as one, we react as one, we struggle as one!"[14] Searching for the opposite of white, Chicanos initially came up with black.

Because the early Chicano movement aggressively took on the mantle of blackness, one movement legacy was an increased willingness among Mexicans to work with the African American community. For example, one study found that twice as many Mexicans favored cooperation with blacks in East Los Angeles in 1972 as compared with 1965.[15] But still, Mexicans open to associating with African Americans in 1972 remained a distinct minority, numbering only 39 percent.[16] "This is an impressive finding," the study's authors contended, "when one takes into account traditional animosities marring black–Mexican American relations."[17] That may be, but the 39 percent figure also shows that, though Mexican animosity toward blacks substantially waned, it never came close to disappearing. By late 1969 and early 1970, lingering prejudice, coupled with ideas that linked Mexican identity to indigenous ancestry, stemmed Chicano assertions of a functionally black identity.

As Chicano activists moved to distinguish themselves from blacks, they analogized their identity to that of Native Americans, as Oscar Acosta did in 1971:

> The black man came here as a slave. He is not of this land. He is so removed from his ancestry that he has nothing but the white society to identify with. We have history. We have culture. We had a land. We do feel solidarity with the American Indians because we are Indians . . . I look upon them as my blood brothers. It is the Indian aspect of our ancestry that gives meaning to the term "La Raza." We are La Raza. Of course there is Spanish and European blood in us, but we don't always talk about it because it is not something we are proud of. For me, my native ancestry is crucial.[18]

Mexicans stressed their native ties partly in order to distance themselves from the black experience in the United States. This is the significance of Acosta's reference to slavery. By asserting that Chicanos were always here and by contrasting this with blacks' arrival as an enslaved population, Acosta suggested that Mexicans should be free of the inferiority imputed to blacks. In this assertion, Acosta accepted the notion that slavery reflects fault on the part of, and therefore stigmatizes, the black community.[19] Though Chicanos did not want to be white, neither did they want to be black.

Acosta's remarks also reflected an independent desire to link Chicano and Native American racial identity. Indigenous descent allowed Chicanos to lay special claim to the Southwest. It also provided a source for a Chicano culture presumably untainted by Anglo norms. Both claims were supremely racial in nature.

Consider first the assertion that Chicanos deserved the Southwest by right of prior possession; this claim resurrected the worn belief that divine provenance allocated the world's continents to different races. Acosta asserted the nexus between race and land in these terms: "The concepts of integration, assimilation and acculturation describe historical relationships between Africans, Orientals and Europeans, persons all foreign to this land . . . The Mexican-American claims the Southwest by right of prior possession, by right of his ancestry."[20] A former Brown Beret in East Los Angeles made the same claim more starkly: "This is motherland. God put the brown man on this continent. Just like God put the black man on his continent, he put the white man on his continent, he put the Asian man on his continent. But this is motherland."[21] When Chicanos claimed the Southwest by descent, they did so on the ground of racial entitlement.

Chicano activists also invoked their indigenous descent to celebrate pre-contact Indian civilizations as the wellspring of Chicano culture. David Sánchez offered this history: "In the beginning . . . there were beautiful lands with all the living resources

. . . It was a paradise where the balance of nature kept everyone alive . . . We were a proud people who perfected medicines."[22] Teatro Campesino's Luís Valdez promoted a similar Chicano origin myth: "This was not a new world at all. It was an ancient civilization based on a distinct concept of the universe. Tula, Teotihuacan, Monte Alban, Uxmal, Chichen Itzá, México-Tenochtitlan were all great centers of learning, having shared the wisdom of thousands of generations of pre-Columbian man."[23] "It is presumptuous, even dangerous," Valdez warned, "for anyone to pretend that the Chicano, the 'Mexican-American,' is only one more in a long line of hyphenated-immigrants to the New World. *We are the New World.*"[24] Along similar lines, Chicana feminist Mirta Vidal asserted that gender equality characterized precontact American civilization and insisted that gender oppression was a white thing. "In fact, before the Europeans came to this part of the world, women enjoyed a high position of equality with men. The submission of women, along with institutions such as the church and the patriarchy, was imported by the European colonizers, and remains to this day part of Anglo society."[25]

Sánchez linked Chicanos to his romanticized conception of pre-contact civilization, suggesting that the "we" in "We were a proud people" joined together Chicanos and an antediluvian people who lived in perfect harmony with their world. Valdez identified Chicanos with the most accomplished civilizations of meso-America, naming the major archeological ruins scattered across Mexico. He insisted that Chicanos were Americans in a true, continental sense. Vidal extolled pre-Columbian gender politics as the authentic inheritance of Chicanos and criticized the corrupting influence of Anglo society. Like Sánchez, Valdez, and Vidal, many Chicanos emphasized their indigenous ancestry to claim a pure Chicano culture rooted in ancient civilizations.[26]

Nevertheless, the association between Chicanos and Aztecs, Mayans, and so on ultimately involved not just a claim about culture but an assertion of race. East Los Angeles's Mexican residents had no particular insight into civilizations many centuries gone. But what they did have was a developing belief that race transmitted culture in a timeless, constant fashion.

AZTLÁN: RACE AS NATION

In March 1969, as East L.A. Chicanos struggled to give their identity a positive content, Corky Gonzales and his Denver-based Crusade for Justice hosted the first Chicano Youth Liberation Conference.[27] Over fifteen hundred activists from across the country attended, including not only a large Los Angeles contingent but also militants from as far away as Chicago, New York, and Puerto Rico.[28] Tensions in Denver were running high because the preceding week the police had violently accosted students protesting a teacher who told his class, "Mexicans are dumb because they eat beans. If you eat Mexican food you'll become stupid like Mexicans."[29] But optimism among participants soared when at the conference's beginning the school board announced they would transfer the teacher and when the police kept their distance while Chicano activists lowered a U.S. flag flying before the state legislature and hoisted in its place Mexico's flag.[30]

Over five days, the youth conference participants caucused, attempting to hammer out position papers to guide the new movement. In addition to speeches and discussions, poetry and music contributed to the flowering of a vibrant protest culture. One young participant enthused, "Conference is a poor word to describe those five days. It was in reality a fiesta. Days of celebrating what sings in the blood of a people who, colonized into believing they are ugly, discover the truth of the secret whisperings of bronze beauty nourished and guarded during years of occupation and intimidation. Coca Cola, Jackie Onassis, Doris Day, Breck Shampoo, the Playboy Bunny, the Marlboro ad, the jet set, life magazine, the Dodge 'rebellion' are all lies. WE ARE BEAUTIFUL!"[31] For many, the Chicano Youth conference marked a peak moment when everything seemed possible.

The conference published a statement of values, *El Plan Espiritual de Aztlán*, the Spiritual Plan of Aztlán, that the participants hoped would guide the movement. The plan's preamble has become one of the Chicano movement's most cited documents, largely because it offers a romantic vision of Chicano identity. Strikingly, the preamble spoke in terms that mixed race and nation:

> In the spirit of a new people that is conscious not only of its proud historical heritage, but also of the brutal "Gringo" invasion of our territories: We, the Chicano inhabitants and civilizers of the northern land of Aztlan, from whence came our forefathers, reclaiming the land of their birth and consecrating the determination of our people of the sun, declare that the call of our blood is our power, our responsibility, and our inevitable destiny.
>
> Brotherhood unites us and love for our brother makes us a people whose time has come and who struggle against the foreigner "Gabacho," who exploits our riches and destroys our culture. With our heart in our hands and our hands in the soil, We Declare the Independence of our Mestizo Nation. We are a Bronze People with a Bronze Culture. Before the world, before all of North America, before all of our brothers in the Bronze Continent, We are a Nation, We are a Union of free pueblos, We are Aztlan.[32]

The plan invoked Aztlán as the basis for the claim that "we are a nation." Aztlán had its origins in Aztec myth, where it referred to an original northern homeland.[33] In time, the Aztec legend intertwined with the Spanish fable of a golden northern land, El Dorado, to create an evocative rumor of lost lands located in what is today the U.S. Southwest.[34] In the last years of the nineteenth century, Anglo boosters of frontier settlement seized on this fable to promote expansion into New Mexico and beyond.[35] In turn, Chicanos appropriated the Aztlán legend to claim that Mexicans were the original inhabitants of the Southwest.[36] "Aztlán!" emerged as one of the great rallying cries of the Chicano movement, and today it continues to evoke notions of peoplehood and ancestral belonging. The iconography of

Aztlán—often a stalwart Aztec warrior standing over or holding up a swooned Aztec princess—remains popular in Mexican establishments and homes throughout the Southwest.[37]

Not only the preamble but the plan's substantive program stressed nationalism. For instance, the plan's first provision proclaimed: "Nationalism as the key to organization transcends all religions, political, class and economic factions or boundaries. Nationalism is the common denominator that all members of La Raza can agree on."[38] This emphasis on nationalism reflected the influence of Corky Gonzales, who believed in nationalism's ability to bridge divisions among Mexicans. Gonzales argued that all Mexicans at their core felt pride in their Mexican identity and that the movement's task was to stoke that pride: "Everybody in the barrios is a nationalist, you see, whether he admits it to himself or not. It doesn't matter if he's middle class, a *vendido,* a sellout, or what his politics may be. He'll come back home, to La Raza, to his heart, if we will build centers of nationalism for him."[39]

Many scholars look back on the Chicano movement, and in particular to events like the Chicano Youth Liberation Conference and documents like the Plan Espiritual de Aztlán, and contend that nationalism defines Chicano ideology. In a typical comment, one historian argues that "what distinguished the [Mexican American and Chicano] eras was that the younger group turned to cultural nationalism to define identity, instead of assimilation."[40] This assessment's prevalence partly results from the fact that many Chicano Studies scholars, and certainly the deans of the field, came of age during the Chicano movement.[41] As movement participants, they absorbed the idea that Mexicans are and always have been brown. What seems striking to most Chicano scholars, then, are the assertions of national solidarity.

But Chicano nationalism was at root an insistence on racial difference. In 1971 the Chicano intellectual Armando Rendón defined nationalism in quintessentially racial terms: "The essence of cultural nationalism is the full acceptance of this fact, that we are oppressed because of the color of our skin and because of the nature of our being, and that as a consequence, inevitably, our sole means of preservation and equality before all men is in that color and in that raza."[42] Luís Valdez also described Aztlán and "our Mestizo nation" in the language of race: "Aztlán is now the name of our Mestizo nation, existing to the north of Mexico, within the borders of the United States . . . Beyond the two-thousand-mile border between Mexico and the United States we see our universal race extending to the very tip of South America. We see millions upon millions of bronze people, living in Mestizo nations."[43]

Both the claim that Aztlán was the Chicano homeland and the assertion that Chicanos were a nation depended upon seeing Mexicans primarily as descendants of indigenous Americans. In turn, in Chicano ideology descent defined racial identity. The idea that Chicanos were a racial group by virtue of descent permeated the Plan Espiritual de Aztlán. It talked of "our forefathers," called for Chicanos to reclaim "the land of their birth," distinguished Chicanos from "Gringos," called Chicanos "a people whose time has come," extolled the "brotherhood" of all Chicanos, and celebrated Chicano "blood." It also described Mexicans as "a Bronze People with a Bronze Culture . . . brothers in the Bronze Continent," a phrase that Valdez later echoed by calling Chicanos part of a "universal race extending to the very tip of South America [with] millions and millions of bronze people." These claims asserted descent from America's first peoples and once again appealed to the idea that each race had its own continent.

I do not argue that Chicano activists elaborated a national identity solely to assert their racial distinctiveness, for nationalism in general and identification with an indigenous past in particular played important roles in Chicano efforts to build a positive Mexican identity.[44] Nor do I suggest that race and nation are strictly separate phenomena. On the contrary, as the Chicano movement shows, these modern ideas are closely related. The rhetoric of nationhood emphasizes solidarity based upon descent, and notions of descent in turn conjure racial ideas.[45]

Nevertheless, I insist that the Chicano movement consistently asserted only one basis for nationhood and only one argument for its claims on Aztlán: the identity of Mexicans as a people with descent-based ties to the Southwest. Every celebration of Aztlán and every declaration of Chicano irredentism functioned first as a statement about Mexican descent and racial non-whiteness. In the language of the Chicano movement, nation meant race.

MESTIZAJE AND HOMOGENEITY

In fashioning a new racial identity, Chicanos had to grapple with their mixed origins. They themselves emphasized descent, while U.S. society had long slandered Mexicans as a mongrel race. In response, Chicanos began to celebrate themselves as a *mestizo* people—hence the reference in the Plan Espiritual to their being a "Mestizo Nation." Mestizo denotes mixed ancestry; as used by Chicano activists, it referred to Mexican descent from Europeans and indigenous Americans. For instance, Luís Valdez wrote, "We are, to begin with, Mestizos—a powerful blend of Indigenous America with European-Arabian Spain, usually recognizable for the natural bronze tone it lends to human skin."[46] For Chicanos, *mestizaje*—or racial mixture—produced a new race of people readily identifiable through physical features.

In stressing mestizaje, Chicanos drew deeply on the racial ideas of José Vasconcelos, an intellectual who served as education minister in Mexico during the 1920s, just after the Mexican Revolution.[47] To spur national rebuilding, Vasconcelos turned his attention to ameliorating racial tensions in Mexican society. He argued against continuing to celebrate only Spanish ancestry, advocating that the country's people instead honor their mixed origins. Vasconcelos extolled the racial mixing prevalent in Latin America as the precondition for a new race, one that would emerge out of the four "great" races, white, black, yellow, and red, into a fifth, triumphant race that combined only the best attributes of its parent stock—he called this race *la raza cósmica,* the cosmic race.[48] "We in America," Vasconcelos wrote, "shall arrive, before any other part of the world, at the creation of a new race fashioned out of the treasures of all of the previous ones: The final race, the cosmic race."[49]

Vasconcelos's cosmic race provided a ready-made tool for reconceptualizing Mexican racial identity in the United States. Most importantly, it reversed the polarity of Mexican identity, transforming the labels "mongrel" and "degraded" into mestizo and celebrated. But it carried other implications as well. To begin with, for Vasconcelos, mestizaje suggested increasing sameness, the gradual fusion of all people, rather than an increasing differentiation. Vasconcelos supposed that a raza cósmica would emerge from and replace the original races—"the four fundamental races . . . disappear in order to create a fifth superior ethnic specimen."[50] Vasconcelos emphasized increasing cohesion most likely to encourage unity among Mexico's citizens.

Like Vasconcelos, the Chicano activists sought to create a cohesive political community, and they too promoted the notion that mestizaje led to racial sameness. Statements like "We are mestizo" often presumed a monolithic identity in order to mask intra-group differences among Mexicans. Among others, Valdez performed the feat of converting mestizaje into homogeneity:

> That we Mexicans speak of ourselves as a "race" is the biggest contradiction of them all. The *conquistadores,* of course, mated with their Indian women with customary abandon, creating a nation of bewildered half-breeds in countless shapes, colors and sizes. Unlike our fathers and mothers, unlike each other, we mestizos solved the problem with poetic license and called ourselves *la raza.* A Mexican's first loyalty—when one of us is threatened by strangers from the outside—is to that race. Either we recognize our total unity on the basis of *raza,* or the ghosts of a 100,000 feuding Indian tribes, bloods and mores will come back to haunt us.[51]

Valdez starts with the idea that mestizaje has produced great differences among Mexicans. Yet in Valdez's hands, such differences quickly become the source of Mexican commonality. By mid-paragraph, Valdez converts heterogeneity into solidarity, insisting that all Mexicans have a primary allegiance to la raza—to a race that demands loyalty and total unity, in Valdez's words. Difference had become sameness.

The Chicano movement's vision of mestizaje contrasts with the way that Chicana feminists now use that idea. Many feminists use mestizaje to emphasize that identity involves a complex negotiation across lines established by gender, race, class, sexuality, culture, language, nation, and so on.[52] In this usage, which focuses primarily on the individual, to be mestizo is to be divided into a welter of conflicting selves. But for the Chicanos, mestizo referred to the group, and mixed origins became the basis for a unified racial identity. As mestizos, the variation that supposedly differentiated Mexicans from one another now defined a single positive identity. Mestizaje connoted a monolithic Mexican identity rooted in the idea that all Mexicans similarly shared mixed antecedents.

It bears emphasizing that the Chicano conception of mestizaje depended upon understanding race as a matter of descent. To this extent, nature determined racial identity, making one Chicano by birth, not by choice. It was nature, and not a common history or religion or language, that most firmly bound Mexicans to one another. Mestizaje—the biology of race—made all Mexicans the same.

CULTURE AND DESTINY

José Vasconcelos also argued that white traits would predominate in the new cosmic race, not by force but by consent: "Perhaps the traits of the white race will predominate among the characteristics of the fifth race, but such a supremacy must be the result of the free choice of personal taste, and not the fruit of violence or economic pressure. The superior traits of culture and nature will have to triumph."[53] One sees here Vasconcelos's debt to the idea newly popular in the United States of a melting pot that would produce an amalgamation nevertheless dominated by white attributes and norms. One also sees a resurrection of nineteenth-century ideas concerning the power of race to determine not just physical features but the character of whole peoples— their temperaments, propensities, skills, cultures, indeed their histories and destinies.

Chicanos rejected Vasconcelos's contention that the white element would predominate in the new mestizo. Just the opposite, Chicanos frequently stressed the essentially Indian nature of their identity. Thus, after writing that "miscegenation went joyously wild, creating the many shapes, sizes, and hues of La Raza," Luís Valdez quickly added that "the predominant strain of the mestizaje remained Indio. By the turn of the nineteenth century, most of the people in Mexico were mestizos with a great deal of Indian blood."[54] Similarly, Acosta explained that "there is Spanish and European blood in us, but we don't always talk about it because it is not something we are proud of. For me, my native ancestry is crucial."[55] For most Chicanos, the term mestizo translated technically into a claim of mixed origins, but functionally into an assertion of indigenous ancestry.

But if Chicanos rejected Vasconcelos's predilection for whites, they applied his idea of a cosmic race to Chicanos, and in so doing accepted that race determined almost all aspects of identity. Luís Valdez drew on Vasconcelos to celebrate Chicano mestizaje: being Chicano, Valdez wrote, "means that Indian mysticism is merging with modern technology to create *un nuevo hombre*. A new man."[56] Chicano intellectual Guillermo Fuenfrios also heralded Chicanos as a new race: "The Chicano stands squarely at the point where both East and West meet. He has access to the occidental modes of rational thought, he is heir to the lyrical and poetic traditions of the Mediterranean, and he has recently discovered the dignity and wonder of the non-rational indigenous mind . . . Oh, Chicano: you are . . . the 'Cosmic Race.' Find your voice and sing and you will save the world."[57]

In describing themselves as a cosmic race, Chicano militants adopted a nineteenth-century vision wherein race determined identity. Indians were mystical, nonrational, and dignified—by race; whites were masters of technology and rational thought—by descent; Mediterranean people were romantic and passionate—by blood.

In turn, race, descent, and blood filled in the details of Chicano identity. Chicanos argued that mestizaje shaped Mexican temperament, culture, politics, and even group destiny. Valdez detailed ancestry's many manifestations in Chicano personality: "*La Raza,* the race, is the Mexican people. Sentimental and cynical, fierce and docile, faithful and treacherous, individualistic and herd-following, in love with life and obsessed with death, the personality of the *raza* encompasses all the complexity of our history . . . [A] million little stubborn mannerisms, beliefs, myths, superstitions, words, thoughts—things not so easily detected— they fill our Spanish life with Indian contradictions." He continued: "The presence of the Indio in La Raza is as real as the barrio. Tortillas, tamales, chile, marijuana, la curandera, el empacho, el molcajete, atole, La Virgen de Guadalupe—these are hard-core realities for our people. These and a thousand other little human customs and traditions are interwoven into the fiber of our daily life."[58]

For Valdez and many others, mestizo identity expressed itself directly in character and culture. Under Chicano racial ideology, everything—from mannerisms to attitudes, food to religion, words to thoughts—flowed from being mestizo. When Chicanos spoke of themselves as a mestizo people, they invoked not just physical difference but also a character, a culture, and a millennial identity rooted in race. Herein lies the significance of the Plan Espiritual's ringing claim that "the call of our blood is our power, our responsibility, and our inevitable destiny." "Blood" functioned as a metonym for race: it reinforced the idea that race was biological, accentuating its supposedly innate, descent-based quality. But "blood" also emphasized that race determined identity and history. Race was indeed destiny.

GENDERING RACE, RACING GENDER

In constructing Chicano identity, the militants relied on racial common sense. But the common sense of gender also played a major role in shaping both the trajectory of the Chicano movement as well as the contours of Chicano identity. Others have examined the role of gender in the Chicano movement.[59] Here, I am particularly interested in how race and gender interacted. Chicano activists combined these social identities in two principal ways: first, they defined racial identity in masculine terms; and second, they used race to justify gender norms. Race was gendered, and gender was raced.

Chicanos fashioned Mexican racial identity in masculine terms partly by making *carnalismo,* or brotherhood, a constituent aspect of Chicano identity. Just as the Brown Berets extolled fraternal relationships among their members, the Plan Espiritual claimed that "Brotherhood unites us and love for our brother makes us a people whose time has come."[60] Carnalismo reflected a larger tendency in the Chicano movement to model social interconnection on the family. Yet carnalismo celebrated not just any familial bond but the specific relation between brothers, and it posited not a relationship between all persons but only among Mexicans. In emphasizing fraternity, Chicanos privileged a masculine behavioral ideal based on autonomy, individualism, and initiative over a feminine or non-gendered ideal that emphasized interdependence, mutual respect, nurturance, and the duty to care for others. At the same time, Chicanos limited carnalismo to members of la raza; whatever duty existed among Mexicans did not extend to others. For many Chicano activists, brotherhood defined a core Chicano value, but Mexican identity defined brotherhood's reach.

Chicano racial identity took on a masculine cast perhaps most forcefully, though, through the rhetoric of *machismo*.[61] This concept played an important role among many Chicano militants who, like Black Power activists, often associated racial oppression with emasculation.[62] Corky Gonzales expressed this sentiment on different occasions, saying, "The politics of the Anglo emasculates the manhood of a man of La Raza. It makes him impotent, a Tío Taco, an Uncle Tom."[63] He also opined, "It's a long road back to yourself when the society has made you into someone else. But I was determined to find my way, to rediscover my roots, to be the man I am, not the emasculated man that the Anglo society wanted me to be."[64] Like Gonzales, many Chicanos understood their marginal social and political position in terms of sexual prowess. Being oppressed became a personal failing akin to being sexually impotent or emasculated.

The equation of racial oppression and emasculation produced a corresponding association between racial emancipation and full manhood. The Brown Berets exhorted student participation in the school walkouts by exclaiming, "Don't be a cherry." Oscar Acosta insinuated that activists would do more to protest police violence if only they were more manly. Condemning police officer James Williston's killing of a young Chicano, Acosta wrote: "Perhaps some day we will have enough power so that perros [dogs] like Williston will not be allowed to carry guns in public . . . perhaps some day, if we cannot obtain justice, we shall have the manhood to insure that perros like Williston pay for their wrongs."[65] Masculine norms permeated the Chicano movement such that opposing oppression became identified with being a man.[66]

Equating activism with manhood in turn led Chicanos to give political significance to traditional male gender roles in personal and familial relationships. For Gonzales, machismo involved not only standing up to Anglos but also ruling one's home: "*Machismo* means manhood. To the Mexican man *machismo* means to have the manly traits of honor and dignity. To have courage to fight. To keep his word and protect his name. To run his house, to control his woman, and to direct his children. This is *machismo* . . . To be a man in your own eyes."[67] Gonzales, like many Chicanos, linked participating in a broad movement supposedly aimed at empowering all Mexicans with maintaining traditional gender norms at home.

In more general terms, activists equated being Chicano with being a real man. As Oscar Acosta asserted, machismo was the "omnipotent and omnipresent central theme to [Chicano] lifestyle"; it was the "instinctual and mystical source of manhood, honor and pride that alone justifies all behavior."[68] In crafting Chicano racial identity, movement activists imbued it with a strongly masculine aspect.

On the other side of the coin, Chicanos also gave a racial cast to gender. They did so partly by insisting that proper family structure undergirded the Chicano movement. Corky Gonzales insisted that "nationalism comes first out of the family."[69] The Plan Espiritual asserted that "our cultural values of life, family, and home will serve as a powerful weapon to defeat the gringo dollar value system."[70] The Chicana intellectual Enriqueta Longeaux y Vasquez proclaimed that "the Mexican-American movement is not that of just adults fighting the social system, but it is a total commitment of a family unit living what it believes to be a better way of life in demanding social change for the benefit of mankind." She added: "When a family is involved in a human rights movement, as is the Mexican-American, there should not have to be a Woman's liberation movement within it."[71]

As these comments show, many Chicano activists insisted that proper family structure ensured nothing less than the well-being of the race. In turn, though, patriarchy determined proper family relations. The endorsement of *la familia* as central to the strength of the race did not allow familial roles to be redefined but instead solidified traditional norms. Chicano activists assigned racial significance to family roles, such that being a good Chicano also meant being a strong husband or a dutiful wife.

ace and patriarchy also combined in many activists' efforts
efine a woman's role in terms of motherhood. Time and
again, Chicano militants celebrated Mexican women as the
mothers of the race, literally and also figuratively. In an extreme
version of this, *La Causa* argued that public promoters of birth
control aimed to reduce the Mexican population and thus endan-
gered the movement. Summing up its position, *La Causa* warned
that "the pill the would-be mother pops today, prevents the revolutionary of tomorrow."[72] A year later, *La Causa* again denounced "genocidal programs such as 'family planning,' or
'planned parenthood,'" insisting that "La Raza's future depends
on the health of all Chicanas in order for them to be able to continue to bear healthy Chicanitos."[73]

Even a newspaper dedicated to encouraging women's participation in the Chicano movement argued that a woman's duty to
the race prominently included motherhood. *El Rebozo's* founders explained the meaning behind the newspaper's title as follows: "*El Rebozo* [the shawl]—the traditional garment of the
Mexican woman, with its many uses, symbolizes the three roles
of the Chicana portraying her as '*la señorita*,' feminine yet humble; as '*la revolucionaria*,' ready to fight for '*La Causa*,' and
finally portraying the role of '*La Madre*,' radiant with life. This
newspaper has tried to portray the women of *La Raza* in their
different roles, for all three roles make up *la mujer completa* [the
complete woman]."[74]

The depth of the consensus that women represented the nation through reproduction is striking. Unlike *La Causa* with its
aggressively masculine stance, *El Rebozo* dedicated itself to
reaching out to women. Yet even *El Rebozo* argued that rearing
the next Chicano generation formed an essential duty of the
complete Chicana. A *La Raza* article also promoted women in
terms of their role as mothers, at the same time appealing to men
for guidance: "We are the mothers and teachers of your children.
We are the ones that greatly influence them in everyday life. Help
us to teach them to be revolutionary Chicanos for La Causa.

Help us to organize! Train us and develop us."[75] For many activists, women served the movement principally as the physical and cultural progenitors of raza men.

El Rebozo's celebration of "*la señorita,* feminine yet humble," raises a related point—that the racial meanings given to gender often extended to sexuality. The preoccupation with masculinity had its corollary in a similar emphasis on women's sexual attractiveness. Rendón made this connection when he argued that in "Anglo culture . . . the male is castrated and the female desexed."[76] Corky Gonzales addressed female attractiveness when commenting on feminism in the Chicano movement: "I want to get back to the women's situation . . . I recognize too much of an influence of white European thinking in the discussion. I hope that our Chicana sisters can understand that they can be front runners in the revolution, they can be in the leadership of any social movement, but I pray to God that they do not lose their *Chicanisma* or their womanhood and become a frigid *gringa*. So I'm for equality, but still want to see some sex in our women."[77] Both Rendón and Gonzales made sexual attractiveness to men integral to Chicana identity.

The Chicano celebration of la familia, la madre, and la señorita used race to define proper gender roles. By the same token, movement activists used race to police those roles, often criticizing gender transgressions in racial terms. Gonzales used race to attack feminists by accusing them of too much "white European thinking" and by warning them against becoming "a frigid *gringa*." Noting such criticism, Longauex y Vasquez lamented that women who aspired to lead the movement faced charges of racial inauthenticity: "If she does a good job, she will have to walk lightly around the men for she may find herself accused of being 'Agringada' or 'Agabachada.'"[78] Just as Chicanos used racial terms as a shorthand for suspect political views, they used such rhetoric to control what they viewed as sexual deviance. Women who sought to remake the meaning of gender, whether in the movement or at home, often encountered resistance expressed in racial terms—they were accused of trying to be white.[79]

In 1968 some East Los Angeles residents set out to improve the Mexican community's situation by seeking to reform schools and end police violence. Yet under the common sense of the times, these efforts and the police repression they engendered convinced many activists that race explained their social position. The Chicano movement's goals expanded to include developing a positive racial self-conception among Mexicans. In effect, though, Chicanos ended up using racial common sense to remake the common sense of race.

Intending to contest the negative characteristics imputed to Mexicans, Chicanos promoted the idea that Mexicans were a mestizo race. They did not think that they were inventing this identity but rather that they were uncovering a fact long denied by the prior generation. Even as they worked assiduously to craft a new sense of self, Chicanos continued to emphasize that race was a matter of descent, not choice. Chicanos embraced the idea that nature made them a race and that race located them in history, not only politically as the victims of Anglo domination but also culturally as possessors of a proud, humanistic tradition.

But this new race differed little as a category from the old Mexican race constructed by Anglos. In both cases, membership depended upon descent and was measured by skin color. Worse, in attempting to give their new racial identity a positive content, Chicanos resurrected worn understandings of racial properties. Chicanos believed that race rendered group members fundamentally the same as one another and strictly distinct from all others; they concluded that race defined individual and group attributes ranging from features and faces to philosophies and destinies; and they assumed that race established appropriate political beliefs and gender relations within the Mexican community.

These racial understandings were promoted most stridently by Chicano activists who came from the most acculturated segments of the Mexican community, like Oscar Acosta, Luís

Valdez, and David Sánchez. They drew on Mexico's José
Vasconcelos, it is true. But much more than that, they drew on
racial common sense as it had developed in the United States.
Common sense influenced more than legal discrimination and
the Chicano movement's protest dynamics. It also provided the
very ideas of race that the activists both challenged and relied
upon in attempting to remake Mexican racial identity.

EPILOGUE

The loose ends of this story do not tie together neatly. Nevertheless, for the important lessons they offer, there are five strands we should follow a bit further: the fate of Oscar Acosta, the legacy of the Chicano Power movement, the ongoing discrimination in L.A. grand jury selection, the diminishing protection offered by Equal Protection doctrine, and continuing legal violence on streets and in courtrooms throughout the nation.

OSCAR ACOSTA

Two final episodes of Acosta's East Los Angeles career should be mentioned before we let him leave the scene. The first, from the spring of 1970, involves his efforts to win election as the sheriff of Los Angeles County. In a flamboyant campaign, Acosta pledged that if elected he would bring about "the ultimate dissolution of the Sheriff's Department"; "the immediate withdrawal of concentrated forces in the barrios and ghettos"; and "the immediate investigation into criminal activities of law enforcement officers."[1] Just three months before his own death, Rubén Salazar described Acosta's quixotic run: "During the campaign, he defended establishment-shaking Catolicos por La Raza, spent a couple of days in jail for contempt of court, and vowed if elected he would do away with the sheriff's department as it is now constituted. Acosta [is] easily recognized in court by his loud ties and flowered attaché case with a Chicano Power sticker."[2]

Acosta lost, of course. The incumbent was reelected with a total of 1,300,000 votes. Still, Acosta garnered an astounding 100,000 votes—more, in the end, than a local chief of police who also ran for sheriff.[3] Salazar described "Acosta's impressive loss [as] an enigmatic ray of sunshine" for the Chicano community.[4] To more fully grasp the significance of the votes for Acosta, consider his campaign statement, issued in February 1970:

> The history of Los Angeles County is one of violence, vice and corruption in high places. Neither the expenditure of huge sums of money nor an increase in the personnel of all the law enforcement agencies throughout the county has diminished the decay inherent in our communities. On the contrary, history is replete with examples that prove that the privilege of bearing guns and their use under color of law has in all probability increased the incidence of violence . . . Because the forces of oppression and suppression—the law enforcement agencies—continue to harass, brutalize, illegally confine and psychologically damage the Chicano, the black, the poor and the unrepresented, I hereby declare my candidacy for the office of Sheriff of Los Angeles County.[5]

Some among the 100,000 citizens who voted for Acosta were not familiar with the details of his campaign platform. But most probably knew that Acosta vowed to abolish the sheriff's department. In 1968 East Los Angeles had a population of just over 105,000 residents; in this context, the votes for Acosta testify to a surprisingly widespread hostility to L.A. law enforcement.[6] The support Acosta garnered indicates that the Chicano movement was generally successful in mobilizing community attention and support; more particularly, the vote constitutes a striking ratification of the view that legal violence oppressed the Chicano people.

In his campaign for sheriff, Acosta attempted to use the polling booth to send a revolutionary message. He stressed that law no longer served as a cornerstone of democracy but instead—as embodied in the actions of the police—contributed to social violence and decay.[7] Acosta also preached that adjudication did not produce justice. He argued that "rules of law and procedure are simply not working, and it is apparent to me that they will no longer work in a society such as we have created in between our numerous wars."[8] For Acosta, writing in 1970, the end of society seemed near. "I am convinced that we are in the final years of a relatively peaceful society," he wrote, and urged "that if we are to survive the holocaust of imminent disintegration and destruction, that we must prepare now for a structure, a way of life that might hopefully turn back the tide."[9] Acosta's words reflect his tendency toward bombast, but they also express the increasing bitterness and frustration of a lawyer trying to defend Mexican activists in a context of rising police oppression and overwhelming judicial bias. Later that year—when riots tore through East Los Angeles and the police killed Rubén Salazar and Whittier Boulevard burned—Acosta's sense that social collapse was imminent almost certainly deepened.

In late 1971, after *Biltmore Six,* Acosta quit the practice of law, telling Judge Alarcon, "I don't know if I ever was a lawyer or whether I acted like one during the trial." Judge Alarcon retorted, "I have to agree with you that you never acted like a lawyer in this court."[10] In part, Acosta's decision to withdraw from the case stemmed from his own legal troubles. In August 1971, as the *Biltmore* trial proceeded, the police arrested Acosta on drug possession charges. According to the *Los Angeles Times,* "Deputies claim that when Acosta stepped from his car a crumpled cigarette packet containing white tablets fell to the ground." The *Times* noted that "Acosta suggested the arrest was part of the 'harassment' he claims he had been subject to by police because of the trial."[11] After an eight-day trial in February 1972, a jury deliberated for less than two hours before acquitting Acosta.[12]

In addition, Acosta was fed up with being a movement lawyer. On several occasions he ran into conflict with his clients, with both sides wondering about the other's true commitment.[13] And he had also tired of practicing a profession that he hated. After several years as a movement lawyer, Acosta described himself and his bitter disdain for law as follows: "I'm the only Chicano lawyer here. By that I mean the only one that has taken a militant posture, to my knowledge, in the whole country . . . I relate to the court system first as a Chicano and only seldom as a lawyer in the traditional sense. I have no respect for the courts and I make it clear to them from the minute I walk in that I have no respect for the system. That I am against it and would destroy it in one second if I had the physical power to do it."[14]

And perhaps Acosta did try to destroy the law, or at least kill one judge. In the last few pages of *Revolt of the Cockroach People*, his semi-autobiographical tale of his career as a radical Chicano lawyer in L.A., Acosta tells of planting a bomb in a Los Angeles courthouse to assassinate a Superior Court judge, one that killed an unintended victim instead.[15] Acosta's book largely tracks events that transpired, though he fictionalized *Revolt* somewhat by combining incidents and altering the names of participants—albeit in a manner that still allows their easy identification.

In *Revolt* Acosta described planting the bomb after a trial in which he defended Corky Gonzales on a misdemeanor gun possession charge.[16] According to Acosta, the jury found Gonzales guilty, and the judge, a Mexican by the name of "Alacran," Spanish for scorpion, sentenced Gonzales to forty days in jail, an unusually long sentence given the crime. Acosta recounted that as people milled about the courtroom, he hurried down to the bathroom on the floor below to join other militants busy assembling a time bomb. "I slipped around the corner and ran down the steps to this john in one corner of the building. Alacran's chambers are directly above me and he is in them," Acosta wrote. The plan, Acosta continued, was "to blow a hole in this cement-concrete-steel building, right under that motherfucking greaser."[17] Acosta and his Chicano militant accomplices set the bomb to go off in a half-hour and left the building. When news of the blast came over the radio, Acosta had "Elena" call the police and read a statement: "Attention . . . The bomb that just exploded today in the Hall of Justice was done in memory of Roland Zanzibar and the Day of the Chicanos . . . This is the Chicano Liberation Front." In the next radio report on the bombing, Acosta learned of a victim: "One person has been found dead in the rubble," he quoted the radio as saying. "We repeat, one young man of presumably Latin descent has been found dead in the wreckage of the toilet in the Hall of Justice." Acosta then wrote: "No, I don't feel guilty about the kid that got killed. I feel terrible. But not guilty. Lots more will die before this fight is over."[18]

Did this bombing occur? Acosta did defend Gonzales, who did receive a sentence of forty days in jail.[19] Alacran almost certainly refers to Superior Court Judge Arthur Alarcon, a well-known judicial figure who was subsequently elevated to the U.S. Court of Appeals; he was the Mexican judge who presided over *Biltmore Six,* and in *Revolt* Acosta conflated that case with Gonzales's trial.[20] Roland Zanzibar is the pseudonym Acosta used for Rubén Salazar. Finally, a group identified as the Chicano Liberation Front did conduct bombings; indeed, according to the historian Edward Escobar, "The bombings began on January 29, 1971, when 'a sophisticated and highly explosive device' exploded in the men's washroom in the federal building in downtown Los Angeles, killing an innocent bystander."[21]

It is unlikely that the bombing transpired exactly as Acosta described in *Revolt.* But it seems quite plausible that Acosta planted a bomb that killed someone. And it may even be that Acosta attempted to assassinate Judge Alarcon. At any rate, it seems likely he was involved in the bombings that swept East L.A. in 1971. Hunter Thompson would later say of his friend, "There were times—all too often, I felt—when Oscar Acosta would show up in front of the courthouse at nine in the morning with the stench of fresh gasoline on his hands and a green crust of charred soap-flakes on the toes of his $300 snakeskin cowboy boots."[22] For his part, sometime in 1972 Acosta wrote to Thompson: "Perhaps after I write it all out, all of you will come to understand exactly what you did by coming down to L.A. I think I can make a pretty good argument that it was you, or God through you, that called a halt to the bombings . . . Which means you'll be remembered as the Benedict Arnold of the cockroach revolt."[23] Escobar reports that "toward the end of 1971, the bombings came to an end . . . Since no one has ever come forward to explain the bombings, we do not know why they ended."[24]

If we accept the idea that Acosta planted at least one bomb, the move from sheriff's candidate in spring 1970 to bomber in spring 1971 deserves some attention. On one level, it was not a dramatic change, since Acosta probably understood both actions as simply different forms of protest against a legal establishment that he considered fundamentally unjust. From another perspective, though, a world of difference divides Acosta the sheriff's candidate from Acosta the bomber. In the former incarnation, Acosta challenged social injustice through creative means that at once disrupted and highlighted the business-as-usual nature of social oppression. Moreover, Acosta's tactics ultimately affirmed humanity, insofar as he demanded justice for all and insisted that social actors and organizations live up to the ideals they professed. In contrast, as a person who planted bombs, Acosta took a destructive path, using unfocused terror to vent rage and frustration. Here, the message of an alternative future was lost, buried under rubble that spoke only of desperation.

In spring 1972, with his major cases over, Acosta fled East Los Angeles—"to stay whole and human, to survive intact, to carry on the species and my own Buffalo run as long as I can," he wrote.[25] His run did not last much longer. After completing *Revolt of the Cockroach People,* Acosta traveled in 1974 to

Mazatlán, Mexico, where, it was reported, he tried drug-running to make some quick money.[26] After that June, no one heard from him again. Rumors regarding his death included reports that he drowned off the Mexican coast during an ill-fated smuggling mission or that he was murdered at the hands of drug lords or U.S. government agents.[27] Acosta was thirty-nine when he dropped out of sight.

Acosta was a volatile person caught in a tempest of political protest and legal repression, and his actions reflected his personality. Nevertheless, Acosta's emotional and political trajectory over four years in East Los Angeles, from the detachment of a would-be writer to the desperate passions of a violent militant, tells us about more than Acosta himself. The path he traveled illustrates the determination of many within the Mexican community to fight for dignity and justice in their lives and reflects the desperation engendered by the grinding violence of routine marginalization and immiseration. Acosta's life also emphasizes how radicalization follows when politically moderate, morally compelling demands are met with force. The Chicano movement, especially at its inception, sought relatively little in the way of change. It adopted a largely reformist stance that called principally for decent schools and an end to police harassment. The use of state power to reject and suppress such temperate demands contributed directly to the desperation many felt and to their growing sense that force and disorder were necessary to achieve liberation. Acosta's story reminds us that violence in many communities is measured in human lives. Blood is a metaphor not just for race but for human suffering.

THE CHICANO MOVEMENT

As a social movement, Chicano Power suffered a relatively quick demise. Mexican political mobilization took different forms across the Southwest, but especially in East Los Angeles the initial reformism of 1968 all too quickly devolved into violence. By

1972 people, organizations, energy, and hope were largely dissipated. When the high school students took to the streets in spring 1968, the lessons of Mexican history and the black movement's contemporary salience pushed race to the fore as a framework for understanding themselves, their goals, and society's response. Law enforcement in turn reacted with its own race-informed interpretations, and the resulting mix produced spiraling violence that soon destroyed activists and activism.

In evaluating the Chicano movement, we can lament that an excessive focus on race led activists to emphasize identity issues over material concerns, cultural purity over coalition building, masculinity over gender equality, and group autonomy over structural reform.[28] We should not suppose, though, that these features of the movement reflect anything so simple as missed choices or incomplete strategizing. Instead, the movement was both empowered and constrained by common sense. Taken-for-granted ideas facilitated Chicano mobilization, providing everything from ways of understanding the social situation to ideas regarding protest tactics and appropriate goals. But background ideas also trapped Chicanos into thinking about their strategies, politics, and even identity in limited, often oppressive ways. The Chicano movement was molded by the common sense of race.

The movement left its most robust legacy in that area of Mexican life most under the militants' control—which is to say, in the area of self-conception. To be sure, the Chicano movement changed the political scene for Mexicans, though not by generating a broad and unified Mexican voting block but by creating space for the rise to elected and appointed positions of relatively more moderate Mexicans, usually members of the Mexican American generation.[29] Similarly, regarding education, the Chicano movement achieved notable successes at the college level through the institutionalization of Chicano Studies programs; but it largely failed to achieve any lasting improvement in primary and secondary education, and high school dropout rates

among Mexicans continue at near 60 percent.[30] Periodically, new
walkouts give vent to continued frustration with educational
apartheid.[31]

On another front, the Chicano movement also contributed,
albeit in a tense and conflicted manner, to the development of
feminism in the Mexican community.[32] In addition, the Chicano
movement played an instrumental role in creating a transna-
tional consciousness among Mexicans in the United States, leading many to reject the Mexican American generation's hostility
toward recent Mexican immigrants in favor of a politics of solidarity based on cultural affinities and shared class interests.[33]

Despite these broad, various, and important contributions,
the principal legacy of the movement probably lies in the notion
of a Chicano racial identity. It is not true, of course, that the
movement completely changed the racial self-conception of East
L.A.'s Mexican residents from white to brown. There was no
unanimity regarding a white identity before 1968, and certainly
none regarding a Chicano self-conception after 1972. Perhaps
the simplest story one can tell is that within the Mexican community, competing notions of racial identity have long existed. On
the eve of the Chicano movement, the middle-class leadership
tended to both emphasize the importance of race and espouse a
white identity, while other segments of the community, particularly among the working class, probably rejected white pretensions and stressed nonracial bases of self-conception. In this context, the Chicano movement mobilized the working-class
members of the Mexican community and transformed a diffuse
social and political alienation into a positive program of empow-
erment centered on a claim of being non-white.[34] Many of those
who had most keenly embraced whiteness changed their views,
but many others did not.[35] This schism continues, with roughly
half of all Mexicans polled identifying themselves as white in
1992 and about the same percentage of Latinos doing so in the
2000 census.[36]

Nevertheless, it remains the case that the architects of Chicano ideology directly challenged the stereotypes surrounding Mexican racial identity. They repudiated the common sense depiction of Mexicans as dark, dirty, lazy, criminal, and so on and elaborated instead a vision of Mexicans as noble, cultured, connected to ancient civilizations, humanistic, family-oriented, and community-minded. The Chicano movement's achievements in this regard should not be underestimated. In society at large, and even in the Mexican community itself, this depiction of Mexican identity has not come close to fully displacing the tainted one that originated in Anglo prejudice in the mid-nineteenth century; nevertheless, it has provided a way for succeeding generations of Mexicans to dispute, particularly among themselves, this cultural drumbeat of common sense racism that constantly pounds out the message of their inferiority. For those within the Mexican community who have been most consistently racialized in negative ways, and especially for communities such as East Los Angeles and successive groups of Mexican university students, the pride in Mexican identity articulated during the Chicano era is an enduring resource and, quite possibly, the Chicano movement's most important legacy.[37]

CONTINUED GRAND JURY DISCRIMINATION

To make their case, the *East L.A. Thirteen* and *Biltmore Six* activists relied on numbers, the judges' actual nominations reduced to small data points that in composite delineated a vivid portrait of that community's almost total exclusion. In the decade leading up to those cases, Mexicans accounted for no more than 1.7 percent of Los Angeles's grand jurors, despite the fact that the Mexican community comprised roughly 14 percent of the county's population. This pattern was repeated across California. In the last three decades, little has changed.

To begin with, California's judiciary remains almost all white. At the Superior Court level, just 4.3 percent of the judges are Latinos, even though this group today comprises one-third of the state's population.[38] In addition, the system for selecting grand jurors remains functionally the same now as during the 1960s. A contemporary survey of the twenty California counties studied by California Rural Legal Assistance in its 1970 report reveals that in virtually every one of those counties, judges continue to exercise considerable discretion over the selection of potential grand jurors.[39]

Eleven counties continue to rely principally on initial nominations by judges. Other counties now allow or even actively invite citizens to volunteer for grand jury service, and a few counties cull potential grand jurors from the trial jury pool, which in turn is randomly drawn from voter registration rolls and motor vehicle department lists.[40] Despite these changes, virtually every county has instituted a screening mechanism in which one or more judges vet all candidates before admitting them to a small pool from which the grand jury is finally drawn. Irrespective of whether counties generate the names of potential jurors by judicial nomination, by application, or randomly, almost all counties require judges to winnow nominees to establish a restricted group, usually no more than thirty, from among whom the actual grand jurors are then randomly selected. Of the twenty counties, there are only three exceptions to this system of judicially vetted pools.[41]

One exception is Los Angeles, which, in a triumph of inertia, continues to rely primarily on judges to nominate their friends and acquaintances. Of course, there has been some forward movement: Los Angeles County now accepts applications for grand jury service. But the Superior Court does not automatically place such applicants in the grand jury pool. Instead, according to the County of Los Angeles Grand Jury website, "Each applicant is interviewed by a member of the Grand and Trial Jurors Committee. The Judge assigns a qualification rating to each volunteer interviewed. The volunteers' application forms are then circulated among the Superior Court judges for *possible* nomination."[42] In short, nomination by a judge continues to be a prerequisite for grand jury service in Los Angeles County.

The L.A. judges' continuing discretion in nominating grand jurors suggests a potential for high levels of discrimination—and the numbers bear this out. During the 1990s in Los Angeles, out of 23 seated grand jurors, Latinos numbered 0 in 1991 and 1999, 1 in 1990, 1993, 1994, and 1998, and 2 in 1992 and 1995. Over the decade, Latinos made up 6.5 percent of the grand jurors in Los Angeles County.[43] It is true that Latino participation on Los Angeles grand juries more than trebled from the 1960s to the 1990s, from under 2 to over 6 percent. But Mexicans accounted for 14 percent of Los Angeles County's total population in the 1960s; in the 1990s Latinos numbered closer to 41 percent.[44] Thus, proportional to their presence in the county as a whole, Los Angeles County excluded Latinos from grand jury service by an eight-to-one ratio during the 1960s, and by six-to-one during the 1990s.

The exclusion of this community from grand jury service in Los Angeles County continues, as do legal challenges to the Superior Court's discrimination against Latinos.[45] Most likely, common sense racism explains this extraordinary rate of exclusion. After all, judges believe that only the most qualified persons should sit as grand jurors, and it is common sense to them that qualified persons resemble themselves—which means, in no small part, that grand jurors even today are usually white and rarely Mexican.

NO EQUAL PROTECTION

Oscar Acosta and the Chicano defendants attempted to fight law with law, thereby exposing law's dual relationship to racial inequality in our society. On the one hand, law has been a principal source of racial oppression. Statutes and cases have authorized every injustice from slavery and Native American dispossession to Jim Crow segregation and Japanese internment. Likewise, police, prosecutors, and courts have long victimized minority communities. On the other hand, the U.S. Constitution's radical proclamation of equality and the efforts of the Reconstruction amendments and myriad civil rights cases to breathe life into that unfulfilled promise sometimes place law on the side of those seeking to end racism's scourge. In the context of contentious times, Acosta did not believe that law would defeat racism; he thought succor, if any, would come from the social movements then marching across the United States.[46] In subsequent decades, though, the potential for law to ameliorate racism has only diminished.

The Los Angeles Superior Court judges ruled against the defendants' discrimination claim on the ground that they had not shown intentional discrimination. Several years later, the U.S. Supreme Court embraced this parsimonious understanding of the Equal Protection clause, ruling in *Washington v. Davis* that the Constitution, with few exceptions, prohibits government officials only from engaging in purposeful racism.[47] Despite its limited conception of racism, under *Davis* the Court barred at least some racism. In contrast, recent Supreme Court decisions have redefined racism to include only those instances when race is explicitly invoked. As a result, Equal Protection doctrine allows racist action that does not mention race but forbids race-conscious remedies designed to counteract racial inequality.

In *Davis* the Court reasoned as though the absence of purposeful racial animus demonstrated that race played no role in producing disparate outcomes. This sort of reasoning led to *McCleskey v. Kemp* in 1987.[48] The findings of a massive sentencing study showed that race—of the defendant and of the victim— figured prominently in who lived and who died at the hands of the Georgia criminal justice system. In particular, blacks who killed whites were sentenced to death twenty-two times more often than blacks who killed blacks.[49] Nevertheless the Court upheld Georgia's imposition of the death penalty on a black man accused of killing a white police officer because the Court could not discern purposeful racism.

Such reasoning predominated through the 1980s; but in the

1990s the Court issued a series of primarily five-to-four decisions that altered its definition of racism. The Court moved from a search for purposeful racism to an inquiry into whether decisionmakers consciously considered race. This shift is most evident in challenges to government affirmative action programs, for instance in cases such as *Richmond v. Croson* and *Adarand v. Pena.*[50] In these cases the Court concluded that any mention of race requires the government to justify its actions under a standard of strict scrutiny that no government decision has ever met (except the first government act judged under the strict scrutiny standard, the internment of the U.S. Japanese population). Where race appears openly in government action, the Court has effectively dispensed with any need to show purposeful racism before striking that action down.

But increasingly the Court sees racism *only* when state actors consciously consider race—that is, discrimination explained on any ground other than race does not constitute racism. In a 1991 jury discrimination case, *Hernandez v. New York,* the Court rejected an Equal Protection challenge to the actions of a prosecutor who struck from service every Latino member of a trial jury on the ground that as Spanish speakers they could not fully accept an interpreter's English translation when witnesses testified in Spanish.[51] The Court was untroubled by the fact that the prosecutor did not say "would not," which suggests doubt about individual character, but specifically emphasized "could not," implying concern with a fixed inability of the group; the Court also seemed indifferent to the fact that the prosecutor questioned only the prospective Latino jurors and no others about their Spanish-language ability.[52]

Concurring in the finding of no discrimination, Justice Sandra Day O'Connor commented: "[The strikes] may have acted like strikes based on race, but they were not based on race. No matter how closely tied or significantly correlated to race the explanation for a peremptory strike may be, the strike does not implicate the Equal Protection Clause unless it is based on race."[53] Under Justice O'Connor's reasoning, purposeful racism does not exist unless a government agent actually says the word "race."

In emphasizing race's explicit invocation, the Court deviates from *Davis* by rendering purposeful racism irrelevant to constitutional analysis. Under O'Connor's reasoning in *Hernandez,* purposeful racism cannot be shown unless the state actor openly considers race. But under *Croson* and *Adarand,* open references to race already trigger heightened review. Thus, once a government actor invokes race, the Supreme Court presumes the existence of racism and strikes the action down. But if race is not mentioned, then no matter how egregiously disproportionate the impact on minorities, the Court upholds the conduct. Any actual showing of purposeful racism is superfluous. The bare majority of Justices on the Supreme Court have transmuted the thoughtful search for racism into a simplistic search for explicit considerations of race. References to race emerge, under current doctrine, as the measure of racism.

One does not need common sense theory to see the error in this doctrine. Justice Stevens's dissent in *Adarand* points out the absurdity in equating race-conscious remedies with the worst excesses of racism. "There is no moral or constitutional equivalence between a policy that is designed to perpetuate a caste system and one that seeks to eradicate racial subordination," the Justice wrote, adding, "The consistency the Court espouses would disregard the difference between a 'No Trespassing' sign and a welcome mat."[54]

Understanding the common sense underpinnings of racism, though, clarifies our understanding of why current Court doctrine fails. The Court seems to be developing an Equal Protection jurisprudence that defines racism both too narrowly (race must be openly considered) and too broadly (every explicit consideration of race constitutes racism). The Supreme Court errs when it suggests that racism—exclusively and always—involves the forthright mention of race. Indeed, by disregarding common sense racism, the Court errs fundamentally by understanding racism exactly backwards. Racism easily occurs without any conscious thought given to race, and conscious consideration of race may stem from a desire to ameliorate rather than perpetuate racism. The Court's new understanding of racism is dead wrong, and our society suffers for it.

RACE AND THE WAR ON CRIME

When the Chicano movement arose in East Los Angeles in the spring of 1968, community protest, legal repression, and race were so interwoven on the level of common sense that the political mobilization and resultant legal crackdown contributed decisively to the development of a brown racial identity. The influence of this tripartite linkage seems now to have dissipated, as sustained political mobilization in minority communities has collapsed. Nevertheless, a new connection linking race directly to crime evolved out of the tumult of the sixties, and this new common sense dramatically informs the racial identities of today.

Criminality has long been a staple characteristic associated with people considered to be non-white; the Mexican version of this emphasized a penchant for thievery coupled with an ardor for knife fights and blood letting. Race remains real, both to those caught in the criminal justice system and to those afraid of society's "criminals," because race and crime have been strongly shackled together—historically, but also with special ferocity over the last few decades. We are in the midst of an especially vicious era of state violence against minorities, rationalized primarily through the language of criminal law. The statistics, although familiar, remain chilling: in 1972, at the end of the Chicano movement, 200,000 persons were incarcerated in state and federal prisons; in 1997, that number stood at 1.2 million, with another 500,000 persons in local jails awaiting trial or serving short sentences and yet another 100,000 juveniles locked up in youth detention facilities across the country.[55] The United States now incarcerates people—mainly minorities—at six to ten

times the rate of other industrialized nations.[56] Half of all in-
mates are black and probably one-fourth are Latino.[57]

What does this mean for our children? A boy born in 1991
faces the following probability of being imprisoned at some time
in his life: if he is white, a 4 percent chance; if he is Latino, then a
16 percent likelihood; and if he is black, then a 29 percent risk.[58]
At home, around the block, and in the community, these numbers translate into shattered lives, disrupted families, and deci-
mated generations. The cold statistics also find expression in an
unprecedented deployment of police forces, all too often accompanied by high levels of brutality.[59]

The current era can be traced back to the civil rights movement; legal violence formed part of the political and legal
response to minority demands for dignity and equal treatment.[60]
The South initially treated political protests as no different from
street crime; this approach relied on Jim Crow criminal statutes,
which had given racial debasement a legal superstructure. When
protesters transgressed the racial etiquette of white supremacy,
they almost invariably found themselves on the wrong side of the
law and, almost as often, in jail. Responding to political protesters as if they were common criminals allowed southern leaders to
avoid questions regarding their own politics and values while
tarring the insurgents with the brush of criminality (and, for
good measure, usually of communism as well).

J. Edgar Hoover embraced this strategy and promoted it on a
national level; herein lies one impetus to the police and prosecutorial crackdown on protesters in East Los Angeles in 1968. But
it was not just the law enforcement establishment that saw an advantage to conflating protest and crime. Politicians took the
same route, starting on a national level with Barry Goldwater
and continuing with Richard Nixon.[61] The year after Nixon's
successful 1968 law and order campaign, four out of five of those
polled "believed that law and order had broken down, and the
majority blamed 'Negroes who start riots' and 'communists.'"[62]
Nixon's law and order campaign has now become a centerpiece

of party politics, utilized successfully by Ronald Reagan, George Bush, and Bill Clinton, among others. Crime constitutes a way to campaign for the votes of whites uneasy about or openly hostile to increasing minority power.[63] In the post-civil rights context, race and racial fears cannot be openly mentioned. Crime-mongering, however, has proved to be a more than adequate substitute, in tirades about illegal immigrants, welfare cheats, and crack addicts.[64]

One result of this politics of crime has been an unprecedented wave of legal violence directed primarily, though not exclusively, at urban minority communities. To be sure, many whites have also been caught up in the rage to punish.[65] But the most direct results have been suffered by the minorities who constantly face the aggressive vigilance of patrol cars, find themselves lit up under the thirty million candlepower nightsuns aimed down from police helicopters, and are arrested, arraigned, tried, convicted, and put away for years under mandatory minimums and three strikes laws. Criminal conduct is a reality in every community and a pressing problem especially in those areas suffering from the negative effects of deindustrialization, segregation, and drastically diminished social services. But the level and tenor of policing in many minority communities, and indeed the use of criminal processes as substitutes for social and health services generally, often have less to do with improving community residents' quality of life than with fulfilling a prophecy of crime rooted principally in a common sense of minority criminality.

In turn, legal violence continues to construct racial identities. The residents of minority communities under siege by law enforcement authorities see themselves in extremely racialized terms. On the popular level, we see it in the themes of rap and hip hop music and in the glorification of lifestyles that emphasize alienation, violence, masculinity, material wealth, law breaking, and hostility toward the police, all in a cultural package that aggressively asserts non-whiteness. East L.A. rapper Kid Frost pounds out rap songs such as "I Got Pulled Over," "Penitentiary," and "Chaos on the Streets of East Los Angeles" that feature sirens, gun shots, and racist LAPD radio conversations as a backdrop to his lyrics about gang-banging and drive-by-shootings.[66] It is no surprise that in this context Frost's songs frequently declaim racial pride, for instance in "Another Firme Rola (Bad Cause I'm Brown)," and in "La Raza," where Frost over and over declares himself "brown and proud."[67]

Urban minorities, especially youth, increasingly develop their identities in environments deformed by massive unemployment, declining social investment, high levels of antisocial behavior, and extreme police violence, and they do so in a cultural context that tightly equates race and criminality. What we now see in rap and hip hop culture, not only among Latinos but among blacks and other urban minorities, is an insistence on non-white identities, often embedded in a complicated dance of words denouncing police violence and boasting of virility, material wealth, and law-breaking.[68] In turn, these new, super-charged identities as rappers, gangstas, homies, gang bangers, hip hoppers, and so on confirm the racialized, bigoted views many Anglos hold regarding minority youth. Thus, since the 1960s legal violence has gained in its power to make race real. It is a matter of virtually unquestioned common sense that there should be a war on crime and that this war should especially target urban minority youth.

The racial identities of those historically constructed as non-white have grown more complicated over the last few decades. The integrationist spirit of the civil rights era and the militancy of minority communities opened up a space for some minorities to functionally attain white identities. Among Latinos and Asians especially, but also among blacks and Native Americans, there are sizable groups who, by virtue of relatively fair features, education, professional standing, athleticism, or artistic accomplishment, can escape many of the burdens otherwise imposed on non-whites. The increasing prominence of persons from historically non-white groups suggests to many that racism and races themselves are relics of the past. But this is not true. Large segments of our society remain deeply racialized as non-white—and so are viewed and treated as criminal, inferior, undeserving, and dangerous. Our prisons and our cities testify immediately to the terrible vigor of race.

Meanwhile, the majority in our society know that they are unquestionably white. This knowledge comes from history, from material privilege, from social status, from common sense. It comes, in part, from the way they are treated by the police and the courts—as if they *should* sit on grand juries, as if they deserve respect and courtesy, as if they are innocent until proven guilty, as if, even when convicted, their conduct represents unfortunate circumstances rather than a criminal disposition, as if, finally, they could potentially be friends or neighbors or in-laws. But there is no fixed white group, just as there is no set Mexican race. Instead, there are cultural practices and material patterns, mediated by common sense, that continue to make race self-evident. Those who think they are white deserve no more, but no less, dignity and fair treatment than anyone else.

Our country is in crisis, but we do not recognize the devastation around us because it has come to seem natural and inevitable that things should be this way. Racial common sense assures us—particularly those of us who assume that we are white—that everything is normal and all right. It assures others, especially those of us who identify with gangstas and homies, that race defines our destiny.

LOOKING TO THE FUTURE

At root, I understand the Chicano movement as an effort to respond to the problem of race in this country. In the United States, racial knowledge and its material consequences strongly shape our culture and define the relative positions of different groups. Responding to the inequalities imposed through the logic of race is one of the greatest challenges this country faces. Because of the harm done in the name of race, it may seem that the most appropriate response is to repudiate race entirely, to demand unequivocally that we eschew this atavistic myth of human difference. This sort of argument has an appealing ring to it. Indeed, perhaps in the very long run our society will evolve to the point where talk of races has meaning only among historians of the distant past. I, for one, would embrace such a future, for it seems to me that race has primarily played a tragic role. Though I strongly support the celebration of group differences and human variation, I would prefer to see such celebration occurring under some concept other than race.

Nevertheless, we must recognize that we are still, and long will be, living in that distant past, the one in which race powerfully defines social and material relations in the United States. At this point in our history, I support the emphasis on race by those constructed as non-white, for it is the only way to directly challenge and remake racial knowledge. Race is not now a primarily conscious concept, subject to change or erasure through revamped education or quick, deliberate policy choices. Instead, it exists in the background, in our daily practices, our social structures, our understanding of what is normal, sane, and natural. As we look to the future, we must purposefully and self-consciously engage with the common sense of race in the present. Rubén Salazar insisted that justice is the most important word in race relations in order to stress that the quality of justice administered by the state shaped relations between races. I seek to add another meaning to that phrase: injustice creates races, especially where such injustice seems like common sense.

NOTES   ACKNOWLEDGMENTS   INDEX

NOTES

PROLOGUE

1. U.S. Department of Commerce, Census Bureau, *Census 2000 Brief, The Hispanic Population*, May 2001, 7.

2. The following statistics, unless otherwise indicated, are from U.S. Department of Commerce, Census Bureau, *Census 2000 Brief, Overview of Race and Hispanic Origin*, March 2001, and Census Bureau, *Census 2000 Brief, The Hispanic Population*. The census uses the term Hispanic but indicates that Latino is an acceptable synonym. Most persons placed into that category prefer the latter term, as do I. See David Hayes-Bautista and Jorge Chapa, "Latino Terminology: Conceptual Bases for Standardized Terminology," 77 *American Journal of Public Health* 61, 65–67 (1986). See also Jack D. Forbes, "The Hispanic Spin: Party Politics and Governmental Manipulation of Ethnic Identity," 75 *Latin American Perspectives* 59 (1992), and Laura E. Gómez, "The Birth of the 'Hispanic' Generation: Attitudes of Mexican-American Political Elites toward the Hispanic Label," 75 *Latin American Perspectives* 45 (1992).

3. Jorge J. E. García and Pablo De Greiff, eds., *Hispanics/Latinos in the United States: Ethnicity, Race, and Rights*, 1 (2000).

4. Hayes-Bautista and Chapa, 64. See also Clara E. Rodríguez, *Changing Race: Latinos, the Census, and the History of Ethnicity in the United States* (2000).

5. In 1992, 46.9 percent of foreign-born and 55.4 percent of U.S.-born persons of Mexican descent classified themselves as white. Rodolfo F. Acuña, *Anything But Mexican: Chicanos in Contemporary Los An-*

geles, 9 (1996). In 1980, 51.9 percent of the Mexican-origin population in California described themselves as racially "other," while 47.7 percent described themselves as white. Hayes-Bautista and Chapa, 65. Jack Forbes points out that Mexican residents of regions with comparatively larger Mexican populations were more likely to self-identify as members of another race and less likely to claim to be white. Forbes, "The Hispanic Spin," 70.

6. Given the chance to choose the racial identity that best described them, 48 percent of Latinos selected white, while 42 percent opted for "some other race"; among non-Latinos, only 0.2 percent indicated the other-race category. Census Bureau, *Census 2000 Brief, Overview of Race and Hispanic Origin*, 10.

7. Floya Anthias, "Connecting 'Race' and Ethnic Phenomena," 26 *Sociology* 421, 422-23 (1992).

8. To be sure, various groups have been socially constructed as races to differing degrees.

9. Rubén Salazar made this point, which I use as the epigraph for this book, just a few months before the police killed him during a riot in East Los Angeles. See Ruben Salazar, "Mexican-Americans' Problems with the Legal System Viewed," *L.A. Times*, May 1, 1970, Part 2, at 7. On the killing of Salazar, see Mario García, "Introduction," in Mario García ed. *Ruben Salazar, Border Correspondent: Selected Writings, 1955-1970*, 2-3 (1995); Edward J. Escobar, "The Dialectics of Repression: The Los Angeles Police Department and the Chicano Movement, 1968-1971," 79 *Journal of American History* 1483, 1484–1485, 1501–1504 (1993); and Hunter Thompson, "Strange Rumblings in Aztlan," in Hunter Thompson, *The Great Shark Hunt: Strange Tales from a Strange Time*, 119 (1979).

INTRODUCTION

1. For a fuller discussion of nomenclature, with particular attention to whether Mexican identity should be conceptualized in racial terms, see Ian Haney López, "Race, Ethnicity, Erasure: The Salience of Race to LatCrit Theory," 85 *California Law Review* 1143 (1998). For other discussions regarding whether Latinos should be thought of in racial or ethnic terms, see Jorge García and Pablo De Greiff, eds., *Hispanics/Latinos in the United States: Ethnicity, Race, and Rights* (2000), and Christopher Rodríguez, *Latino Manifesto: A Critique of the Race Debate in the U.S. Latino Community* (1996).

The use of "Mexican" here shares some of the same motivations as those animating its usage by Rudy Acuña. Acuña advocates the use of "Mexican" because it accepts, reclaims and valorizes an otherwise slighted identity. On the other hand, Acuña also favors the use of "Mexican" because it connotes a non-white identity, a connotation I avoid in my usage of the term. Rodolfo Acuña, *Anything But Mexican: Chicanos in Contemporary Los Angeles* 1, 8–9 (1996).

2. Aída Hurtado and Carlos Arce, "Mexicans, Chicanos, Mexican Americans, or Pochos . . . ¿Qué somos? The Impact of Language and Nativity on Ethnic Labeling," 17 *Aztlán: A Journal of Chicano Studies* 103 (Spring 1986).

3. Oscar Z. Acosta, *The Revolt of the Cockroach People* 222 (Vintage 1989 [1973]). See also Oscar Z. Acosta, *Autobiography of a Brown Buffalo* (Vintage 1989 [1972]).

4. Edward A. Villalobos, Comment, "Grand Jury Discrimination and the Mexican American," 5 *Loyola University of Los Angeles Law Review* 87, 109–110 (1972).

5. See generally Ian Haney López, "The Social Construction of Race: Some Observations on Illusion, Fabrication, and Choice," 29 *Harvard Civil Rights–Civil Liberties Law Review* 1 (1994).

6. Portions of Part Two draw on Ian F. Haney López, "Institutional Racism: Judicial Conduct and a New Theory of Racial Discrimination," 109 *Yale Law Journal* 1717 (2000).

7. See Robert Cover, "Violence and the Word," 95 *Yale Law Journal* 1601 (1986).

8. Edward J. Escobar, *Race, Police, and the Making of a Political Identity: Mexican Americans and the Los Angeles Police Department, 1900–1945* (1999).

9. The initial portion of Part Three draws on Ian Haney López, "Protest, Repression, and Race: Legal Violence and the Chicano Movement," 150 *University of Pennsylvania Law Review* 205 (2001).

1 THE CHICANO MOVEMENT CASES

1. Leo Grebler, Joan Moore, and Ralph Guzman, *The Mexican-American People: The Nation's Second Largest Minority*, 15 (1970).

2. Rodolfo Acuña, *A Community Under Siege: A Chronicle of Chicanos East of the Los Angeles River, 1945–1975*, 184 (1984).

3. Ibid.

4. Ibid. A look at just the Spanish-surnamed population of East Los Angeles reveals an even bleaker picture of poverty and educational handicap. The median income of this group was lower by over $1,000 than the median income in East Los Angeles as a whole, and barely a fifth had finished high school. Ibid.

5. U.S. Bureau of the Census, *Census 2000 Brief: The Hispanic Population*, table 4, 7 (May 2001).

6. Film producers regularly stage their depictions of East L.A. by spreading rubbish about and scrawling graffiti prior to filming their renditions of barrio life. Mary Pardo, *Mexican American Women Activists: Identity and Resistance in Two Los Angeles Communities,* 65–68 (1998).

7. Acuña, *Community Under Siege,* 184.

8. U.S. Commission on Civil Rights, *Mexican Americans and the Administration of Justice in the Southwest,* x (1970). See also David Gutiérrez, *Walls and Mirrors: Mexican Americans, Mexican Immigrants, and the Politics of Ethnicity,* 183 (1995).

9. Gerald Rosen, "The Development of the Chicano Movement in Los Angeles from 1967 to 1969," 4 *Aztlán: A Journal of Chicano Studies* 155, 164 (1973).

10. U.S. Commission on Civil Rights, *Education and the Mexican American Community in Los Angeles County, Report Prepared by the California State Advisory Committee,* 3 (April 1968). See also "The Mexican American Child: How Have We Failed Him?" excerpted in Luis Valdez and Stan Steiner, eds., *Aztlan: An Anthology of Mexican American Literature,* 298 (1972) (originally published by U.S. Office of Education, 1968).

11. Henry Gutierrez, "The Chicano Education Rights Movement and School Desegregation, Los Angeles, 1962–1970," 56 (Ph.D. diss., University of California, Irvine, 1990).

12. Quoted in Juan Inda, *La Comunidad en Lucha: The Development of the East Los Angeles High School Blowouts,* 3, Stanford Center for Chicano Research, Working Paper Series, no. 29 (March 1990).

13. David Gomez, *Somos Chicanos: Strangers in Our Own Land,* 112 (1973). The inadequate education of Mexicans in East Los Angeles reflected similar patterns throughout the Southwest. See U.S. Commission on Civil Rights, *Mexican American Education Study: Ethnic Isolation of Mexican Americans in the Public Schools of the Southwest* (1971); U.S. Commission on Civil Rights, *Mexican American Education Study: The Unfinished Education: Outcomes for Minorities in the Five Southwestern States* (1971); U.S. Commission on Civil Rights, *Mexican American Education Study: The Excluded Student: Educational Practices Affecting Mexican Americans in the Southwest* (1972); U.S. Commission on Civil Rights, *Mexican American Education Study: Differences in Teacher Interaction with Mexican American and Anglo Students* (1973).

14. Inda, *Comunidad,* 4.

15. Juan Gómez-Quiñones, *Chicano Politics: Reality and Promise, 1940–1990,* 79–80 (1990).

16. Juan Gómez-Quiñones, *Mexican Students por La Raza: The Chicano Student Movement in Southern California 1967–1977*, 21–22 (1978).

17. Dial Torgerson, "Latin Groups Fight 'Anglo Integration,'" *Los Angeles Times*, Part 2, 1 (Feb. 23, 1968).

18. Ruben Salazar, "Brown Berets Hail 'La Raza' and Scorn the Establishment," in Mario García, ed., *Ruben Salazar, Border Correspondent: Selected Writings, 1955–1970*, 212, 217 (1995). First published in *Los Angeles Times*, June 16, 1969. Gómez-Quiñones, *Mexican Students*, 17. See also "Brown Beret: Serve, Observe, Protect," *La Raza*, 13 (June 7, 1968) ("The Brown Beret was chosen because it is a symbol of the love and pride we have in our race and in the color of our skin.").

19. "Pickets vs. Pickets," *La Raza*, 5 (Oct. 15, 1967); "L.A. Schools Strike Out," *La Raza*, 3 (Nov. 15, 1967); "Garfield High: Another Manual Arts?" *La Raza*, 3 (Nov. 15, 1967); "Questions???" *La Raza*, 8 (Dec. 2, 1967); "Time of Studies and Statistics Over! Time for Action and Revolution Now!" *La Raza*, 3 (Dec. 2, 1967).

20. "Questions???"

21. "Merry Christmas from the L.A. School Board," *La Raza*, 4 (Dec. 2, 1967).

22. People v. Castro, No. A-232902, Reporter's Transcript of Grand Jury Proceedings, 456–57 (California Superior Court, Los Angeles County, 1968). During the Grand Jury investigation, the prosecutor entered into the record a taped radio interview given by Castro. Quotes from the Grand Jury transcript attributed to Castro are from that recorded interview and are not testimony given under direct questioning.

23. Cf. Gómez-Quiñones, *Mexican Students*, 31 (arguing that "Organizers and leadership came from the college groups; the strikers were high school kids."). During the walkouts, Gómez-Quiñones was a doctoral candidate at the University of California, Los Angeles, and a member of UMAS. He participated in the strikes at Roosevelt High School and was called before the 1968 Los Angeles Grand Jury. Transcript of Grand Jury Proceedings, 68–100.

24. Inda, *Comunidad*, 13.

25. Ibid.

26. Ibid.

27. "Education, Not Concentration Camps," *La Raza*, 1 (March 31, 1968); Stan Steiner, *La Raza: The Mexican Americans*, 210 (1970).

28. Transcript of Grand Jury Proceedings, 463. In 1988, on the twentieth anniversary of the walkouts, the *Los Angeles Times* reported that "although he said he denied it at the time to avoid going to jail, to-

day Castro freely takes credit for masterminding the walkouts." Elaine Woo, "60s 'Blowouts' Leaders of Latino School Protest See Little Change," *Los Angeles Times,* Part 2, 1 (March 7, 1988).

29. Inda, *Comunidad,* 14; Transcript of Grand Jury Proceedings, 143–145.

30. Transcript of Grand Jury Proceedings, 475.

31. Ibid., 474–475.

32. Ibid., 464–465.

33. Edward Escobar, "The Dialectics of Repression: The Los Angeles Police Department and the Chicano Movement, 1968–1971," 79 *Journal of American History* 1483, 1496–1497 (1993).

34. Inda, *Comunidad,* 16; Rosen, "Development of the Chicano Movement," 166.

35. Ridgely Cummings, "Intimidation Charged: Teachers Rap School Board on 'Walkouts,'" *Belvedere Citizen,* 1 (April 4, 1968); Eric Malnic, "Angry Teachers Accuse Board of Laxity on Boycott," *Los Angeles Times,* Part 1, 1 (March 29, 1968).

36. Rosen, "Development of the Chicano Movement," 166–167. See also Jack McMurdy, "Frivolous to Fundamental: Demands Made by East Side High School Students Listed," *Los Angeles Times,* Part 1, 1 (March 17, 1968).

37. "Educational Issues," *La Raza,* 14 (May 11, 1968). See also Joe Kretschmer, "Letters to the Times," *Los Angeles Times,* Part 2, 4 (March 19, 1968).

38. "An Open Letter to Mexican-American Parents from an Anglo Elementary School Teacher," *La Raza,* 14 (May 11, 1968).

39. Ibid.

40. "Reddin, Younger's Dog Pack Loose in East L.A.," *La Raza,* 5 (June 7, 1968). See also Ron Einstoss, "13 Indicted in Disorders at 4 L.A. Schools; Arrests Underway," *Los Angeles Times,* Part 1, 1 (June 2, 1968).

41. "Conspiracy to Educate," *La Raza,* 6B (July 10, 1968); Transcript of Grand Jury Proceedings, 403 (testimony of Father John Luce).

42. "Conspiracy to Educate," 6B; F. Arturo Rosales, *Chicano! The History of the Mexican American Civil Rights Movement,* 192 (1996).

43. Armando Morales, *Ando Sangrando (I Am Bleeding): A Study of Mexican American-Police Conflict,* 78 (1972).

44. "Reddin, Younger's Dog Pack."

45. Ibid.

46. "Conspiracy to Educate," 6B.

47. "Reddin, Younger's Dog Pack."

48. Carlos Muñoz Jr., *Youth, Identity, Power: The Chicano Movement,* 65 (1989); "Conspiracy to Educate," 6C.

49. "Reddin, Younger's Dog Pack"; Rosales, *Chicano!* 193.

50. "Conspiracy to Educate," 6C; Muñoz, *Youth, Identity,* xii, 68.

51. "Conspiracy to Educate," 6C; see also Ron Einstoss, "Bail Reduced for 9 in Walkouts at 4 Schools," *Los Angles Times,* Part 1, 3 (June 4, 1968).

52. "Conspiracy to Educate," 6C.

53. Muñoz, *Youth, Identity,* 68; "Conspiracy to Educate," 6C.

54. "Conspiracy to Educate," 6C; see also Ron Einstoss, "Bail Reduced for 9 in Walkouts at 4 Schools," *Los Angles Times,* Part 1, 3 (June 4, 1968).

55. "Conspiracy to Educate," 6C.

56. Ibid.

57. "Reddin, Younger's Dog Pack."

58. "Conspiracy to Educate," 6C.

59. Ibid.

60. Einstoss, "13 Indicted," 11. The U.S. Commission on Civil Rights cited the bail originally set for the East L.A. Thirteen in concluding that "the system of bail in the Southwest frequently is used more severely against Mexican Americans than against Anglos as a form of discrimination." U.S. Commission on Civil Rights, *Administration of Justice,* 48, 52.

61. Einstoss, "Bail Reduced." See also Rosales, *Chicano!* 192 (reporting that Sánchez feared that if arrested he would miss his prom; this prompted him to jump out a bathroom window at the Berets' office, only to be arrested at home).

62. Dave Larsen, "Timing of Arrests in School Walkouts Called Political," *Los Angeles Times,* Part 2, 1 (June 5, 1968).

63. People v. Castro, No. A-232902 (California Superior Court, Los Angeles County, 1968).

64. "Political Prisoners Speak," *La Raza,* 7 (June 7, 1968); "Arrests Were Political," *La Raza,* 7 (June 7, 1968).

65. Oscar Acosta, "Autobiographical Essay," in Ilan Stavans, ed., *Oscar "Zeta" Acosta: The Uncollected Works,* 4, 5 (1996).

66. Ilan Stavans, *Bandido: Oscar "Zeta" Acosta and the Chicano Experience,* 22–23 (1995).

67. Acosta, "Autobiographical Essay," 5. See also Stavans, *Bandido,* 20.

68. Acosta, "Autobiographical Essay," 5.

69. Ibid.

70. Ibid., 6.

71. Ibid.

72. Ibid.

73. Stavans, *Uncollected Works,* xix.

74. Acosta, "Autobiographical Essay," 7.

75. Newspaper clipping from *La Voz Latina,* Oscar Zeta Acosta Papers, Department of Special Collections, California Ethnic and Multicultural Archives, University of California, Santa Barbara.

76. Acosta, "Autobiographical Essay," 7.

77. Ibid.

78. Ibid., 8.

79. Hunter Thompson, *Fear and Loathing in Las Vegas: A Savage Journey to the Heart of the American Dream,* 11 (1971); Hunter Thompson, *Fear and Loathing in America: The Brutal Odyssey of an Outlaw Journalist, 1968–1976,* xix-xx, 29 (2000). Correspondence between Acosta and Thompson appears in *Fear and Loathing in America.*

80. Acosta, "Autobiographical Essay," 8.

81. Ibid.

82. Ibid., 5.

83. See Acosta, "Autobiographical Essay"; Oscar Acosta, *The Revolt of the Cockroach People* (Vintage, 1989 [1973]).

84. Oscar Acosta, "ELA 13 and Biltmore 6," *La Raza,* 2 (Dec. 1969); "Lawyers File Motions for 13," *La Raza,* 8 (Aug. 15, 1968). The National Lawyers Guild supplied Neil Herring and Samuel Rosenwein, and A. L. Wirin and Fred Okrand from the ACLU also greatly helped out. Ibid. Other attorneys involved in the Chicano cases included Herman Sillas, Paul Posner, Hugh Manes, Al Michaelson, Ralph Segura, Joe Ortega, Elnora Livezey and Joan Anderson. Acosta, "ELA 13"; "The East Los 13 v. Superior Court," *La Raza,* 8 (Feb. 7, 1969); "Nuevas Vistas 10," *La Raza,* 13 (July 1969); Ron Einstoss, "Judge Jails Three Defense Attorneys in Biltmore Trial," *L.A. Times,* Part 2, 1 (Aug. 11, 1971).

85. Acosta, "Autobiographical Essay," 13.

86. Acosta, "ELA 13."

87. "Chicano Legal Defense Fund," *La Raza,* 9 (Aug. 15, 1968).

88. Ibid. Notably, Derrick Bell, who would pioneer critical race theory in U.S. law schools, also served as a sponsor for the Chicano fund.

89. "Lawyers File Motions."

90. Ridgely Cummings, "Ask Dismissal of Walkout Charges," *Belvedere Citizen,* 1 (Sept. 12, 1968).

91. "Brown Beret: Serve, Observe, Protect," *La Raza,* 13 (June 7,

1968). See also "Chicano Leaders Arrested," *La Raza,* 6A (July 10, 1968).

92. Castro v. Superior Court, 9 Cal. App. 3d 675 (1970).

93. Oscar Acosta, "Racial Exclusion," in Stavans, *Uncollected Works,* 280, 285. In 1969, an additional 23 grand jurors served, none of whom were Mexican. Thus, in the period from 1958 to 1969, Mexicans made up just 4 of 233 Los Angeles grand jurors.

94. Acuña, *Community Under Siege,* 184; Edward Villalobos, Comment, "Grand Jury Discrimination and the Mexican American," 5 *Loyola University of Los Angeles Law Review* 87, 110 (1972).

95. See People v. Castro, No. A-232902, Motion to Quash Indictment (California Superior Court, Los Angeles County, 1968).

96. "La Raza Nueva 13," *La Raza,* 11 (Sept. 3, 1968).

97. Acosta, "Autobiographical Essay," 14.

98. Acosta, "Racial Exclusion," 280, 288.

99. "Educational Issues," *La Raza,* 14 (May 11, 1968). In reporting on the removal of Castro from his teaching position, *La Raza* pointedly noted that "Mr. Davis, the teacher whom parents want out because of his racist statements, remains in the classroom." "Castro Out of Classroom," *La Raza,* 12 (June 7, 1968).

100. Gerald Rosen, "Political Ideology and the Chicano Movement: A Study of the Political Ideology of Activists in the Chicano Movement," 177–78 (Ph.D. diss., University of California, Los Angeles, 1972). See also Jack McMurdy, "Lincoln High Pickets Protest Absence of Indicted Teacher," *Los Angeles Times,* Part 1, 3 (Sept. 17, 1968); Jack McMurdy, "Student-Parent Sit-In Continuing on Weekend," *Los Angeles Times,* Part 3, 1 (Sept. 28, 1968); Jack McMurdy, "School Board Sit-In Extended as Teacher Ruling Is Delayed," *Los Angeles Times,* Part 1, 1 (Oct. 1, 1968); Jack McMurdy, "Arrests of 35 End 2nd Sit-In at School Board," *Los Angeles Times,* Part 1, 3 (Oct. 3, 1968). Castro was eventually restored to his teaching job at Lincoln High, only to be subsequently transferred to a high school that had a predominantly Anglo student body. Jack McMurdy, "Castro Restored to Teaching Job," *Los Angeles Times,* Part 1, 1 (Oct. 4, 1968); Jack McMurdy, "Action against L.A. Teacher Upheld," *Los Angeles Times,* Part 2, 4 (Dec. 2, 1969).

101. Rodolfo Acuña, *Occupied America: A History of Chicanos,* 342 (3rd ed., 1988).

102. See "Chicano Legal Defense: The Dominguez Family Case," *La Raza,* 2 (Oct. 15, 1968); "Hung Jury in Second Dominguez Trial," *La Raza,* 7 (Nov. 1969); "Do We Also Have to Pay for It?" *La Raza,* 13 (Dec. 1969).

262															NOTES TO PAGES 34-37

103. Muñoz, *Youth, Identity,* 68.

104. Ernesto Vigil, *The Crusade for Justice: Chicano Militancy and the Government's War on Dissent,* 136 (1999).

105. Muñoz, *Youth, Identity,* 68.

106. Acuña, *Occupied,* 350. See also Vigil, *Crusade,* 135–138, 150–153.

107. Ron Einstoss, "Hotel Fire Indictments Reveal Heroism of Rookie Policeman," *Los Angeles Times,* Part 1, 1 (June 7, 1969).

108. Acuña, *Occupied,* 350; see also Vigil, *Crusade,* 137; "El Frito Vendido," *La Raza,* 12 (July, 1969).

109. "Ronnie's Show Flops as Biltmore Burns," *La Raza,* 3 (April 30, 1969).

110. "Fires, Protests Jar Reagan Talk," *Los Angeles Herald Examiner,* § A, 1 (April 25, 1969); Tom Newton, "Demonstration Disrupts Talk by Governor," *Los Angeles Times,* Part 1, 1 (April 25, 1969).

111. "Help Us Help You, Reagan Tells Hispano Educators," *Los Angeles Herald Examiner* (n.d.), newspaper clipping, Oscar Zeta Acosta Papers, Department of Special Collections, California Ethnic and Multicultural Archives, University of California, Santa Barbara.

112. "Nuevas Vistas 10," *La Raza,* 13 (July 1969).

113. Ibid. See also Acosta, "ELA 13," 2. The other three to stand trial were Rene Nuñez and Ernest Cebada Eichwald, both with the Los Angeles Educational Clearinghouse, and Juan Rojas, also known as Juan Robles, a student at East Los Angeles College. See also "Nuevas Vistas 10."

114. "Nuevas Vistas 10."

115. "4 Activists Surrender in Biltmore Fire Case: Attorney for Indicted Mexican-Americans Denies They Were Involved, Assails Police," *Los Angeles Times,* Part 1, 28 (June 10, 1969).

116. Ibid.

117. Ron Einstoss, "No Bias Found Against Latins on Grand Juries," *Los Angeles Times,* Part 1, 3 (April 1, 1971). The other Mexican Superior Court judges were Leopoldo Sánchez, Carlos Teran, and Edward Guirado. People v. Montez, Offer of Proof, No. A-244906, (California Superior Court, Los Angeles County, 1969).

118. This is my conjecture based upon a conversation with Judge Alarcon in 1992.

119. "4 Activists."

120. Montez v. Superior Court, 10 Cal.App. 3d 343, 347 (1970).

121. I have not been able to locate a transcript of this hearing.

122. Einstoss, "No Bias Found."

123. Acosta, *Revolt*, 221–22.

124. People v. Ramirez, et. al., No. A-244906, Findings of Fact, Conclusions of Law, and Order, 8 (California Superior Court, Los Angeles County, 1969) (issued March 31, 1971). See also Einstoss, "No Bias Found."

125. Ron Einstoss, "Undercover Officer Describes Role at Biltmore Fire Trial," *Los Angeles Times*, Part 1, 3 (Aug. 4, 1971).

126. People v. Montez, No. A-244906, Transcript, 617, 624, 628, 674, 678 (California Superior Court, Los Angeles County, 1969) (Aug. 9, 1971) (partial transcript recording the cross-examination of Fernando Sumaya, on file with author).

127. Ibid., 635.

128. Ibid. (emphasis added).

129. Ibid. Officer Sumaya insisted that despite months of service as an undercover agent among the Brown Berets, he "never made any field notes or written reports of any kind." Vigil, *Crusade*, 150.

130. Einstoss, "Judge Jails." After jailing Acosta, Judge Alarcon ordered Acosta's two co-counsel, Elnora Livezey and Joan Anderson, to proceed with the case. When they refused on the ground that they were too "emotionally upset" to continue, Judge Alarcon ordered them jailed for one night each. Ibid.

131. "Lawyer Gets Five-Day Term in Biltmore Case," *Los Angeles Times*, Part 2, 5 (Aug. 13, 1971).

132. "Defendant Cleared in Biltmore Case," newspaper clipping, Oscar Zeta Acosta Papers.

133. Ron Einstoss, "Two Acquitted after Biltmore Jurors Deadlock; Remaining Two Granted Mistrial by Judge; Jury Cites Witness Credibility," *Los Angeles Times*, Part 2, 1 (Sept. 14, 1971).

134. Ron Einstoss, "Acosta Quits Defense for Two Brown Berets: Judge Delays Retrial, Names Two New Lawyers in Biltmore Hotel Arson Case," *Los Angeles Times*, Part 1, 22 (Nov. 16, 1971).

135. William Farr, "2 Freed in Hotel Fire; Lack of Evidence Cited," *Los Angeles Times*, Part 2, 8 (May 18, 1972).

136. Ernesto Chávez, "Creating Aztlán: The Chicano Movement in Los Angeles, 1966–1978," 85 (Ph.D. diss., University of California, Los Angeles, 1994).

137. See also "Catolicos Por La Raza," *La Raza*, 5–12 (Feb. 1970). See People v. Cruz, 101 Cal. Rep. 711 (California Superior Court, Los Angeles County, 1972).

138. Vigil, *Crusade*, 146–148.

264

139. "St. Basil Attorney Jailed by Judge," newspaper clipping, Oscar Zeta Acosta Papers.

140. Vigil, *Crusade,* 146; "Judge Jails Attorney in East L.A. Riot Case: Acosta Found in Contempt during Jury Selection for Concealed Weapons Trial," newspaper clipping, Oscar Zeta Acosta Papers.

141. Vigil, *Crusade,* 146–148.

2 PROVING MEXICANS EXIST

1. Hernandez v. Texas, 347 U.S. 475 (1954).

2. Brown et al. v. Board of Education of Topeka, Shawnee County, Kansas, et al., 347 U.S. 483 (1954).

3. Hernandez v. Texas, 347 U.S. 475, 478.

4. Ibid., 479.

5. Ibid.

6. Both Acosta and the district attorney cited to *Hernandez.* See People v. Castro, No. A-232902, Motion to Quash Indictment (Grand Jury Illegally Constituted; Arbitrary Discretion to Proceed by Indictment), 5 (California Superior Court, Los Angeles County, 1968) (filed Aug. 6, 1968); People v. Castro, No. A-232902, Reporter's Transcript of Proceedings, Motion to Quash Indictment, 896–97 (California Superior Court, Los Angeles County, 1968).

7. Transcript of Proceedings, Motion to Quash, 79 (George Marr, Los Angeles County Regional Planning Commission), 99 (George Sabagh, professor of sociology, University of California, Los Angeles), 176 (Richard Villalobos, County of Los Angeles Commission on Human Relations), 188 (Joan Moore, associate professor of sociology, University of California, Riverside).

8. The report was subsequently published as Leo Grebler, Joan Moore, and Ralph Guzman, *The Mexican-American People: The Nation's Second Largest Minority* (1970). See also Joan Moore and Alfredo Cuéllar, *Mexican Americans* (1970).

9. Transcript of Proceedings, Motion to Quash, 202.

10. Ibid., 200–201, 218–219. See also Moore and Cuéllar, *Mexican Americans,* 64–65; U.S. Bureau of the Census, *Characteristics of the South and East Los Angeles Area, November 1965, Current Population Report,* Series P-23, No. 18 (June 28, 1966).

11. Transcript of Proceedings, Motion to Quash, 200–201, 214, 218–219.

12. Ibid., 217. See also Moore and Cuéllar, *Mexican Americans,* 115.

13. U.S. Bureau of the Census, *United States Census of Population: 1960, Persons of Spanish Surname: Social and Economic Data for White Persons of Spanish Surname in Five Southwestern States, Final Report,* Subject Reports, PC(2)-1B (1960).

14. Transcript of Proceedings, Motion to Quash, 199.

15. In 1940, the census dropped "Mexican" as a separate race and required census enumerators to classify Mexicans as white unless they were "definitely Indian or of other Nonwhite races." Clara Rodríguez, *Changing Race: Latinos, the Census, and the History of Ethnicity in the United States,* 102 (2000).

16. Transcript of Proceedings, Motion to Quash, 203, 204.

17. Ibid., 204–205.

18. Ibid., 246.

19. Ibid.

20. Ibid., 247.

21. Ibid., 551–554.

22. Ibid., 606, 615.

23. Ibid., 662.

24. Ibid., 666–670.

25. Ibid., 673.

26. Ibid., 673–674.

27. Ibid., 675–676.

28. Ibid., 688–689.

29. Ibid., 715–716.

30. For an example of another judge who sought to nominate members of the Mexican "race," see ibid., 769, 772–776, 778 (testimony of Judge Bernard S. Selber).

31. Ibid., 422–43. Judge Dockweiler later admitted that he had only one Mexican acquaintance: "The only man I know is the man who runs the gasoline station at Larchmont and First Street. He is of Mexican extraction." Ibid., 419.

32. Ibid., 425.

33. Ibid., 1005.

34. Ibid., 61.

35. Ibid.

36. Ibid.

37. Ibid., 675–66.

38. Ibid., 551–54.

39. Ibid.

40. Ibid., 924.

41. The principal exception is the work of Carey McWilliams, in

particular Carey McWilliams, *North from Mexico: The Spanish-Speaking People of the United States* (1949).

3   THE MEXICAN RACE IN EAST L.A.

1. See generally Robert Heizer and Alan Almquist, *The Other Californians: Prejudice and Discrimination under Spain, Mexico, and the United States to 1920* (1971).

2. Richard Griswold del Castillo, *The Los Angeles Barrio, 1850–1890: A Social History*, 12 (1979). See also Heizer and Almquist, *Other Californians*, 16.

3. Carey McWilliams, *Southern California: An Island on the Land*, 52 (1983).

4. Griswold del Castillo, *Los Angeles Barrio*, 22–23; Joan Moore and Alfredo Cuéllar, *Mexican Americans*, 4 (1970).

5. Douglas Monroy, *Thrown Among Strangers: The Making of Mexican Culture in Frontier California*, 158 (1990).

6. Tomás Almaguer, *Racial Fault Lines: The Historical Origins of White Supremacy in California*, 4, 59 (1994).

7. McWilliams, *Southern California*, 95.

8. Suzanne Oboler, *Ethnic Labels, Latino Lives: Identity and the Politics of (Re)Presentation in the United States*, 23, 25 (1995).

9. Arnoldo De León, *They Called Them Greasers: Anglo Attitudes toward Mexicans in Texas, 1821–1900*, 4 (1983).

10. Quoted in ibid., 22.

11. Note that a census taken in 1834 reported that four out of five of the Anglo settlers in Texas came from slave states. Cecil Robinson, *With the Ears of Strangers: The Mexican in American Literature*, 67 (1963).

12. Quoted in Reginald Horsman, *Race and Manifest Destiny: The Origins of Racial Anglo-Saxonism*, 238 (1981).

13. Quoted in ibid., 246.

14. Quoted in Moore and Cuéllar, *Mexican Americans*, 47.

15. Quoted in Horsman, *Race and Manifest Destiny*, 238.

16. Quoted in ibid., 239.

17. Quoted in Bill Piatt, *Black and Brown in America: The Case for Cooperation*, 22 (1997).

18. Quoted in Horsman, *Race and Manifest Destiny*, 243–244.

19. Ibid.

20. Quoted in ibid., 243.

21. Quoted in Heizer and Almquist, *Other Californians*, 140.

22. Ibid.

23. Horsman, *Race and Manifest Destiny*, 208.

24. Ibid., 245.

25. Quoted in De León, *Greasers*, 16. See also Ozzie Simmons, "The Mutual Images and Expectations of Anglo-Americans and Mexican-Americans," 90 *Daedalus* 286, 290 (1961).

26. Douglas Monroy, *Rebirth: Mexican Los Angeles from the Great Migration to the Great Depression*, 107 (1999). Anglos also frequently ascribed dirtiness to California's indigenous population. James Rawls, *Indians of California: The Changing Image*, 195 (1986). For a discussion of how the term "dirty Mexican" functioned in Texas, see David Montejano, *Anglos and Mexicans in the Making of Texas, 1836–1886*, 225–233 (1987).

27. The prevalent "attitude toward the Californio is summed up in a single word—indolent, which is itself repeated time and again in the American observations as a blanket condemnation of all classes of Californian males." David Langum, "Californios and the Image of Indolence," 9 *Western Historical Quarterly* 181 (1978).

28. Quoted in Robinson, *Ears of Strangers*, 34.

29. Quoted in ibid.

30. Quoted in Langum, "Image of Indolence," 183.

31. Quoted in Robinson, *Ears of Strangers*, 42.

32. Quoted in ibid., 48.

33. Quoted in ibid., 44.

34. Ibid., 54.

35. Quoted in ibid., 58.

36. Larry Trujillo, "La Evolución del 'Bandido' al 'Pachuco': A Critical Examination and Evaluation of Criminological Literature on Chicanos," 9 *Issues in Criminology* 43, 47 (1974); Blaine Lamb, "The Convenient Villain: The Early Cinema Views of the Mexican-American," 14 *Journal of the West* 75 (1975).

37. Chon Noriega, "Citizen Chicano: The Trials and Titillations of Ethnicity in the American Cinema, 1935–1962," 58 *Social Research* 413, 425 (1991).

38. Quoted in Roger Lipshultz, "Attitudes toward the Mexican," in Matt Meier and Feliciano Rivera, eds., *Readings on La Raza: The Twentieth Century*, 64, 68 (1974).

39. Quoted in Rodolfo Acuña, *Anything But Mexican: Chicanos in Contemporary Los Angeles*, 111–12 (1996).

40. Quoted in David Gutiérrez, *Walls and Mirrors: Mexican Americans, Mexican Immigrants, and the Politics of Ethnicity*, 54 (1995).

41. See Juan Gómez-Quiñones, *Chicano Politics: Reality and Promise, 1940–1990*, 42 (1990).

42. Almaguer, *Racial Fault Lines*, 62.

43. Quoted in ibid., 61.

44. Monroy, *Thrown among Strangers*, 202–3; McWilliams, *Southern California*, 58.

45. Heizer and Almquist, *Other Californians*, 50.

46. Ibid., 131. See also Almaguer, *Racial Fault Lines*, 57.

47. Heizer and Almquist, *Other Californians*, 23–64; Almaguer, *Racial Fault Lines*, 135–141.

48. McWilliams, *Southern California*, 60; Monroy, *Thrown among Strangers*, 209. See also Griswold del Castillo, *Los Angeles Barrio*, 106.

49. Rodolfo Acuña, *A Community Under Siege: A Chronicle of Chicanos East of the Los Angeles River, 1945–1975*, 5, 7 (1984).

50. Griswold del Castillo, *Los Angeles Barrio*, 35.

51. Ibid., 48.

52. Ibid., 143, 145.

53. Ibid., 174; Mario García, *Mexican Americans: Leadership, Ideology, and Identity, 1930–1960*, 14 (1989). I draw on García's notion of overarching political generations—cohorts bound together by unique self-conceptions generated by specific epochs of community history—as a useful way to examine the rise of East Los Angeles as a Mexican enclave. See ibid., 3–4.

54. Gutiérrez, *Walls and Mirrors*, 29 (1995).

55. Griswold del Castillo, *Los Angeles Barrio*, 133, 139.

56. Ibid., 61; George Sánchez, *Becoming Mexican American: Ethnicity, Culture, and Identity in Chicano Los Angeles, 1940–1945*, 90 (1993).

57. Ricardo Romo, *East Los Angeles: History of a Barrio*, 89–111 (1983).

58. Sánchez, *Becoming Mexican American*, 88.

59. Romo, *East Los Angeles*, 10; Sánchez, *Becoming Mexican American*, 83.

60. Sánchez, *Becoming Mexican American*, 90.

61. Quoted in Monroy, *Rebirth*, 110.

62. Romo, *East Los Angeles*, 127.

63. Quoted in ibid., 139. See also Charles Wollenberg, "Mendez v. Westminster: Race, Nationality and Segregation in California Schools," 53 *California Historical Society Quarterly* 317 (1974). The principal California legislation that facilitated the school segregation of Mexican students treated that community as Native Americans. Martha Menchaca, "Chicano Indianism: A Historical Account of Racial Repression in the United States," 20 *American Ethnologist* 583, 598 (1993). In 1946 Mendez v. Westminster, 64 F. Supp. 544 (So. D. Ca. 1946),

brought the de jure segregation of Mexican students to an end on the ground that such segregation was not specifically authorized by the legislature; nevertheless, the segregation of Mexican students remained widespread. Ibid., 599.

64. Romo, *East Los Angeles*, 85.

65. Sánchez, *Becoming Mexican American*, 72.

66. Romo, *East Los Angeles*, 61–62, 69–70.

67. Sánchez, *Becoming Mexican American*, 201.

68. Romo, *East Los Angeles*, 64–67.

69. Quoted in George Lipsitz, *The Possessive Investment in Whiteness: How White People Profit from Identity Politics*, 6 (1998). See also Romo, *East Los Angeles*, 9–10.

70. Sánchez, *Becoming Mexican American*, 70.

71. Mario García describes this as the "immigrant generation." García, *Mexican Americans*, 15.

72. Ibid., 210.

73. Ibid., 212.

74. Ibid., 211–213.

75. Quoted in Edward Escobar, *Race, Police, and the Making of a Political Identity: Mexican Americans and the Los Angeles Police Department, 1900–1945*, 86, 89 (1999).

76. Sánchez, *Becoming Mexican American*, 12.

77. Romo, *East Los Angeles*, 162.

78. Sánchez, *Becoming Mexican American*, 221.

79. García, *Mexican Americans*, 16.

80. Sánchez, *Becoming Mexican American*, 245, 254.

81. Ibid., 255–57. See also Carlos Muñoz Jr., *Youth, Identity, Power: The Chicano Movement*, 29–44 (1989).

82. Quoted in Sánchez, *Becoming Mexican American*, 257.

83. Quoted in ibid., 258.

84. Ibid., 245–247.

85. García, *Mexican Americans*, 152; Gutiérrez, *Walls and Mirrors*, 111–114; Sánchez, *Becoming Mexican American*, 245–247. Almost uniquely, El Congreso also urged "women's equality," "that she may receive equal wages, enjoy the same rights as men in social, economic, and civil liberties, and use her vote for the defense of the Mexican and Spanish American people, and of American democracy." Sánchez, *Becoming Mexican American*, 248; see also García, *Mexican Americans*, 164. El Congreso also initiated several citizen's arrests against police officers who used the threat of arrest for prostitution to coerce sex from Mexican women, mainly waitresses. Escobar, *Race, Police*, 153. El Congreso owed much of its success to the organizing efforts of two charismatic

women, Luisa Moreno and Josefina Fierro de Bright. Sánchez, *Becoming Mexican American,* 244, 246.

86. Gómez-Quiñones, *Chicano Politics,* 40.

87. Ibid., 34.

88. Romo, *East Los Angeles,* 167, citing Raúl Morin, *Among the Valiant: Mexican-Americans in WW II and Korea* (1966).

89. Romo, *East Los Angeles,* 165; Lipsitz, *Possessive Investment,* 199.

90. Carey McWilliams, *North from Mexico: The Spanish-Speaking People of the United States,* 227 (1949). McWilliams observed, "In Los Angeles . . . it was a foregone conclusion that Mexicans would be substituted as the major scapegoat group once the Japanese were removed." Ibid.

91. Ibid., 229; Mauricio Mazón, *The Zoot-Suit Riots: The Psychology of Symbolic Annihilation,* 20 (1984).

92. McWilliams, *North from Mexico,* 229.

93. Ibid.

94. Mazón, *Zoot-Suit Riots,* 21.

95. Sánchez, *Becoming Mexican American,* 266; McWilliams, *North from Mexico,* 231; García, *Mexican Americans,* 171.

96. McWilliams, *North from Mexico,* 231.

97. Ibid.

98. Ibid., 233.

99. Ibid., 234.

100. Quoted in ibid.

101. Quoted in Mazón, *Zoot-Suit Riots,* 22.

102. McWilliams, *North from Mexico,* 238.

103. Mazón, *Zoot-Suit Riots,* 7–8; McWilliams, *North from Mexico,* 242.

104. McWilliams, *North from Mexico,* 248.

105. Ibid., 247, 249.

106. Mazón, *Zoot-Suit Riots,* 75.

107. Mazón uses the term "symbolic annihilation" in discussing the zoot-suit riots to express a sense that what transpired was a *ritual* of destruction rather than the actual destruction of a supposedly distinct out-group. Ibid., 12. On a separate point, the turmoil in Los Angeles anticipated a number of white race riots, many much more violent, in cities such as Detroit, Evansville, New York, and Philadelphia. Ibid., 78.

108. Quoted in García, *Mexican Americans,* 172.

109. See Ricardo Romo, "Southern California and the Origins of Latino Civil-Rights Activism," 3 *Western Legal History* 379 (1990). In

response to LULAC's legal success, California repealed its school segregation laws on June 14, 1946. Romo, *East Los Angeles,* 168.

110. Julie Pycior, *LBJ and Mexican Americans: The Paradox of Power,* 68–73 (1997). See also Gutiérrez, *Walls and Mirrors,* 154 (1995).

111. Gómez-Quiñones, *Chicano Politics,* 53.

112. Mary Pardo, *Mexican American Women Activists: Identity and Resistance in Two Los Angeles Communities,* 61–62 (1998); Gómez-Quiñones, *Chicano Politics,* 53, 73. César Chávez served initially as a CSO organizer. John Hammerback, Richard Jensen, and Jose Gutierrez, *A War of Words: Chicano Protest in the 1960s and 1970s,* 36, 103 (1985).

113. Neil Foley, "Becoming Hispanic: Mexican Americans and the Faustian Pact with Whiteness," in Neil Foley, ed., *Reflexiones 1997: New Directions in Mexican American Studies,* 53 (1997).

114. Hernandez v. Texas, 347 U.S. 475 (1954).

115. Ibid., 479.

116. Ibid., 479–480.

117. Brief of Petitioner, 38, Hernandez v. Texas, 347 U.S. 475 (1954).

118. "Mexican Americans as 'whites' believed no substantive racial factor existed to justify racial discrimination against them." García, *Mexican Americans,* 43.

119. Foley, "Becoming Hispanic," 54.

120. Ibid., 63.

121. Ibid., 63–64.

122. García, *Mexican Americans,* 233–238.

123. Ibid., 237.

124. Quoted in Muñoz, *Youth, Identity,* 33.

125. Ernesto Chávez, "Creating Aztlán: The Chicano Movement in Los Angeles, 1966–1978," 35 (Ph.D. diss., University of California, Los Angeles, 1994) (emphasis in original).

126. Paul Coronel, "The Pachuco Problem," *The Mexican Voice,* 3 (1943). Coronel also chastised "Our American people" because they "have not regarded the Mexican-American as an equal, racially and economically," and for "segregating the Mexican from the normal processes of American life." Ibid.

127. See also Neil Foley, *The White Scourge: Mexicans, Blacks, and Poor Whites in Texas Cotton Culture* (1997).

128. Indicative of this differing emphasis, political groups founded in the late 1950s to push for political power included the Mexican American Political Association (MAPA) in California and the Political

Association of Spanish-Speaking Organizations (PASSO) in Texas. Despite shared goals, the organizations were unable to amalgamate because of conflict over a common name: Texas constituents opposed as too ethnic the label "Mexican American," and the California group rejected as unpalatable the euphemism "Spanish-speaking." Moore and Cuéllar, *Mexican Americans*, 148.

129. See Robin Kelley, *Race Rebels: Culture, Politics, and the Black Working Class*, 6 (1994) (warning against treating mainstream middle-class leaders as if they speak for or represent entire communities).

130. Monroy, *Rebirth*, 259.

131. García, *Mexican Americans*, 282.

132. Quoted in ibid.

133. María Herrera-Sobek, *Northward Bound: The Mexican Immigrant Experience in Ballad and Song*, 216–219 (1993). See also María Herrera-Sobek, *The Bracero Experience: Elitelore versus Folklore* (1979), and Guillermo Hernandez, *Canciones de la Raza: Songs of the Chicano Experience* (1978).

134. Gregory Rodríguez uses the history of boxing in Los Angeles to explore the national and class aspects of conflict in the Mexican community in the twentieth century. Gregory Rodríguez, "'Palaces of Pain'—Arenas of Mexican-American Dreams: Boxing and the Formation of Ethnic Mexican Identities in Twentieth-Century Los Angeles" (Ph.D. diss. University of California, San Diego, 1999). See also Gutiérrez, *Walls and Mirrors*.

135. Regarding the music and dance in particular, see Steven Loza, *Barrio Rhythm: Mexican American Music in Los Angeles*, 80–83, 161–162 (1993).

136. Octavio Paz, in his famous if problematic comments regarding Pachuco culture, stressed the largely negative content of that identity. Of interest here, Paz suggested that "the pachucos do not attempt to vindicate their race or the nationality of their forbears. Their attitude reveals an obstinate will-to-be, but this will affirms nothing specific except their determination . . . not to be like those around them." Octavio Paz, *The Labyrinth of Solitude: Life and Thought in Mexico*, 14 (Lysander Kemp, trans., 1961).

137. See Mathew Frye Jacobson, *Whiteness of a Different Color: European Immigrants and the Alchemy of Race* (1998).

138. Werner Sollors, "Foreword: Theories of American Ethnicity," in Werner Sollors, ed., *Theories of Ethnicity: A Classical Reader*, x (1996).

139. U.S. Bureau of the Census, *Characteristics of the Population, 1940*, 3 (1943).

140. Hernandez v. State, 251 S.W.2d 531, 533, 535 (Tex. Crim. App., 1952). For a fuller exploration, see Ian Haney López, "Race, Ethnicity, Erasure: The Salience of Race to Latcrit Theory," 85 *California Law Review* 1143 (1998). In the late 1960s and early 1970s, Texas school officials avoided meaningful desegregation by assigning African Americans and Mexicans to the same school, using the white designation of Mexicans to argue that such schools were integrated. See Tasby v. Estes, 517 F.2d 92, 106 (5th Cir. 1975) (discussing the Dallas Independent School District's policy of integrating Mexican and Black students to circumvent the desegregation requirements of Brown v. Board of Education).

141. Romo, *East Los Angeles*, 169. On the impact of the freeways, see Pardo, *Mexican American Women*, 61–62 (1998).

142. Juan Ramon García, *Operation Wetback: The Mass Deportation of Mexican Undocumented Workers in 1954*, 183 (1980).

143. Ibid., 143.

144. Moore and Cuéllar, *Mexican Americans*, 29. Rodolfo Acuña, *Occupied America: A History of Chicanos*, 268 (3rd ed., 1988). Paradoxically, during these same years legal immigration from Mexico increased dramatically, especially in the form of farm workers in the Bracero program. Indeed, the U.S. government through this program granted permission to many of those deported to re-enter the United States—they were, in a parlance that included the routine use of the term "wetback," "dried out." García, *Operation Wetback*, 235–237. See also Kitty Calavita, *Inside the State: The Bracero Program, Immigration, and the I.N.S.* (1992).

145. Thomas Martínez, "Advertising and Racism: The Case of the Mexican-American," in Edward Simmen, ed., *Pain and Promise: The Chicano Today, Vivid Accounts of the Reawakening of a Proud and Oppressed People*, 94, 104 (1972). Rubén Salazar reported on this study in the *Los Angeles Times*. Ruben Salazar, "Latins' Image in Advertising Held 'Inferior,'" in Mario García, ed., *Ruben Salazar, Border Correspondent: Selected Writings, 1955–1970*, 232 (1995). First published in *Los Angeles Times*, October 20, 1969.

146. Martínez, "Advertising and Racism," 94.

147. Ruben Salazar, "Judge's Latin Slurs Bring Call for Removal," in García, *Border Correspondent*, 225. First published in *Los Angeles Times*, Oct. 2, 1969.

148. "In the Superior Court of the State of California in and for the County of Santa Clara," in Livie Isauro Duran and H. Russell Bernard, eds., *Introduction to Chicano Studies: A Reader*, 482 (1973).

149. Ruben Salazar, "Maligned Word: Mexican," in García, *Border*

Correspondent, 250–251. First published in *Los Angeles Times,* April 17, 1970. In the wake of the furor, Judge Chargin offered the following comment to the *Los Angeles Times:* "I am pleased to say that my entire adult life, both in the law and on the Superior Court bench, has been an effort and a striving for justice for all. The most recent example of this is my nomination of the only Mexican-American individual presently serving on the County Grand Jury." Salazar, "Latin Slurs," 226.

150. U.S. Bureau of the Census, *United States Census of Population: 1960, Persons of Spanish Surname: Social and Economic Data for White Persons of Spanish Surname in Five Southwestern States, Final Report,* Subject Reports, PC(2)-1B (1960). For an overview of the socioeconomic characteristics of Mexicans in the Southwest in the 1960s, see Leo Grebler, Joan Moore, and Ralph Guzman, *The Mexican-American People: The Nation's Second Largest Minority,* 14–23 (1970).

151. Sánchez, *Becoming Mexican American,* 77, 198.

152. Moore and Cuéllar, *Mexican Americans,* 56.

4   JUDGES AND INTENTIONAL RACISM

1. People v. Castro, No. A-232902, Reporter's Transcript of Proceedings, Motion to Quash Indictment, 1005–1006 (California Superior Court, Los Angeles County, 1968).

2. Marvin Frankel and Gary Naftalis, *The Grand Jury: An Institution on Trial* (1975).

3. Ibid., 3.

4. California Legislature, Assembly Interim Committee on Governmental Efficiency and Economy, *Hearing on the California County Grand Jury System, Part II, Los Angeles, 1967,* 53 (1967) (testimony of Evelle Younger, District Attorney, County of Los Angeles).

5. California Legislature, Assembly Select Committee on the Administration of Justice, *Hearings on Police-Community Relations, East Los Angeles, April 21, 1972,* 52 (1972). See also California Penal Code, § 935. For critiques regarding the lack of grand jury independence, see Deborah Day Emerson, *Grand Jury Reform: A Review of Key Issues,* 21 (1983); and Andrew Leipold, "Why Grand Juries Do Not (and Cannot) Protect the Accused," 80 *Cornell Law Review* 260, 264 (1995).

6. Frankel and Naftalis, *Grand Jury,* 16.

7. Leroy Clark, *The Grand Jury: The Use and Abuse of Political Power,* 24–25 (1975). See also Frankel and Naftalis, *Grand Jury,* 55.

8. For California cases involving Huey Newton and Sirhan Sirhan, see respectively People v. Newton, 8 Cal.App. 3d 359 (1970), and People v. Sirhan, 7 Cal.3d 710 (1972).

9. California Code of Civil Procedure, § 198. Current qualifications for grand jurors are now listed in California Penal Code, § 893.

10. California Penal Code, § 903.

11. California Penal Code, § 903.4. Not surprisingly, jury commissioners rarely bothered to compile jury lists, and courts did not require them to do so. People v. Goodspeed, 22 Cal. App. 3d 690, 701 (1972).

12. California Penal Code, §§ 900, 903.

13. The Chicano cases did not constitute the first attempt to challenge discrimination in the selection of California grand juries. For example, in 1964 the California legislature heard testimony from the Los Angeles NAACP urging "a better cross section of citizens within the county on the grand jury." California Legislature, Assembly Interim Committee on Criminal Procedure, *Problems of the California Grand Jury System*, 25 (1964) (testimony of Thomas G. Neusome). One author traces the impetus for grand jury reform to 1963, when the California Assembly passed a resolution calling for the study of whether current selection methods ensured the representation of a cross-section of the community on grand juries. Patricia Mar, "The California Grand Jury: Vestige of Aristocracy," 1 *Pacific Law Journal* 36, 38 (1970) (citing House Resolution 266, 1963 Regular Session).

14. Kenneth Arnold, *California Courts and Judges Handbook*, 292 (1968).

15. Transcript of Proceedings, Motion to Quash, 378–381.

16. Ibid., 395, 396.

17. Ibid., 370, 375, 376–377.

18. Ibid., 561–565 (testimony of Judge Kenneth Chantry regarding nomination of acquaintances from the Wilshire Country Club).

19. Ibid., 660–666.

20. These numbers are drawn from a table compiling the judges' nominees, excerpting the judges' description of their relationship to the persons that they nominated, and characterizing those relationships in several ways, as well as on a table summarizing the results. The percentages given are measured in terms of total nominations, rather than in terms of individual nominees. Ian Haney López, "Institutional Racism: Judicial Conduct and a New Theory of Racial Discrimination," 109 *Yale Law Journal* 1717, 1845–1876 (2000).

21. The data regarding judicial nominees for grand jury service derived from the *East L.A. Thirteen* transcript track the following calculations derived by the defense in the 1969 trial of Sirhan Sirhan for the assassination of Robert F. Kennedy: "Fifty-one percent of the nominees were personal friends or neighbors of the judges who nominated them. Another 42 percent were either professional acquaintances, fellow

members of a social or service group, or recommended by a friend of the judge. The addresses of the nominees were clustered around the addresses of the judges in the most affluent areas of the county. Few of the nominees were selected from areas where minority groups are concentrated." Patricia Mar, "The California Grand Jury: Vestige of Aristocracy," 1 *Pacific Law Journal* 36, 42 (1970) (citations omitted).

22. Transcript of Proceedings, Motion to Quash, 736.

23. Ibid., 390.

24. Ibid., 386–387.

25. Similarly, "80 percent of whites claim that they have close personal friends who are black," though if this is true, "every American black, even those most isolated from whites, has five or six close white friends." George Lipsitz, *The Possessive Investment in Whiteness: How White People Profit from Identity Politics,* 172 (1998).

26. Transcript of Proceedings, Motion to Quash, 310–311, 316, 419, 722.

27. California Legislature, *Grand Jury System,* 59–60.

28. In Taylor v. Louisiana, 419 U.S. 522 (1975), eight justices reasoned that "the fair-cross-section requirement is violated by the systematic exclusion of women . . . [A] flavor, a distinct quality is lost if either sex is excluded." Ibid., 531–532. Now Chief Justice William Rehnquist entered the lone dissent, chastising the majority because "this 'flavor' is not of such importance that the Constitution is offended if any given petit jury is not so enriched. This smacks more of mysticism than of law." Ibid., 542 (citation omitted).

29. Rodolfo Acuña, *A Community Under Siege: A Chronicle of Chicanos East of the Los Angeles River, 1945–1975,* 184 (1984); Edward Villalobos, Comment, "Grand Jury Discrimination and the Mexican American," 5 *Loyola University of Los Angeles Law Review* 87, 110 (1972).

30. According to papers Acosta submitted in the *Biltmore Six* case, Judge Carlos Teran had nominated ten persons with Spanish surnames; in comparison, Judges Arthur Alarcon and Edward Guirado had each nominated one person of Spanish surname, and Judge Leopoldo Sanchez had never nominated such persons. People v. Montez, No. A-244906, Offer of Proof (California Superior Court, Los Angeles County, 1969).

31. Edwin Lemert, "The Grand Jury as an Agency of Social Control," 10 *American Sociological Review* 751, 753 (1945).

32. U.S. Commission on Civil Rights, *Mexican Americans and the Administration of Justice in the Southwest* (1970).

33. California Rural Legal Assistance, "A Study of Grand Jury Ser-

vice by Persons of Spanish Surname and by Indians in Selected California Counties," in U.S. Commission on Civil Rights, *Administration of Justice,* 112.

34. Ibid., 123–124.

35. Ibid., 114.

36. Ibid., 119.

37. Commission on Civil Rights, *Administration of Justice,* 88–89.

38. Transcript of Proceedings, Motion to Quash, 400.

39. Ibid., 680–681.

40. Ibid., 890 (emphasis added).

41. Ibid., 909 (emphasis added).

42. Ibid., 923–924.

43. Ibid., 1006.

44. Judge Arthur Alarcon held that "no evidence was presented that any Judge of the Los Angeles Superior Court consciously, deliberately, intentionally or arbitrarily discriminated *against* persons of the class of persons identifiable as Mexican-Americans in the selection of nominees for the 1969 Grand Jury." People v. Ramirez, et. al., No. A-244906, Findings of Fact, Conclusions of Law, and Order, 12 (California Superior Court, Los Angeles County, 1969) (issued March 31, 1971); see also Lorenzo Arredondo and Donato Tapia, "El Chicano Y the Constitution: The Legacy of Hernandez v. Texas Grand Jury Discrimination," 6 *University of San Francisco Law Review* 129, 142 (1971). By emphasizing "against," Judge Alarcon highlighted his contention that the Los Angeles Superior Court judges intentionally favored Mexicans by seeking their inclusion on the 1969 grand jury. People v. Ramirez, Findings of Fact, 13.

45. Hernandez v. Texas, 347 U.S. 475, 482 (1954). *Hernandez* echoed the Court's earlier ruling that "if there has been discrimination, whether accomplished ingeniously or ingenuously, the conviction cannot stand." Smith v. Texas 311 U.S. 128, 132 (1940). See also Reece v. Georgia, 350 U.S. 85, 88 (1955).

46. Akins v. Texas, 325 U.S. 398, 403–404 (1945). See also Cassell v. Texas, 339 U.S. 282, 290 (1950); Swain v. Alabama, 380 U.S. 202, 209 (1965).

47. Washington v. Davis, 426 U.S. 229 (1976). The requirement that one prove "a racially discriminatory purpose" was soon extended to cases involving discrimination in the selection of jury venires, and then to the selection of actual jurors. Castañeda v. Partida, 430 U.S. 482, 493 (1977); Batson v. Kentucky, 476 U.S. 79, 93 (1986).

48. Washington v. Davis, 426 U.S. 237.

49. For compelling critiques of this state of affairs, see Alan Free-

man, "Legitimizing Racial Discrimination through Antidiscrimination Law: A Critical Review of Supreme Court Doctrine," 62 *Minnesota Law Review* 1049 (1978); Neil Gotanda, "A Critique of 'Our Constitution is Colorblind,'" 44 *Stanford Law Review* 1 (1991); and Reva Siegel, "Why Equal Protection No Longer Protects: The Evolving Forms of Status-Enforcing State Action," 49 *Stanford Law Review* 1111 (1997).

50. Gary Becker, *The Economics of Discrimination,* 6 (1957). Becker asserted that racial discrimination is costly and that a perfect market would drive out discriminators. See ibid., 35–37. John Donohue has argued to the contrary, as has Cass Sunstein. See John Donohue III, "Is Title VII Efficient?" 134 *University of Pennsylvania Law Review* 1411 (1986); Cass Sunstein, "Why Markets Don't Stop Discrimination," 8 *Social Phiosophy and Policy* 22 (1991).

51. Edmund Phelps, "The Statistical Theory of Racism and Sexism," 62 *American Economics Review* 659 (1972). Legal scholar and federal appellate judge Richard Posner subscribes to both theories, writing that "some people do not like to associate with the members of racial, religious, or ethnic groups different from their own and will pay a price to indulge their tastes," and also that "to the extent that race or some attribute similarly difficult to conceal (sex, accent, etc.) is positively correlated with the possession of undesired characteristics, or negatively correlated with desired characteristics, it is rational for people to use the attribute as a proxy for the underlying characteristic with which it is correlated ('statistical discrimination')." Richard Posner, *Economic Analysis of Law,* 715, 725 (5th ed., 1998). Similarly, Richard Epstein relies on both models in arguing that employment discrimination laws are inefficient and should be repealed. Richard Epstein, *Forbidden Grounds: The Case against Employment Discrimination Laws,* 33–35, 40–47 (1992).

52. Dinesh D'Souza, *The End of Racism: Principles for a Multiracial Society,* 24 (1995).

53. For an extended response to such arguments, see Jody David Armour, *Negrophobia and Reasonable Racism: The Hidden Costs of Being Black in America* (1997).

54. Transcript of Proceedings, Motion to Quash, 913.

5 RACE AND RACISM AS COMMON SENSE

1. People v. Castro, No. A-232902, Reporter's Transcript of Proceedings, Motion to Quash Indictment, 399–400 (California Superior Court, Los Angeles County, 1968).

2. Ibid., 923–924.

3. To develop this idea, I draw most directly on the sociology of knowledge developed by Harold Garfinkel, Peter Berger, and Thomas Luckmann. For a fuller exploration of these theories, and for a comparison to other social science theories of behavior, see Ian Haney López, "Institutional Racism: Judicial Conduct and a New Theory of Racial Discrimination," 109 *Yale Law Journal* 1717 (2000). Harold Garfinkel, *Studies in Ethnomethodology* (1967); Peter Berger and Thomas Luckmann, *The Social Construction of Reality* (1966).

4. The following is adapted from Paul DiMaggio and Walter Powell, introduction to Walter Powell and Paul DiMaggio, eds., *The New Institutionalism in Organizational Analysis*, 1, 37 n. 24 (1991).

5. The sociological genre of New Institutionalism provides a more focused analysis of the role of common sense in organizational settings. I discuss this genre in Haney López, "Institutional Racism." See also Powell and DiMaggio, *New Institutionalism;* Mark Suchman and Lauren Edelman, "Legal Rational Myths: The New Institutionalism and the Law and Society Tradition," 21 *Law and Social Inquiry* 903 (1996).

6. All of these methods, it should be noted, found use after the scandal over grand jury nomination practices reached critical proportions in the few years following *East L.A. Thirteen* and *Biltmore Six.*

7. Transcript of Proceedings, Motion to Quash, 594.

8. California Code of Civil Procedure, § 198.

9. Smith v. Texas, 311 U.S. 123, 132 (1940).

10. Cassell v. Texas, 339 U.S. 282, 290 (1950). See also Hill v. Texas, 316 U.S. 400, 404 (1942).

11. Cassell, 339 U.S. 282, 289 (citation omitted).

12. People v. White, 43 Cal. 2d 740, 754 (1954) (involving a petit jury panel selected from prominent social clubs).

13. Letter from Presiding Judge Lloyd S. Nix (July 26, 1967), quoted in Transcript of Proceedings, Motion to Quash, 289, 299. See also Edward Villalobos, Comment, "Grand Jury Discrimination and the Mexican American," 5 *Loyola University of Los Angeles Law Review* 87, 108 (1972).

14. Ellen Langer, "The Mindlessness of Ostensibly Thoughtful Action: The Role of 'Placebic' Information in Interpersonal Interaction," 36 *Journal of Personality and Social Psychology* 635 (1978).

15. Ibid., 637.

16. Scripts are something like Alfred Schutz's "cook-book knowledge": "The cook-book has recipes, lists of ingredients, formulae for mixing them, and directions for finishing off. This is all we need to make an apple pie, and also all we need to deal with the routine matters of daily life . . . Most of our daily activities from rising to going to bed are

280   NOTES TO PAGES 116–122

of this kind. They are performed by following recipes reduced to automatic habits or unquestioned platitudes." Alfred Schutz, "The Problem
of Rationality in the Social World," in Arvid Brodersen, ed., 2 *Alfred
Schutz, Collected Papers: Studies in Social Theory* 64, 73–74 (1964).

17. Transcript of Proceedings, Motion to Quash, 368–369.

18. Ibid., 529.

19. Sixteen judges recalled receiving the letter, while four did not.

20. Robert Abelson, "Psychological Status of the Script Concept,"
36 *American Psychologist* 715, 717 (1981).

21. Transcript of Proceedings, Motion to Quash, 596.

22. Ibid., 649–650. See also ibid., 453 (testimony of Judge Sidney
Kaufman).

23. Ibid., 330.

24. Berger and Luckmann, *Social Construction,* 66.

25. Mark Suchman, "On Beyond Interest: Rational, Normative and
Cognitive Perspectives in the Social Scientific Study of Law," 1997 *Wisconsin Law Review* 475, 499 (1997).

26. Stereotypes do not exhaust what I mean by the "characteristics"
associated with racial groups. In addition, generalizations abound regarding group identities. Unlike stereotypes, generalizations purport to
describe typical, not fixed and inescapable, characteristics.

27. Oscar Acosta, "The East L.A. 13 vs. the L.A. Superior Court," 3
El Grito 12, 15 (Winter 1970), also published as Oscar Acosta, "Racial
Exclusion," in Ilan Stavans, ed., *Oscar "Zeta" Acosta: The Uncollected
Works,* 280, 285 (1996).

28. Even "low prejudiced" individuals nevertheless "readily associate positive traits with whites." Samuel Gaertner and John McLaughlin,
"Racial Stereotypes: Associations and Ascriptions of Positive and Negative Characteristics," 46 *Social Psychology Quarterly* 23, 24 (1983).
Linda Krieger summarizes other studies demonstrating white in-group
biases. Linda Krieger, "Civil Rights Perestroika: Intergroup Relations
after Affirmative Action," 86 *California Law Review* 1251, 1322–1324
(1998).

29. Cf. Krieger, "Civil Rights," 1319 ("[In-group favoritism] largely
underlies the kind of discrimination that results in the systematic advan-
taging of white males").

30. Persons tend to over-attribute the behavior of others they perceive as unlike themselves to dispositional traits rather than to situa-
tional factors. See Lee Ross, "The Intuitive Psychologist and His Short-
comings: Distortions in the Attribution Process," in Leonard Berkowitz,
ed., 10 *Advances in Experimental Social Psychology* 173 (1977). If this
attribution error held true, those judges who claimed Mexican acquain-

tances but named gardeners and servants most likely attributed the menial or servile position of their acquaintances not to social factors but to Mexican "character." Lee Ross and Richard Nisbett, *The Person and the Situation: Perspectives on Social Psychology,* 150 (1991).

31. Jack Balkin offers a theory similar to what I mean by common sense, though he uses the language of memes and cultural software. J. M. Balkin, *Cultural Software: A Theory of Ideology* (1998). See also Suchman, "Beyond Interest."

32. Harold Garfinkel suggests icebergs as a metaphor: "In the conduct of his everyday affairs, in order for the person to treat rationally the one-tenth of this situation that, like an iceberg, appears above water, he must be able to treat the nine-tenths that lies below as an unquestioned and, perhaps even more interestingly, as an unquestionable background of matters that are demonstrably relevant to his calculation, but which appear without even being noticed." Garfinkel, *Ethnomethodology,* 173.

33. Transcript of Proceedings, Motion to Quash, 400.

34. Ibid., 399–400.

35. Ibid., 289, 393, 457, 493, 508, 519, 556, 597, 650 (emphases added). Notice that in *Hernandez,* the Texas jury discrimination case, the jury selectors there too justified the total exclusion of Mexicans on the grounds that "their only objective had been to select those whom they thought were best qualified." Hernandez v. Texas, 347 U.S. 475, 481 (1954).

36. Linda Krieger, "The Content of Our Categories: A Cognitive Bias Approach to Discrimination and Equal Employment Opportunity," 47 *Stanford Law Review* 1161, 1215 (1995).

37. Transcript of Proceedings, Motion to Quash, 653 (testimony of Judge Richard Fildew).

38. Ibid.

39. Ibid.

40. This approach corresponds to the representativeness heuristic in psychology, which describes how persons assign others to categories. Persons do not carefully scrutinize others and compare their characteristics against exactly assembled criteria for category membership. Instead, they contrast those aspects of others perceived as salient against facets of the category that stand out. See Daniel Kahneman and Amos Tversky, "On the Psychology of Prediction," in Daniel Kahneman, et al., eds., *Judgment Under Uncertainty: Heuristics and Biases,* 48, 49–57 (1982).

41. "There can be no timeless and absolute standard for what constitutes racism." Michael Omi and Howard Winant, *Racial Formation in the United States: From the 1960s to the 1990s,* 71 (2d. ed., 1994).

42. Status conflict is a common component in definitions of racism. In the legal field, status-based approaches are advocated by J. M. Balkin, "The Constitution of Status," 106 *Yale Law Journal* 2313 (1997) (developing a general model of status subordination); Kenneth Karst, *Law's Promise, Law's Expression: Visions of Power in the Politics of Race, Gender, and Religion,* 67–111 (1993) (using a status model to explore the Supreme Court's treatment of race); Rachel Moran, "Bilingual Education as a Status Conflict," 75 *California Law Review* 321 (1987) (using a status model to assess conflicts over bilingual education); Reva Siegel, "'The Rule of Love': Wife Beating as Prerogative and Privacy," 105 *Yale Law Journal* 2117 (1996) (discussing gender discrimination as a form of status hierarchy); and Reva Siegel, "Why Equal Protection No Longer Protects: The Evolving Forms of Status-Enforcing State Action," 49 *Stanford Law Review* 1111 (1997) (discussing gender and racial discrimination as status hierarchies).

43. George Fredrickson, *White Supremacy: A Comparative Study in American and South African History,* xi (1982).

44. George Lipsitz argues that "the practice of pursuing policies designed to have detrimental effects on nonwhites while at the same time disingenuously disavowing any racial intent is characteristic of traditional 'Americanism.'" George Lipsitz, *The Possessive Investment in Whiteness: How White People Profit from Identity Politics,* 216 (1998).

45. The common sense basis of purposeful racism suggests that studies of intentional racism should attend to racism's cultural context. Cf. David Goldberg, *Racist Culture: Philosophy and the Politics of Meaning,* 90 (1993).

46. Joe Feagin notes that many social science theories of racism treat that phenomenon as largely irrational, and so relatively easily remedied. Joe Feagin, *Discrimination American Style,* 5 (2d ed., 1986).

47. Krieger, "Civil Rights," 1286. Krieger doubts the ability of individual actors to successfully counteract cognitive biases. Ibid., 1286–1291.

48. Patricia Williams writes that "the solution to racism lies in our ability to see its ubiquity but not to concede its inevitability." Patricia Williams, *Seeing a Color-Blind Future: The Paradox of Race,* 68 (1997). This seems particularly true with respect to common sense racism.

49. See Charles Lawrence III, "The Id, the Ego, and Equal Protection: Reckoning with Unconscious Racism," 39 *Stanford Law Review* 317, 323 (1987) ("When an individual experiences conflict between racist ideas and the social ethic that condemns those ideas, the mind ex-

cludes his racism from consciousness."). See also Joel Kovel, *White Racism: A Psychohistory* (1970); Paul Wachtel, *Race in the Mind of America: Breaking the Vicious Cycle between Blacks and Whites* (1999).

50. Kovel, *White Racism*, 191–211; see also John Dovidio and Samuel Gaertner, "The Aversive Form of Racism," in John Dovidio and Samuel Gaertner, eds., *Prejudice, Discrimination, and Racism*, 1 (1986).

51. Haney López, "Institutional Racism," 1727–1728.

52. Stokely Carmichael and Charles Hamilton, *Black Power: The Politics of Liberation in America* (1967).

53. Ibid., 4–5.

54. See Nijole Benokraitis and Joe Feagin, "Institutional Racism: A Perspective in Search of Clarity and Research," in Charles Willie, ed., *Black/Brown/White Relations: Race Relations in the 1970s*, 121, 122 (1977).

55. In the legal academy, critical race theory has long insisted on the importance of institutional racism, broadly conceived. Kimberlé Crenshaw, et al., eds., introduction to *Critical Race Theory: The Key Writings that Formed the Movement*, xvi (1995). Among the important critical race theory works directly addressing racism are the following: Jody Armour, *Negrophobia and Reasonable Racism: The Hidden Costs of Being Black in America* (1997); Derrick Bell, *And We Are Not Saved: The Elusive Quest for Racial Justice* (1987) (especially chapter 9); Derrick Bell, *Faces at the Bottom of the Well: The Permanence of Racism* (1992) (especially chapters 5 and 8); John Calmore, "Race/ism Lost and Found: The Fair Housing Act at Thirty," 57 *University Miami Law Review* 1067 (1998); Anthony Cook, "Cultural Racism and the Limits of Rationality in the Saga of Rodney King," 70 *Denver Law Review* 297 (1993); Peggy Davis, "Law as Microaggression," 98 *Yale Law Journal* 1559 (1989); and Lawrence, "Unconscious Racism."

56. See Benokraitis and Feagin, "Institutional Racism," 128.

57. Gertrude Ezorsky, *Racism and Justice: The Case for Affirmative Action*, 9 (1991) ("Institutional racism occurs when a firm uses a practice that is race-neutral [intrinsically free of racial bias] but that nevertheless has an adverse impact on blacks as a group."). For yet others, institutional racism means any discrimination engaged in by large scale, stable social arrangements, whether generated through individual action or not. See Louis Knowles and Kenneth Prewitt, *Institutional Racism in America*, 5 (1969). If one thought it appropriate to label these arrangements racist, one could apply the term "structural racism." Cf. Marion Young, *Justice and the Politics of Difference*, 40 (1990) (describing "structural oppressions").

58. Oscar Acosta, "Autobiographical Essay," in Stavans, *Uncollected Works,* 13.

6 LAW ENFORCEMENT AND LEGAL VIOLENCE

1. Edward Escobar, *Race, Police, and the Making of a Political Identity: Mexican Americans and the Los Angeles Police Department, 1900–1945,* 28 (1999); Joseph Woods, "The Progressives and the Police: Urban Reform and the Professionalization of the Los Angeles Police," 498 (Ph.D. diss., University of California, Los Angeles, 1973).

2. Edward Escobar, "The Dialectics of Repression: The Los Angeles Police Department and the Chicano Movement, 1968–1971," 79 *Journal of American History* 1483, 1493–94 (1993).

3. Woods, "Progressives and the Police," 457; Rodolfo Acuña, *Anything But Mexican: Chicanos in Contemporary Los Angeles,* 271 (1996).

4. Escobar, "Dialectics," 1494.

5. O. W. Wilson, ed., *Parker on Police* (1957).

6. Ibid., 161. Parker added: "When I am told that intense police activity in a given area is psychologically disturbing to its residents, I am forced to agree . . . Is the police administrator, then, to discard crime occurrences and statistics and deploy his men on the basis of social inoffensiveness? This would be discrimination indeed!" Ibid.

7. Escobar, *Race, Police,* 122, 124.

8. "Beginning in the 1920s the LAPD began linking race and crime. The very fact that the department kept increasingly detailed and sophisticated statistics of arrests by race shows a growing interest in explaining crime in racial terms." Ibid., 130–131.

9. Ibid., 131.

10. "Edward Duran Ayres Report," in Matt Meier and Feliciano Rivera, eds., *Readings on La Raza: The Twentieth Century,* 127, 131 (1974).

11. Escobar, *Race, Police,* 13.

12. Ibid.

13. Ibid., 162.

14. Escobar suggests that such racism reflected personal rather than organizational factors: "The police practices that most angered Mexican Americans included verbal abuse, sexual harassment, indiscriminate searches, unwarranted arrests, and, most important, excessive use of force or police brutality. It should be remembered that while these practices were pervasive within the LAPD, they were for the most part the consequence of individual officers' prejudices rather than of departmental policy." Ibid., 172. This distinction between personal prejudice and

departmental policy misses the way that organizational culture encouraged common sense racism among Los Angeles law enforcement personnel.

15. Woods, "Progressives and the Police," 457, 458.

16. Ibid., 462.

17. "In the 1950s and 1960s Chief of Police William H. Parker described the LAPD as 'the thin blue line' that stood between civilization and chaos. No one who heard his words doubted that to Parker, 'civilization' meant whites and 'chaos' meant the Chicano and black communities of Los Angeles." Escobar, *Race, Police,* 286.

18. Quoted in Steve Herbert, *Policing Space: Territoriality and the Los Angeles Police Department,* 81 (1997).

19. Quoted in Joan Moore and Alfredo Cuéllar, *Mexican Americans,* 92–93 (1970).

20. Woods, "Progressives and the Police," 464.

21. Ibid., 472.

22. Armando Morales, *Ando Sangrando (I Am Bleeding): A Study of Mexican American-Police Conflict,* 53–54 (1972).

23. Ibid., 54.

24. Ibid. Morales also compared the LAPD's statistics for the Hollenbeck Division, covering a portion of East Los Angeles, and the Wilshire Division, a predominantly white area, finding that in the three years studied, 1965, 1966, and 1969, major crimes as a ratio of total population was consistently greater in the Wilshire area. Ibid., 52.

25. Ibid. These numbers include CHP officers.

26. Ibid., 55.

27. Quoted in Escobar, *Race, Police,* 123.

28. Ibid., 127, 128.

29. "From the 1890s to the 1930s, perhaps as many as 20 percent to 25 percent of incoming Mexican immigrants were arrested or accosted by the police, often brutally." F. Arturo Rosales, *¡Pobre Raza! Violence, Justice, and Mobilization among México Lindo Immigrants, 1900–1936,* 75 (1997).

30. California Legislature, Assembly Select Committee on the Administration of Justice, *Hearings on Police-Community Relations, East Los Angeles, April 28, 1972,* 4.

31. Ibid., 10–11.

32. Ibid., 64.

33. Acuña, *Anything But Mexican,* 264.

34. American Civil Liberties Union of Southern California, *Law Enforcement: The Matter of Redress* (1969).

35. Ibid., 15.

36. Ibid., 55, 56.

37. Ibid., 56.

38. Ibid., 60, 61.

39. Ibid., 60.

40. Ibid.

41. Ibid.

42. Ibid., 61.

43. Ibid., 62–63.

44. East Los Angeles journalist Roberto Rodríguez has written about the long nightmare, including the criminal prosecution for assaulting police, that began when sheriffs beat him for photographing their attack on another person. Roberto Rodríguez, *Justice: A Question of Race* (1997).

45. American Civil Liberties Union of Southern California, *Law Enforcement,* 57, 59.

46. Ibid.

47. Ibid., 69.

48. Ibid., 21.

49. Ibid., 77 n. 14.

50. California Legislature, *East Los Angeles, April 28, 1972,* 9.

51. U.S. Commission on Civil Rights, *Mexican Americans and the Administration of Justice in the Southwest,* 88 (1970).

52. Ibid., 87.

53. Steve Herbert argues that the police routinely draw on a variety of extralegal considerations when enforcing the law, citing among other influential normative orders a tendency on the part of the police to understand themselves as "moral" and those they oppose as "evil." Herbert, *Policing Space,* 36, 144.

54. Woods, "Progressives and the Police," 475.

55. Ibid., 483.

56. Ibid., 491.

57. Ibid., 487, 490.

58. Acuña, *Anything But Mexican,* 271.

59. Quoted in Escobar, "Dialectics," 1494, 1495.

60. "Police Chief Claims Latin Youths Being Used by Reds," *Belvedere Citizen* (Jan. 21, 1970). See also Dial Torgerson, "Reds Seek to Use Latin Youths as 'Prison Fodder,' Davis Says," *Los Angeles Times,* Part 1, 1 (Jan. 15, 1970).

61. Quoted in David Gomez, *Somos Chicanos: Strangers in Our Own Land,* 136 (1973).

62. Acuña, *Anything But Mexican,* 271–272.

63. Carlos Muñoz Jr., *Youth, Identity, Power: The Chicano Movement*, 68 (1989).

64. Quoted in ibid., 172–73 (last ellipses added, all others appear in Muñoz).

65. Ernesto Vigil, *The Crusade for Justice: Chicano Militancy and the Government's War on Dissent*, 137 (1999).

66. Escobar, "Dialectics," 1495.

67. Vigil, *Crusade*, 152.

68. Ibid. Police Chief Davis would claim, commenting on Martínez's success in provoking the arrest of Moratorium members, "We were knocking them off right and left . . . But what they didn't know is that in the Mexican community the great bulk of the people are very law abiding and very anti-Marxist and very supportive of the police and very respectful of the uniform." Quoted in ibid., 153. See also Muñoz, *Youth, Identity*, 173.

69. Vigil, *Crusade*, 152.

70. "Davis Blames Subversives for East L.A. Riot," *Los Angeles Times*, Part 1, 14 (Aug. 31, 1970).

71. California Legislature, *East Los Angeles, April 28, 1972*, 42.

72. Ibid.

73. Escobar, "Dialectics," 1498.

74. In the worldview of the police, "public order became not an effect of democracy but a prerequisite." Christopher Wilson, *Cop Knowledge: Police Power and Cultural Narrative in Twentieth-Century America*, 101 (2000).

75. Armando Morales, "A Study of Mexican American Perceptions of Law Enforcement Policies and Practices in East Los Angeles," 51, 223 (Ph.D. diss., University of Southern California, 1972).

76. Ibid., 322.

77. Morales anticipated finding that persons who identified as "'Chicanos,' the popular contemporary term used in connection with . . . a current, active political movement, would be the most critical of police practices." Ibid., 224.

7 THE CHICANO MOVEMENT AND EAST L.A. THIRTEEN

1. Acosta also alleged racism on the part of the district attorney. Acosta noted, for instance, that the prosecutor "reminded the judges that, after all, the Grand Jury performs many sophisticated functions nowadays, including accounting and business matters; that since a large part of the Mexican population was undereducated and poor and unable to speak English properly, that the figures alone did not mean anything . . . In a word, Mexicans are too dumb to serve on the Grand

Jury!" Acosta added: "True or not, the Chicano militants interpreted the District Attorney's argument to say that the Mexican was perhaps too stupid and too poor for service on the Grand Jury of Los Angeles. This 'explanation' can simply serve as further evidence of the racist society which compels him to seek his destiny in an identity and a rage that this society can ill afford." Oscar Acosta, "The East L.A. 13 vs. The L.A. Superior Court," 3 *El Grito* 12, 14 (1970); also published as Oscar Acosta, "Racial Exclusion," in Ilan Stavans, ed., *Oscar "Zeta" Acosta: The Uncollected Works*, 280, 288 (1996).

2. John Chávez, *The Lost Land: The Chicano Image of the South-west*, 135, 137 (1984); Ignacio García, *Chicanismo: The Forging of a Militant Ethos Among Mexican Americans*, 88 (1997).

3. García, *Chicanismo*, 30–31 (notes omitted).

4. See also John Hammerback, Richard Jensen, and Jose Gutierrez, *A War of Words: Chicano Protest in the 1960s and 1970s*, 33–36 (1985).

5. Oscar Acosta, *The Revolt of the Cockroach People*, 45 (Vintage 1989 [1973]). Acosta quotes César Chávez as identifying "Risco and Ruth"; these are most likely Eliezer Risco and Ruth Robinson. See *La Raza*, "página dos" (Sept. 16, 1967). Risco was an *East L.A. Thirteen* defendant.

6. Acosta, *Revolt*, 47.

7. F. Arturo Rosales, *Chicano! The History of the Mexican American Civil Rights Movement*, 154–170 (1996); Juan Gómez-Quiñones, *Chicano Politics: Reality and Promise, 1940–1990*, 115 (1990).

8. Rodolfo Acuña, *Occupied America: A History of Chicanos*, 340 (3rd ed., 1988).

9. Ibid.; Carlos Muñoz Jr., *Youth, Identity, Power: The Chicano Movement*, 57 (1989).

10. On the early history of Mexican resistance to Anglo hegemony in the Southwest, see Robert Rosenbaum, *Mexicano Resistance in the Southwest: "The Sacred Right of Self-Preservation"* (1981).

11. Rosales, *Chicano!* 154.

12. Ernesto Vigil, *The Crusade for Justice: Chicano Militancy and the Government's War on Dissent*, 8 (1999).

13. Muñoz, *Youth, Identity*, 57.

14. Ramón Gutiérrez, "Unraveling America's Hispanic Past: Internal Stratification and Class Boundaries," 17 *Aztlán: A Journal of Chicano Studies* 79, 94–98 (1986).

15. Muñoz, *Youth, Identity*, 61. "I Am Joaquín" did not address the African strain in Mexican identity.

16. Rodolfo Gonzales, "I Am Joaquin," *La Raza*, 4–5 (Sept. 16,

1967). Carlos Muñoz comments, "Gonzales did not advocate a specific identity for Mexican Americans in his poem: at the time he wrote *I Am Joaquín* he believed it possible to organize a movement regardless of the question of a specific identity." Muñoz, *Youth, Identity*, 62. In contrast, and tellingly, when Luís Valdez produced a film version of "I Am Joaquín" in 1969, he stressed the indigenous ancestry of Mexicans. Rosa Linda Fregoso, *The Bronze Screen: Chicana and Chicano Film Culture*, 7 (1993).

17. Gonzales, "I Am Joaquin."

18. Vigil, *Crusade*, 41, 50, 148. Oscar Acosta described Gonzales as "a poet, a street-fighter, a theorist and an organizer," adding, "He is recognized by a lot of Chicanos as the boss, the leader." Oscar Acosta, "Autobiographical Essay," in Stavans, *Uncollected Works*, 4, 10.

19. Acosta, *Revolt*, 40.

20. Gómez-Quiñones, *Chicano Politics*, 103. See also Alfredo Cuéllar, "Perspective on Politics," in Joan Moore and Alfredo Cuéllar, *Mexican Americans*, 137, 151 (1970).

21. Rosales, *Chicano!* 189.

22. I use social movement theory to assess the Chicano movement in Ian Haney López, "Protest, Repression, and Race: Legal Violence and the Chicano Movement," 150 *University of Pennsylvania Law Review* 205 (2001). Doug McAdam offers a good summary of social movement theory as it has developed in the United States, as does Ed Rubin. Doug McAdam, *Political Process and the Development of Black Insurgency, 1930–1970*, 6–19 (2nd ed., 1999); Edward Rubin, "Passing Through the Door: Social Movement Literature and Legal Scholarship," 150 *University of Pennsylvania Law Review* 1 (2001). Doug McAdam's notion of initiator and spin-off movements, as well as Sidney Tarrow's concept of a cycle of protest, and David Snow and Robert Benford's insights regarding protest framing, all help to explain the Chicano movement. See, for example, Doug McAdam, "'Initiator' and 'Spin-off' Movements: Diffusion Processes in Protest Cycles," in Mark Traugott, ed., *Repertoires and Cycles of Collective Action*, 217, 218 (1995); Sidney Tarrow, *Power in Movement: Social Movements, Collective Action, and Politics*, 153 (1994); and David Snow and Robert Benford, "Master Frames and Cycles of Protest," in Aldon Morris and Carol McClurg Mueller, eds., *Frontiers in Social Movement Theory*, 133 (1992).

23. Ruben Salazar, "Brown Berets Hail 'La Raza' and Scorn the Establishment," in Mario García, ed., *Ruben Salazar, Border Correspondent: Selected Writings, 1955–1970*, 216 (1995). First published in *Los Angeles Times*, June 16, 1969. See Stokely Carmichael and Charles Hamilton, *Black Power: The Politics of Liberation in America* (1967).

See also Manning Marable, *Race, Reform, and Rebellion: The Second Reconstruction in Black America, 1945–1990,* 94 (1991).

24. Enrique Trueba, *Latinos Unidos: From Cultural Diversity to the Politics of Solidarity,* 18 (2000) ("The training ground for political organization in Latino communities was the Civil Rights Movement of the 1960s and 1970s.").

25. Acosta, "Autobiographical Essay," 7.

26. "Reddin, Younger's Dog Pack Loose in East L.A.," *La Raza,* 5 (June 7, 1968).

27. See generally Doug McAdam and Ronnelle Paulsen, "Specifying the Relationship between Social Ties and Activism," in Doug McAdam and David Snow, eds., *Social Movements: Readings on Their Emergence, Mobilization, and Dynamics,* 145 (1997).

28. Muñoz, *Youth, Identity,* 55.

29. "Brown and Black Together," *La Raza,* 5 (Oct. 29, 1967). García, *Chicanismo,* 33–34; Rosales, *Chicano!* 159.

30. Quoted in Vigil, *Crusade,* 10.

31. Ruben Salazar, "Negro Drive Worries Mexican-Americans," in García, *Border Correspondent,* 113. First published in *Los Angeles Times,* July 14, 1963. Ruben Salazar, "Latin-Negro Unity Move Launched," in García, *Border Correspondent,* 146. First published in *Los Angeles Times,* July 5, 1964.

32. Chávez, *Lost Land,* 133.

33. Ruben Salazar, introduction to U.S. Commission on Civil Rights, *Stranger in One's Land,* iii, 2 (1970).

34. Acosta, "Racial Exclusion," 280, 285 (ellipses in original).

35. García, *Chicanismo,* 135; see also Nancy Whittier, "Political Generations, Micro-Cohorts, and the Transformation of Social Movements," 62 *American Sociological Review* 760, 762 (1997).

36. *East L.A. Thirteen* defendants Joe Razo and Eliezer Risco served on the editorial board of *La Raza.* See *La Raza,* 11 (March 31, 1968). Risco and Razo were handcuffed and arrested in the *La Raza* offices. "Reddin, Younger's Dog Pack."

37. García, *Chicanismo,* 58–59. Cf. Benedict Anderson, *Imagined Communities: The Origins and Spread of Nationalism,* 37–47 (rev. ed., 1991) (discussing the role of print-capitalism in fostering national identities).

38. Edward Escobar, "The Dialectics of Repression: The Los Angeles Police Department and the Chicano Movement, 1968–1971," 79 *Journal of American History* 1483, 1492 (1993). See also Gerald Rosen, "Political Ideology and the Chicano Movement: A Study of the Political

Ideology of Activists in the Chicano Movement," 157 (Ph.D. diss., University of California, Los Angeles, 1972).

39. "Barrio and Ghetto Communities Protest Police Violence," *La Raza*, 5 (Sept. 3, 1968).

40. Ibid. (first ellipses in original; second ellipses added). See also "Justice Under the Law?" *La Raza*, 4 (Sept. 3, 1968) (alleging a "triple standard of justice; one for the Brown and Black minorities, one for Anglos, and one for cops.").

41. Acosta, *Revolt*, 55. See also Escobar, "Dialectics," 1497.

42. "El Pueblo Responde al Grito," *La Raza*, 8 (June 7, 1968).

43. Acosta, "The East L.A. 13," 13–14; Acosta, "Racial Exclusion," 283. See also Jay Lintner, "Day of Collision," *La Raza*, 6C (July 10, 1968).

44. Escobar, "Dialectics," 1488. On the relationship between police abuse and political mobilization in Mexican communities, see ibid.; Edward Escobar, *Race, Police, and the Making of a Political Identity: Mexican Americans and the Los Angeles Police Department, 1900–1945* (1999); and F. Arturo Rosales, *¡Pobre Raza! Violence, Justice, and Mobilization among México Lindo Immigrants, 1900–1936* (1997).

45. Escobar notes this point. "More dramatic and convincing than the rhetoric of any sixties activists, the LAPD's repressive tactics . . . helped convince even conservative Mexican Americans that they, like African Americans, were an oppressed racial minority." Escobar, "Dialectics," 1514. He does not, however, develop this argument.

46. Dave Larsen, "Timing of Arrests in School Walkouts Called Political," *Los Angeles Times*, Part 2, 1 (June 5, 1968). District Attorney Evelle Younger called Risco's allegation "absurd." Ibid. See also Acosta, *Revolt*, 54–55.

47. Armando Morales, *Ando Sangrando (I Am Bleeding): A Study of Mexican American-Police Conflict*, 78 (1972).

48. "Political Prisoners Speak," *La Raza*, 7 (June 7, 1968).

49. *La Raza*, 8 (June 7, 1968).

50. "Noticia a la Jefe Placa," *La Raza*, 1 (June 7, 1968).

51. Richard Griswold del Castillo, *The Los Angeles Barrio, 1850–1890: A Social History*, 133 (1979).

52. Muñoz, *Youth, Identity*, 63; Genaro Padilla, "Myth and Comparative Cultural Nationalism: The Ideological Uses of Aztlán," in Rudolfo Anaya and Francisco Lomelí, eds., *Aztlán: Essays on the Chicano Homeland*, 111 (1989).

53. Luis Valdez, "Organizense Raza against Racism," *La Raza*, 4 (June 7, 1968).

54. "El Pueblo Responde al Grito" (ellipses in original).

55. See, for example, "Chicano Legal Defense Fund," *La Raza*, 6D (July 10, 1968).

56. "La Raza Nueva 13," *La Raza*, 11 (Sept. 3, 1968).

57. "Political Prisoners Speak."

58. Ron Einstoss, "Mexican-American Majority Opposes Boycott—Younger," *Los Angeles Times*, Part 2, 1 (Oct. 9, 1968).

59. "Francisco Martinez Found Guilty," *La Raza*, 12 (Oct. 15, 1968) (although without a direct byline, Oscar Acosta almost certainly wrote this article).

60. Ibid.

61. Ibid.

62. In mid-1969 Acosta successfully appealed Martínez's conviction on free speech grounds. People v. Eduardo Martinez, No. A.-8347 (California Superior Court, Los Angeles County, 1969).

63. "Francisco Martinez Found Guilty."

64. Others, of course, drew different lessons from the conviction of Martínez. District Attorney Evelle Younger cited the guilty verdict as evidence that "the majority of the Mexican-American community in East Los Angeles continues to oppose the March school boycotts and the type of militant activity which they represent." "Younger Declares: Eastside Majority against Boycott," *Belvedere Citizen*, 1 (Oct. 10, 1968). See also Einstoss, "Mexican-American Majority."

65. "Francisco Martinez Found Guilty."

66. Zeta, "The East Los 13 Are Ready," *La Raza*, 12 (Oct. 15, 1968). "Zeta" was used by Acosta as his middle name, and also frequently as his by-line.

67. "La Raza Nueva 13," 11.

68. The need to establish a new identity partly reflected dynamics common to most social movements, while also deriving inspiration from the Black Power movement's emphasis on a renaissance in identity. See Carmichael and Hamilton, *Black Power*, 35 ("We shall have to struggle for the right to create our own terms through which to define ourselves and our relationship to society, and to have those terms recognized.")

69. Acosta, "Racial Exclusion," 283–285.

8 FROM YOUNG CITIZENS TO BROWN BERETS

1. "Brown Berets Serve, Observe, Protect," *La Raza*, 13 (June 7, 1968); Ruben Salazar, "Brown Berets Hail 'La Raza' and Scorn the Establishment," in Mario García, ed., *Ruben Salazar, Border Correspondent: Selected Writings, 1955–1970*, 212, 217 (1995). First published in *Los Angeles Times*, June 16, 1969.

2. Quoted in Gerald Rosen, "Political Ideology and the Chicano

Movement: A Study of the Political Ideology of Activists in the Chicano Movement," 136 (Ph.D. diss., University of California, Los Angeles, 1972).

3. Ernesto Chávez, "Creating Aztlán: The Chicano Movement in Los Angeles, 1966–1978," 59–60 (Ph.D. diss., University of California, Los Angeles, 1994).

4. Juan Gómez-Quiñones, *Mexican Students Por La Raza: The Chicano Student Movement in Southern California 1967–1977*, 17 (1978).

5. Ibid.; Chávez, "Creating Aztlán," 60. (Esparza, Ramírez, and Sánchez would be indicted in *East L.A. Thirteen*.)

6. Chávez, "Creating Aztlán," 60.

7. Gómez-Quiñones, *Mexican Students*, 18.

8. Stan Steiner, *La Raza: The Mexican Americans*, 117 (1970).

9. Chávez, "Creating Aztlán," 61–62.

10. Ibid., 62.

11. Dionne Espinoza, "Pedagogies of Nationalism and Gender: Cultural Resistance in Selected Representational Practices of Chicana/o Movement Activists, 1967–1972," 73 n. 12 (Ph.D. diss., Cornell, 1996).

12. Ibid.; Chávez, "Creating Aztlán," 64.

13. Espinoza, "Pedagogies," 73.

14. Chávez, "Creating Aztlán," 62–63.

15. Quoted in Espinoza, "Pedagogies," 74.

16. "The Sheriff's Department," *La Raza*, 7 (Dec. 25, 1967).

17. "Brown Berets Picket Sheriffs," *La Raza*, 2 (Jan. 15, 1968).

18. "The Sheriff's Department."

19. Ibid.

20. Steiner, *Mexican Americans*, 117–118 (parentheticals in original).

21. F. Arturo Rosales, *Chicano! The History of the Mexican American Civil Rights Movement*, 188 (1996).

22. Chávez, "Creating Aztlán," 64.

23. Espinoza, "Pedagogies," 85; Chávez, "Creating Aztlán," 64.

24. "Sheriffs Harass," *La Raza*, 1 (Jan. 15, 1968).

25. Ibid.

26. Quoted in Steiner, *Mexican Americans*, 118.

27. Quoted in Chávez, "Creating Aztlán," 65 (first parenthetical added, ellipses in original).

28. Quoted in Steiner, *Mexican Americans*, 118. In his autobiography, the prominent Texas Chicano militant José Angel Gutiérrez records a similar political genesis at the hands of the police. José Gutiérrez, *The Making of a Chicano Militant: Lessons from Cristal*, 55 (1998).

29. "Brown Beret and Chicano Movement History," on file with the Oscar Zeta Acosta Papers, Department of Special Collections, California Ethnic and Multicultural Archives, University of California, Santa Barbara. Ernesto Chávez reports that Sánchez was incarcerated for sixty days, though this conflicts with police testimony placing Sánchez at Garfield High School on March 5. Chávez, "Creating Aztlán," 65; People v. Castro, No. A-232902, Reporter's Transcript of Grand Jury Proceedings, 38–40 (California Superior Court, Los Angeles County, 1968). David Sánchez, "The Birth of a New Symbol," on file with the Oscar Zeta Acosta Papers, mimeographed.

30. Sánchez, "New Symbol," 1.

31. Ibid.

32. Ibid.

33. Ibid., 2.

34. Ibid., 1.

35. Ibid., 2. David Montejano explores the emphasis on "visibility" in the elaboration of Brown Beret identity and identity-performance. David Montejano, "Toward an Understanding of the Politicization of Lumpenproletariat: A Dramaturgical First Look," in Reynaldo Macías, ed., Perspectivas en Chicano Studies, 157 (1977). See also Espinoza, "Pedagogies," 89–93.

36. Sánchez, "New Symbol," 3.

37. Espinoza, "Pedagogies," 105.

38. Rodolfo Acuña, Occupied America: The Chicano's Struggle Toward Liberation, 233 (1972); Ignacio García, Chicanismo: The Forging of a Militant Ethos Among Mexican Americans, 106 (1997).

39. Rosales, Chicano! 188.

40. Sánchez, "New Symbol," 1.

41. In spring 1968, Father Luce testified before the Los Angeles Grand Jury that "there are only five Brown Berets, to my knowledge . . . I mean—and then also, if I might say, the Brown Beret thing is really anyone who will go up and buy a brown beret and put it on." Transcript of Grand Jury Proceedings, 407.

42. Espinoza, "Pedagogies," 121.

43. Salazar, "Brown Berets," 215.

44. Transcript of Grand Jury Proceedings, 38–40.

45. Ibid., 175.

46. Ibid.

47. Ibid., 55.

48. "Who Are the Brown Berets?" Chicano Student News, 6 (March 15, 1968). See also Salazar, "Brown Berets," 217.

49. "Who Are the Brown Berets?"

50. "Conspiracy to Educate," *La Raza*, 6B (July 10, 1968).

51. "Brown Berets Serve."

52. Ibid.

53. Ibid.

54. Ibid.

55. Chávez, "Creating Aztlán," 73–74.

56. Acuña, *Struggle Toward Liberation*, 232. See also Armando Navarro, "The Evolution of Chicano Politics," 5 *Aztlán: A Journal of Chicano Studies* 57 (1974).

57. *La Causa*, 19 (April 1971).

58. April 1971 marks the end of *La Causa*'s regular publication. After that, the Berets sporadically published several more *La Causa* issues on various topics.

59. David Sánchez, "La Causa," *La Raza*, 8 (Feb. 7, 1969).

60. "Robert Avila Is a Traitor, Vendido, and Dog," *La Causa*, 5 (May 23, 1969).

61. Hilda Reyes, "Yorty's Pigs on the Job," *La Causa*, 7 (July 10, 1969).

62. Lorraine Escalante, "Establishment Tactics," *La Causa*, 2 (Sept. 16, 1969).

63. People v. Montes, No. A 244 906, Declaration of Carlos Montes, March 1, 1979 (on file with author). See also "Carlos Montes Disappears," *La Causa*, 9 (Feb. 28, 1970); Ernesto Vigil, *The Crusade for Justice: Chicano Militancy and the Government's War on Dissent*, 149 (1999).

64. "Political Prisoners Must be Free," *La Causa*, 1 (July 10, 1969).

65. "Student Unrest Continues for Third Day at Roosevelt High School," *Belvedere Citizen*, 1 (May 12, 1970); "Brown Beret Chief Arrested," *San Francisco Chronicle*, Part 1, 23 (Sept. 10, 1970); "Militant Jailed on Draft Charge," *Los Angeles Times*, Part 2, 3 (March 13, 1971).

66. Montes moved to El Paso, Texas, with his wife, where he worked in construction, raised two children, and bought a house. Opening Statement on the Carlos Montes Trial, October 2, 1979, unpaginated (on file with author). When Montes returned to Los Angeles in 1977, he was arrested and tried on the *Biltmore Six* charges. He was acquitted two years later. Chávez, "Creating Aztlán," 85.

67. García, *Chicanismo*, 107. Sidney Tarrow suggests that violence late in the cycle of social movements is a standard development. Sidney Tarrow, *Power in Movement: Social Movements, Collective Action, and Politics*, 112 (1994). Note that on the whole, recent studies in social

movement theory give relatively little attention to violence and deviance, emphasizing instead, as Frances Fox Piven and Richard Cloward note, a "normalized, overorganized, and conventionalized conception of political protest." Frances Fox Piven and Richard Cloward, "Normalizing Collective Protest," in Aldon Morris and Carol McClurg Mueller, eds., *Frontiers in Social Movement Theory,* 301, 322 (1992).

68. John Dreyfuss, "Crowd Jeers Roosevelt High Administration Supporters," *Los Angeles Times,* Part 1, 3 (March 13, 1970); Johnny Mosqueda, "Student Gives Views and Opinions on Roosevelt High Bombings," *Belvedere Citizen,* 1 (Oct. 8, 1970).

69. "Student Unrest Continues."

70. George Mariscal, ed., *Aztlán and Viet Nam: Chicano and Chicana Experiences of the War,* 3 (1999). *La Causa* reported in May 1970, "The brutal reality that the heaviest burdens of the Vietnam war have fallen on the Chicanos is a growing issue with La Raza . . . Almost three Chicanos are dying for every gabacho in proportion to the population." "Comité Moritorio," *La Causa,* 6 (May 22, 1970).

71. "Comité Moritorio."

72. The committee was initially led by Rosalio Muñoz, a former UCLA student body president, and by the Brown Berets' David Sánchez, though his role soon ended when a rift opened between the organizations. Carlos Muñoz Jr., *Youth, Identity, Power: The Chicano Movement,* 86 (1989).

73. The following is based on Frank Gonzalez, "War Protest March Ends in Death and Destruction," *Belvedere Citizen* (Sept. 3, 1970); Frank del Olmo, "Anatomy of a Riot—Eyewitness Report," *Los Angeles Times,* Part 1, B (Aug. 30, 1970); and William Drummond, "How East L.A. Protest Became a Major Riot," *Los Angeles Times,* Part 1, 1 (Sept. 15, 1970). See also Armando Morales, *Ando Sangrando (I Am Bleeding): A Study of Mexican American-Police Conflict,* 100–107 (1972).

74. Richard Vasquez, "Second Victim of Riot Dies; Militant Chicano Freed on Bail," *Los Angeles Times,* Part 1, 1 (Sept. 2, 1970).

75. "Lynn Ward, Beret Lieutenant, Killed by Exploding Tear Gas Canister," *La Causa,* 10 (Dec. 1970); see also Paul Houston, "Boy, 15, Dies of Riot Injuries; Salazar Inquest to Begin Today," *Los Angeles Times,* Part 1, 1 (Sept. 9, 1970).

76. Charles Powers and Jeff Perlman, "One Dead, 40 Hurt in East L.A. Riot; Times Columnist Ruben Salazar Killed by Bullet," *Los Angeles Times,* Part 1, 1 (Aug. 30, 1970). See generally Hunter Thompson, "Strange Rumblings in Aztlan," in Hunter Thompson, *The Great Shark Hunt: Strange Tales from a Strange Time,* 119 (1979).

77. Robert Kistler, "Eyewitness Give Composite Picture of Salazar's Death," *Los Angeles Times,* Part 1, 1 (Sept. 2, 1970). See also Jerry Cohen, "Fatal Gas Missile Not Intended for Riot-Control Use," *Los Angeles Times,* Part 1, 1 (Sept. 1, 1970).

78. Robert Rawitch, "Thousands Pay Homage to Riot Victim Salazar," *Los Angeles Times,* Part 1, 1 (Sept. 2, 1970).

79. Paul Houston, "TV Channels Will Provide Full Coverage of Salazar Inquest," *Los Angeles Times,* Part 2, 1 (Sept. 9, 1970).

80. Paul Houston and Dave Smith, "Mexican-American Observers Walk Out of Salazar Inquest," *Los Angeles Times,* Part 1, 1 (Sept. 11, 1970); Paul Houston and Dave Smith, "Salazar Inquest Melee Causes Abrupt Recess: Mexican-American Lawyer Ejected from Hearing Room," *Los Angeles Times,* Part 1, 3 (Sept. 16, 1970).

81. David Gomez, *Somos Chicanos: Strangers in Our Own Land,* 143 (1973); Thompson, "Strange Rumblings," 141.

82. Paul Houston, "Jury Splits 4–3 on Salazar Death; DA Will Review Case," *Los Angeles Times,* Part 1, 1 (Oct. 5, 1970).

83. Paul Houston, "Verdict Meant as Criticism of Deputies, 4 Salazar Jurors Say," *Los Angeles Times,* Part 1, 1 (Oct. 8, 1970).

84. Paul Houston, "No Charge Justified in Death of Salazar, Younger Announces," *Los Angeles Times,* Part 1, 1 (Oct. 15, 1970); Thompson, "Strange Rumblings," 142.

85. Houston, "No Charge Justified."

86. "Lynn Ward, Beret Lieutenant."

87. Ibid.

88. Ibid.

89. Ibid.

90. "Brown Beret, Captain Danny Rodriguez, Dies Trying to Save Black Brother," *La Causa,* 9, 10 (Dec. 1970); *La Causa,* 20 (Dec. 1970).

91. *La Causa,* 1 (Dec. 1970).

92. Ibid., 3.

93. Ibid., 8.

94. "Justicia o Revolucion," *La Causa,* 8 (Dec. 1970).

95. "Destroy the White Mind," *La Causa,* 3 (Dec. 1970).

96. Frank Gonzalez, "Reporter Gives Eyewitness View of Rally and Riots," *Belvedere Citizen,* 1 (Feb. 4, 1971). Days before the planned march, Rosalio Muñoz made the Moratorium Committee's concern with police violence clear: "We must not forget the lesson of August 29th," he wrote in a letter to the *Belvedere Citizen,* "that the major social and political issue we face is police brutality . . . Either the people control the police, or we are living in a police state." "Letters on Protest

March," *Belvedere Citizen,* 1 (Jan. 28, 1971). See also Frank del Olmo, "Chicano Group Plans Series of Protests," *Los Angeles Times,* Part 1, 22 (Jan. 7, 1971); Frank del Olmo, "Chicano Groups Converging for East L.A. Rally; Marchers Stop Along the Way to Picket Police Stations as Part of Today's Protest," *Los Angeles Times,* Part 1, B (Jan. 31, 1971).

97. Vigil, *Crusade,* 153, quoting agent Eustacio "Frank" Martínez.

98. Gonzalez, "Eyewitness View"; Morales, *Sangrando,* 119. An intervening riot occurred on September 16, 1970, a few weeks after the first Chicano Moratorium. Armando Morales suggests that this clash reflected "retaliatory behavior by militant youth toward the police for their aggressive actions against Mexican Americans on August 29." Morales, *Sangrando,* 116. In any event, more than 100 persons were injured and three persons, including a deputy, were shot. At least 68 arrests were made. Ibid., 108.

99. Morales, *Sangrando,* 119; "Says Pitchess: Deputies Didn't Shoot to Kill During Riot," *Belvedere Citizen,* 6 (Feb. 4, 1971); Paul Houston and Ted Thackrey Jr., "1 Slain, 25 Hurt in Violence after Chicanos' Rally," *Los Angeles Times,* Part 1, 1 (Feb. 1, 1971). For an eye-witness account of the killing of the "young Chicano," see Rick Browne, "Young Chicano's Death Described," *Los Angeles Times,* Part 1, 3 (Feb. 1, 1971). The victim was later identified as a native of Austria who had been a student at East Los Angeles College. Dial Torgerson, "Chicano Violence Laid to Mob That Ignored Monitors," *Los Angeles Times,* Part 2, 1 (Feb. 2, 1971).

100. "Police Genocide," *La Causa,* 2 (Feb. 1971).

101. Ibid.

102. "Barrio and Block Defense System," *La Causa,* 1, 6 (March 1971).

103. *La Causa,* 6 (March 1971).

104. "Genocide on the Chicano Family," *La Causa,* 3 (March, 1971).

105. "Brown Beret 13 Point Political Program," *La Causa,* 16 (Dec. 1970).

106. "Brown Berets Serve."

107. "Brown Beret 13 Point," 16.

108. Ibid., 16, 17.

109. Ibid., 17.

110. Ibid., 16.

111. For instance, Juan Gómez-Quiñones argues that although the "Berets made contributions to progressive thinking on a number of issues," over time "the Berets became increasingly dominated by lumpen

elements and a juvenile ultra leftism [that rendered them] increasingly marginal to the movement process in Southern California." Gómez-Quiñones, *Mexican Students,* 19.

112. Espinoza, "Pedagogies," 127, 131.

113. Chávez, "Creating Aztlán," 79.

114. Quoted in Espinoza, "Pedagogies," 139. See also Adelaida del Castillo, "Mexican Women in Organization," in Magdalena Mora and Adelaida del Castillo, eds., *Mexican Women in the United States,* 7, 8 (1980).

115. Espinoza, "Pedagogies," 133.

116. Chávez, "Creating Aztlán," 79.

117. "Is There a Frito Bandito in Your House?" *La Causa,* 3 (July 10, 1969).

118. Espinoza, "Pedagogies," 135–139, 142–143.

119. Steve Herbert, *Policing Space: Territoriality and the Los Angeles Police Department,* 80 (1997) ("The masculinist aggressiveness of the LAPD has long distinguished it among American police departments").

120. Morales, *Sangrando,* first page of photos after page 100.

121. Frank del Olmo, "East L.A. Leaders Urge Halt to Chicanos' Massive Rallies," *Los Angeles Times,* Part 1, 1 (Feb. 4, 1971).

122. "Another Scar to Be Healed," *Los Angeles Times,* Part 2, 6 (Feb. 2, 1971).

123. *La Causa,* 13, 16, 19 (April 1971).

124. "La Caravana de La Reconquista Is Coming," *La Causa* (n.d.); Chávez, "Creating Aztlán," 93.

125. "Los Brown Berets Occupy La Isla de Catalina," *La Causa,* 1, 3 (Sept. 16, 1972). See also Dial Torgerson, "Avalon 'Invaders' Now Just Tourist Attraction," *Los Angeles Times,* Part 2, 1 (Sept. 1, 1972) (noting that "tourists alighted from rented jeeps to take pictures of stern-faced youths standing in front of the Mexican flag," and that "when townspeople found out the Brown Berets had no food . . . boxes of foodstuffs from residents began to appear at their camp.").

126. Chávez, "Creating Aztlán," 95. See also Al Martinez, "Judge Asks Berets to Leave—They Do; Chicano Group Quits Catalina without Incident," *Los Angeles Times,* Part 1, 1 (Sept. 23, 1972).

127. Chávez, "Creating Aztlán," 95–96.

128. Dial Torgerson, "Brown Beret Leader Quits, Dissolves Units; Chapters Disbanding to Avoid Factional Strife, Sanchez Says," *Los Angeles Times,* Part 2, 1 (Nov. 2, 1972). Conflict over the legacy of the Brown Berets continues. As recently as 1995, David Sánchez was involved in litigation with another original member of the East Los An-

geles Brown Berets over who owns the copyright to the Brown Beret symbol. Espinoza, "Pedagogies," 145 n. 118.

129. Frank del Olmo, "Latin Leaders Report Few Gains since Riot," *Los Angeles Times*, Part 1, 3 (Aug. 30, 1971).

130. Ibid.

131. Ibid. Doug McAdam notes that riots emerged as a common event in minority communities in the mid 1960s, and he suggests that by 1967 or so the state had decided to respond to such events with massive force. Doug McAdam, "Tactical Innovation and the Pace of Insurgency," in Doug McAdam and David Snow, eds., *Social Movements: Readings on Their Emergence, Mobilization, and Dynamics*, 340, 353–354 (1997). This seems correct insofar as the response to the riots in East Los Angeles in 1970 and 1971 produced further repression, not reform.

132. California Legislature, Assembly Select Committee on the Administration of Justice, *Hearings on Police-Community Relations, East Los Angeles, April 28, 1972*, 77 (1972). The GI Forum reported 92 police killings of Mexicans across the Southwest between 1972 and 1978. Vigil, *Crusade*, 337. See also Muñoz, *Youth, Identity*, 173–174.

9   INVENTING CHICANOS

1. Quoted in Susan Keefe and Amado Padilla, *Chicano Ethnicity*, 93 (1987).

2. Arthur Campa, "The Mexican American in Historical Perspective," in Renato Rosaldo, Robert Calvert, and Gustav Seligmann, comps., *Chicano: The Evolution of a People*, 15, 16 (1973).

3. Quoted in Edward Simmen, ed., *Pain and Promise: The Chicano Today, Vivid Accounts of the Reawakening of a Proud and Oppressed People*, 129 (1972).

4. Gerald Rosen, "Political Ideology and the Chicano Movement: A Study of the Political Ideology of Activists in the Chicano Movement," 110–111 (Ph.D. diss., University of California, Los Angeles, 1972).

5. Ruben Salazar, "Brown Berets Hail 'La Raza' and Scorn the Establishment" in Mario García, ed., *Ruben Salazar, Border Correspondent: Selected Writings, 1955–1970*, 212, 217 (1995). First published in *Los Angeles Times*, June 16, 1969.

6. An idea of *blanqueamiento* or "whitening" may have informed the sense among Chicano militants that some members of the Mexican community not only sought but achieved status by holding themselves out as white. *Blanqueamiento* refers to a process in Mexico by which one gains racial and social status; at some level, this notion persisted among Mexican immigrants to the United States. Neil Foley, *The White*

Scourge: Mexicans, Blacks, and Poor Whites in Texas Cotton Culture, 61 (1999).

7. Ysidro Macías, "The Chicano Movement," in Simmen, *Pain and Promise,* 137, 139.

8. "The emotionalism of nationalist movements is more comprehensible when one recognizes that interruption of everyday business represents a threat to one's way of life: it is a disruption of all that is taken for granted." Hank Johnston, "New Social Movements and Old Regional Nationalisms," in Enrique Laraña et al., eds., *New Social Movements: From Ideology to Identity,* 267, 281 (1994).

9. Quoted in Rosen, "Political Ideology," 121.

10. John Hammerback, Richard Jensen, and Jose Angel Gutierrez, *A War of Words: Chicano Protest in the 1960s and 1970s,* 88 (1985). See also Ignacio García, *Chicanismo: The Forging of a Militant Ethos Among Mexican Americans,* 36 (1997); José Angel Gutiérrez, *The Making of a Chicano Militant: Lessons from Cristal* (1998).

11. Armando Rendon, "Chicano Culture in a Gabacho World," in Livie Isauro Duran and H. Russell Bernard, eds., *Introduction to Chicano Studies: A Reader,* 350, 354 (1973). First published as "Chicano Manifesto," 1971.

12. "La Causa," *La Raza,* 10 (Feb. 7, 1969).

13. Rodolfo Gonzales, "I Am Joaquin," *La Raza,* 4 (Sept. 16, 1967).

14. "Barrio and Ghetto Communities Protest Police Violence," *La Raza,* 5 (Sept. 3, 1968).

15. Biliana Ambrecht and Harry Pachon, "Ethnic Political Mobilization in a Mexican American Community: An Exploratory Study of East Los Angeles, 1965–1972," 27 *Western Political Quarterly* 500, 514 (1974).

16. Ibid.

17. Ibid. One study noted the following indicia of prejudice among Mexicans just prior to the Chicano movement: "Among Mexican Americans in Los Angeles, 1965–1966, 18 percent said they would find it distasteful to eat at the same table with African Americans; and 53 percent said they would find it distasteful to go to a party and find that most people are African American." The authors also noted that 82 percent of the respondents agreed that it would be distasteful to marry an African American. Leo Grebler, Joan Moore, and Ralph Guzman, *The Mexican-American People: The Nation's Second Largest Minority,* 391, 393 (1970).

18. Oscar Acosta, "Autobiographical Essay," in Ilan Stavans, ed., *Oscar "Zeta" Acosta: The Uncollected Works* 4, 12 (1996).

19. Acosta's remarks picked up on sentiments expressed by a Mexi-

can American generation member: "To the Mexican American in the Southwest this is his land and his roots are sunk deep into it. Unlike that of the American Negro, his history is not one of economic slavery by force and chains. In many if not most cases, he preceded those who have and are exploiting him. The Mexican American has a culture with which he is able and does identify." Maclovio Barraza, "Mañana Is Too Late—Labor Standards," in Luis Valdez and Stan Steiner, eds., *Aztlan: An Anthology of Mexican American Literature*, 188, 191 (1972).

20. Oscar Acosta, "Racial Exclusion," in Stavans, *Uncollected Works*, 280, 289.

21. Quoted in Stan Steiner, *La Raza: The Mexican Americans*, 120 (1970).

22. Quoted in García, *Chicanismo*, 44.

23. Luis Valdez, "Introduction: La Plebe," in Valdez and Steiner, *Aztlan*, xvii.

24. Ibid., xiv.

25. Mirta Vidal, "New Voice of La Raza: Chicanas Speak Out" (1971), in Alma García, ed., *Chicana Feminist Thought: The Basic Historical Writings*, 21, 23 (1997).

26. García, *Chicanismo*, 44.

27. Ernesto Vigil, *The Crusade for Justice: Chicano Militancy and the Government's War on Dissent*, 95 (1999).

28. Ibid., 96; Ruben Salazar, "Chicanos Hold 5-State Event in Colorado," in García, *Border Correspondent*, 204, 206. First published in *Los Angeles Times*, March 30, 1969.

29. Steiner, *La Raza*, 389.

30. Salazar, "5-State Event," 205.

31. M. E. Varela, "Denver Conference," *La Raza*, 8 (April 30, 1969).

32. "El Plan Espiritual de Aztlán," rpt. in Valdez and Steiner, *Aztlan*, 402–03. Ernesto Vigil states that Alberto Urista, better known as the poet Alurista, wrote most of this preamble. Vigil, *Crusade*, 99. Vigil also identifies Corky Gonzales as the author of the substantive components of the plan. Ibid. In contrast, Juan Gómez-Quiñones identifies himself as a member of a "drafting committee" along with four others, including Luís Valdez. Gómez-Quiñones does not mention whether Alurista or Gonzales played a role in drafting the plan. Juan Gómez-Quiñones, *Chicano Politics: Reality and Promise, 1940–1990*, 242 n. 23 (1990).

33. John Chávez, *The Lost Land: The Chicano Image of the Southwest*, 8 (1984).

34. Ibid.

35. Ramón Gutiérrez, "Aztlán, Montezuma, and New Mexico: The Political Uses of American Indian Mythology," in Rudolfo Anaya and Francisco Lomelí, eds., *Aztlán: Essays on the Chicano Homeland,* 172 (1989).

36. John Chávez points out that the contemporary use of Aztlán originated with Native American scholar Jack Forbes, who published an article in 1962 arguing that Mexicans "were more truly an Indian than a mestizo people." Chávez, *Lost Land,* 141. With the circulation of Forbes' article, Aztlán "gained popularity, but was not universally accepted by the Chicano movement until, in the spring of 1969, the first Chicano national conference, in Denver, drafted 'El plan espiritual de Aztlán.'" Ibid., 141–142.

37. In its patriarchal quality, such imagery also demonstrates the tendency among Chicanos to fashion their identity in ways that support traditional gender roles. Elizabeth Martínez, "'Chingón Politics' Die Hard: Reflections on the First Chicano Activist Reunion," in Carla Trujillo, ed., *Living Chicana Theory,* 123, 127 (1998).

38. "Plan Espiritual," 404.

39. Quoted in Steiner, *La Raza,* 385. Oscar Acosta in 1971 also advocated a version of nationalism: "Aztlán is the land we're sitting on now. The land where my forefathers lived hundreds of years ago before they migrated to the valley of Mexico . . . We don't kid ourselves anymore. We know we're headed for a head-on collision with the rest of society . . . You can't be a class or a nation without land. Without it, it doesn't have any meaning. It's that simple. So we are beginning to see that what we are talking about is getting land and having our own government. Period. It is that clear cut." Acosta, "Autobiographical Essay," 11–12.

40. F. Arturo Rosales, *Chicano! The History of the Mexican American Civil Rights Movement,* 195 (1996). Even those scholars dissatisfied with how nationalism developed in the Chicano movement nevertheless give that ideology primacy in discussing movement thinking. Thus, Juan Gómez-Quiñones comments that "the implicit common ideology accepted by movement persons was 'nationalism,' but it was bogus. In effect, what was espoused was culturalism and political access to the dominant system." Gómez-Quiñones, *Chicano Politics,* 146.

41. For instance, *East L.A. Thirteen* defendant Carlos Muñoz became an ethnic studies professor at U.C. Berkeley and authored a major book on the Chicano movement. Carlos Muñoz Jr., *Youth, Identity, Power: The Chicano Movement,* xii (1989).

42. Rendon, "Chicano Culture," 350, 356.

43. Valdez, "Introduction," xii, xxxiii–xxxiv.

44. Genaro Padilla, "Myth and Comparative Cultural Nationalism: The Ideological Uses of Aztlán," in Anaya and Lomelí, *Chicano Homeland*, 111, 112.

45. "Both [race and nation] denote something to which one is naturally tied . . . In this way, nation-ness is assimilated to skin-colour, gender, parentage, and birth-era—all those things one cannot help." Benedict Anderson, *Imagined Communities: Reflections on the Origin and Spread of Nationalism*, 143 (rev. ed., 1991). Nevertheless, as Anderson points out, "Nationalism also thinks in terms of historical destinies, while racism dreams of eternal contaminations, transmitted from the origins of time through an endless sequence of loathsome copulations: outside history." Ibid., 149.

46. Valdez, "Introduction," xiv.

47. García, *Chicanismo*, 73.

48. José Vasconcelos, *The Cosmic Race* (1925; Didier Jaén, trans., 1979).

49. Ibid., 40.

50. Ibid., 39.

51. Luis Valdez, "The Tale of La Raza," in Rosaldo, *Chicano*, 293, 294. First published in *Ramparts Magazine*, 1971.

52. Gloria Anzaldúa, *Borderlands/La Frontera: The New Mestiza* (1987); Chelá Sandoval, "Mestizaje as Method: Feminists-of-Color Challenge the Canon," in Trujillo, *Living Chicana Theory*, 352.

53. Vasconcelos, *Cosmic Race*, 25–26.

54. Valdez, "Introduction," xv.

55. Acosta, "Autobiographical Essay," 12.

56. Valdez, "Introduction," xxx.

57. Guillermo Fuenfrios, "The Emergence of the New Chicano," in Valdez and Steiner, *Aztlan*, 284, 287–288.

58. Valdez, "Tale of La Raza," 293, 294; Valdez, "Introduction," xv.

59. See generally García, *Chicana Feminist Thought*.

60. David Montejano, "Toward an Understanding of the Politicization of Lumpenproletariat: A Dramaturgical First Look," in Reynaldo Macias, ed., *Perspectivas en Chicano Studies*, 157, 169 (1977); "Plan Espiritual," 402–403.

61. Patriarchy and hyper-masculinity are not unique to or particularly virulent in Mexican or Latino culture. Rosa Linda Fregoso cautions against the tendency to view sexism as another pathology particu-

lar to racial minorities. Rosa Linda Fregoso, *The Bronze Screen: Chicana and Chicano Film Culture*, 29 (1993).

62. Ramón Gutiérrez, "Community, Patriarchy and Individualism: The Politics of Chicano History and the Dream of Equality," 45 *American Quarterly* 44, 45–46 (March 1993).

63. Quoted in Valdez and Steiner, *Aztlan*, 383.

64. Ibid., 379.

65. "Million $$ Suit for Jesse's Murder," *La Raza*, 9 (June, 1969). Although unsigned, the subject, language and style suggest that this is another Acosta article.

66. Aída Hurtado, *The Color of Privilege: Three Blasphemies on Race and Feminism*, 114 (1996).

67. Quoted in Valdez and Steiner, *Aztlan*, 386.

68. Acosta, "Racial Exclusion," 284. For an extended critique of the sexual politics in Acosta's writing, see Carl Gutiérrez-Jones, *Rethinking the Borderlands: Between Chicano Culture and Legal Discourse*, 129–139 (1995).

69. Rudolfo Gonzales, "Chicano Nationalism: The Key to Unity for La Raza," in Rosaldo, *Chicano*, 424, 425.

70. "Plan Espiritual," 405.

71. Enriqueta Longauex y Vasquez, "The Women of La Raza," *La Raza*, 7 (July 7, 1969).

72. "A Revolutionary Defense of the Pope's Encyclical on Birth Control," *La Causa*, 4 (Feb. 28, 1970).

73. "Genocide on the Chicano Family," *La Causa*, 3 (March 1971). Although this article is signed "Concerned Chicanas," it was written after a number of Chicanas had already left the Brown Berets. Dionne Espinoza, "Pedagogies of Nationalism and Gender: Cultural Resistance in Selected Representational Practices of Chicana/o Movement Activists, 1967–1972," 129 (Ph.D. diss., Cornell, 1996). Note also that in May 1971 the first national conference of Chicanas took place in Houston, Texas, which resulted in a resolution calling for "free, legal abortions and birth control for the Chicano community; controlled by Chicanas." Vidal, "New Voice," 21.

74. "El Reboso Newspaper," *La Raza*, 5 (Dec. 1969).

75. "Chicanas in the Movement," *La Raza*, 5 (Nov. 1969).

76. Rendon, "Chicano Culture," 353.

77. Gonzales, "Chicano Nationalism," 424–425.

78. Longauex y Vasquez, "Women of La Raza," 10. See also Suzanne Oboler, *Ethnic Labels, Latino Lives: Identity and the Politics of (Re)Presentation in the United States*, 76 (1995).

79. See Aída Hurtado, "The Politics of Sexuality in the Gender Subordination of Chicanas," in Trujillo, *Living Chicana Theory,* 383.

EPILOGUE

1. Oscar Acosta, "Declaration of Candidacy," in Ilan Stavans, ed., *Oscar "Zeta" Acosta: The Uncollected Works,* 299 (1996).

2. Ruben Salazar, "Narrowly a Candidate Lost," in Mario García, ed., *Ruben Salazar, Border Correspondent: Selected Writings, 1955–1970,* 258, 259 (1995). First published in *Los Angeles Times,* June 2, 1970.

3. Ibid.

4. Ibid.

5. Acosta, "Declaration."

6. Rodolfo Acuña, *A Community Under Siege: A Chronicle of Chicanos East of the Los Angeles River, 1945–1975,* 184 (1984).

7. Acosta, "Declaration," 300.

8. Ibid.

9. Ibid.

10. Ron Einstoss, "Acosta Quits Defense for Two Brown Berets: Judge Delays Retrial, Names Two New Lawyers in Biltmore Hotel Arson Case," *Los Angeles Times,* Part 1, 22 (Nov. 16, 1971).

11. "Biltmore Trial Lawyer Arrested," *Los Angeles Times,* Part 2, 3 (Aug. 29, 1971).

12. "Ex-Attorney Acquitted of Drug Charge," *Los Angeles Times,* Part 2, 5 (Feb. 17, 1972).

13. Early in *East L.A. Thirteen,* Acosta published a blistering criticism of the community and the defendants for their failure to be sufficiently involved in the case. "The Chicano 13 vs. the Grand Jury," *La Raza,* 12 (Dec. 13, 1968). Acosta also recounted the activists' suspicions regarding his commitment to the Chicano cause after he decided to spend some time away from East Los Angeles. Oscar Acosta, *The Revolt of the Cockroach People,* 196–197 (Vintage, 1989 [1973]).

14. Oscar Acosta, "Autobiographical Essay," in Stavans, *Uncollected Works,* 14.

15. Acosta, *Revolt,* 254–258.

16. Ibid., 253–254.

17. Ibid., 254.

18. Ibid., 256–257.

19. Ernesto Vigil, *The Crusade for Justice: Chicano Militancy and the Government's War on Dissent,* 147–148 (1999).

20. Acosta, *Revolt,* 213–229. Acosta described questioning Superior

Court judges during the defense of Gonzales, though this constituted the core part of the *Biltmore Six* defense. Municipal Judge Joseph Grillo presided over the Gonzales trial. Vigil, *Crusade,* 146.

21. Edward Escobar, "The Dialectics of Repression: The Los Angeles Police Department and the Chicano Movement, 1968–1971," 79 *Journal of American History* 1483, 1508 (1993).

22. Quoted in Douglas Brinkley, editor's note, in Hunter Thompson, *Fear and Loathing in America: The Brutal Odyssey of an Outlaw Journalist, 1968–1976,* xx (2000).

23. Oscar Acosta, "Letter to Hunter S. Thompson," in Stavans, *Uncollected Works,* 105, 106 (ellipses in original).

24. Escobar, "Dialectics," 1508. See also David Gomez, *Somos Chicanos: Strangers in Our Own Land,* 127 (1973) (noting that the Chicano Liberation Front claimed responsibility for twenty-eight bombings, including of City Hall, schools, post offices, and banks).

25. Acosta, *Revolt,* 258.

26. Ilan Stavans, *Bandido: Oscar "Zeta" Acosta and the Chicano Experience,* 118 (1995).

27. Ibid., 118–119; Marco Acosta, afterword, in Acosta, *Revolt,* 259.

28. See Jorge Klor de Alva, "Aztlán, Borinquen and Hispanic Nationalism in the United States," in Rudolfo Anaya and Francisco Lomelí, eds., *Aztlán: Essays on the Chicano Homeland,* 135, 147–148 (1989). See also Juan Gómez-Quiñones, *Chicano Politics: Reality and Promise, 1940–1990,* 141–144 (1990).

29. Mario García, *Mexican Americans: Leadership, Ideology, and Identity, 1930–1960,* 111 (1989).

30. On Chicano studies, see Carlos Muñoz Jr., *Youth, Identity, Power: The Chicano Movement* (1989), especially chapter 5. "While the number of Mexican Americans twenty-five and older completing college has remained 'frozen' at the 5–6 percent level since 1975, the number failing to complete high school has increased several points, to 56.4 percent." David Montejano, "On the Future of Anglo-Mexican Relations in the United States," in David Montejano, ed., *Chicano Politics and Society in the Late Twentieth Century,* 234, 235 (1999). Montejano advances an apocalyptic view of looming conflict when a young, undereducated, underemployed Latino majority is called upon to support a retired population that is largely white. Ibid., 242–243.

31. Elizabeth Martínez, "Be Down with the Brown: Thousands of Raza Youth Blowout of School to Protest Racism," 7 (no. 11) *Z Magazine* 39 (1994).

32. Alma García, "The Development of Chicana Feminist Discourse, 1970–1980," 3 *Gender & Society* 217, 222 (1989).

33. David Gutiérrez, "Sin Fronteras? Chicanos, Mexican Americans, and the Emergence of the Contemporary Mexican Immigration Debate, 1968–1978," 10 *Journal of American Ethnic History* 5, 6–7 (1991).

34. Carlos Muñoz and Ignacio García both stress the working-class origins of the Chicano movement. Muñoz, *Youth, Identity,* 76 (1989); Ignacio García, *Chicanismo: The Forging of a Militant Ethos Among Mexican Americans,* 74 (1997).

35. One study found that in 1976, 43 percent of Mexican youth in Los Angeles had positive attitudes toward nationalism and that, among these, members of the lower class outnumbered their middle-class compatriots by almost two to one. Martín Sánchez Jankowski, "Where Have All the Nationalists Gone? Change and Persistence in Radical Political Attitudes Among Chicanos, 1976–1986," in Montejano, *Chicano Politics and Society,* 201, 204.

36. Rodolfo Acuña, *Anything But Mexican: Chicanos in Contemporary Los Angeles,* 9 (1996); U.S. Bureau of the Census, *Overview of Race and Hispanic Origin, Census 2000 Brief,* table 10 (March 2001).

37. García, *Chicanismo,* 145. See also Biliana Ambrecht and Harry Pachon, "Ethnic Political Mobilization in a Mexican American Community: An Exploratory Study of East Los Angeles, 1965–1972," 27 *Western Political Quarterly* 500 (1974).

38. Cruz Reynoso, "Hispanics and the Criminal Justice System," in Pastora San Juan Cafferty and David Engstrom, eds., *Hispanics in the United States: An Agenda for the Twenty-First Century,* 277, 286 (2000) (the percentage of Latino judges is from a 1997 study); U.S. Bureau of the Census, *Census 2000 Redistricting Data, Summary File, Matrices PL1, PL2, PL3, and PL4* (May 23, 2001).

39. California Rural Legal Assistance, "A Study of Grand Jury Service by Persons of Spanish Surname and by Indians in Selected California Counties," in U.S. Commission on Civil Rights, *Mexican Americans and the Administration of Justice in the Southwest,* 112 (1970). The information provided in this section is from Ian Haney López, "Institutional Racism: Judicial Conduct and a New Theory of Racial Discrimination," 109 *Yale Law Journal* 1717, 1884 (Appendix D) (2000).

40. California Code of Civil Procedure, § 197.

41. San Bernardino County requires judges to directly select grand jurors, while Imperial County gives judges no discretion in the selection of grand jurors.

42. Los Angeles County website, "How is a Person Chosen for the Grand Jury?" http://www.co.la.ca.us/grandjury/ (emphasis added).

43. Haney López, "Institutional Racism," 1756.

44. In 1990, Hispanics constituted 37.8 percent of the population of Los Angeles County. U.S. Bureau of the Census website, *1990 Data Base C90STF1A, Los Angeles County,* http://venus.census.gov/cdrom/lookup/947540548. In 1999 Latinos amounted to 43.9 percent of that population. U.S. Bureau of the Census website, *County of Los Angeles Statistical Data,* http://www.co.la.us/statistics.htm. Given these numbers, we can assume that on average Latinos accounted for 41 percent of the Los Angeles population during the 1990s. During the 1960s, virtually all Latinos in Los Angeles County were Mexican, while in the 1990s Mexicans accounted for approximately 75 percent of Los Angeles's Latinos.

45. Ann O'Neill, "Retaliation for Grand Jury Reform Effort Is Alleged," *Los Angeles Times,* B1 (April 13, 2000).

46. Cornell West argues that progressive lawyers should concentrate on preserving past gains during moments of quiescence and preparing new arguments for the brief, fertile periods that come with popular mobilization. Cornell West, "The Role of Progressive Lawyers," in David Kairys, ed., *The Politics of Law* (2nd ed., 1990).

47. Washington v. Davis, 426 U.S. 229 (1976).

48. McCleskey v. Kemp, 481 U.S. 279, 312 (1987).

49. Ibid., 325. Justice Brennan, in dissent, noted that "Since our [1976] decision upholding the Georgia capital sentencing system . . . the State has executed seven persons. All of the seven were convicted of killing whites, and six of the seven executed were black. Such execution figures are especially striking in light of the fact that, during the period encompassed by the Baldus study, only 9.2 percent of Georgia homicides involved black defendants and white victims." Ibid., 325–327.

50. Richmond v. Croson, 488 U.S. 469 (1989); Adarand Constructors, Inc. v. Pena, 515 U.S. 200 (1995).

51. Hernandez v. New York, 500 U.S. 352 (1991).

52. Ibid., 356–57. See Sheri Lynn Johnson, "The Language and Culture (Not to Say Race) of Peremptory Challenges," 35 *William & Mary Law Review* 21, 53 (1993).

53. Hernandez v. New York, 500 U.S. 352, 375.

54. Adarand, 515 U.S. 200, 245 (Justice Stevens, dissenting).

55. Marc Mauer, *Race to Incarcerate,* 9, 19 (1999).

56. Ibid., 9.

57. Ibid., 119; Reynoso, "Criminal Justice System," 277, 293.

58. Mauer, *Race to Incarcerate,* 125.

59. Jill Nelson, introduction to Jill Nelson, ed., *Police Brutality* (2000).

60. For a full development of this argument, see Katherine Beckett, *Making Crime Pay: Law and Order in Contemporary American Politics* (1997). See also Christian Parenti, *Lockdown America: Police and Prisons in the Age of Crisis* (1999).

61. Beckett, *Making Crime Pay,* 32–33, 38–39.

62. Ibid., 38. Beckett remarks, "Crime, political dissent, and race were thus merged in both the rhetoric and practice of law and order." Ibid. Her linkage of crime, political dissent, and race mirrors the connections I discuss between legal repression, protest, and race, except that "crime" stands in for "legal repression."

63. Indeed, the desire to inject crime into national politics led to the so-called war on drugs. Traditionally, criminal law is a local matter. Drugs constitute one of the few areas of federal jurisdiction. The war on drugs, waged against minorities far out of proportion to actual rates of drug use, constitutes some of the most dramatic evidence that the current "race to incarcerate" turns very much on race. Of course, this war also comes as a "response to the vicious economic restructuring of the Reagan era." Parenti, *Lockdown America,* xii.

64. Beckett, *Making Crime Pay,* 85. In this context, the war on crime and the militarization of U.S. borders, especially that shared with Mexico, go hand-in-hand as attempts by the federal government to animate white voters by seeming to respond to threats posed by non-whites. See Timothy Dunn, *The Militarization of the U.S.-Mexico Border, 1978–1992: Low-Intensity Conflict Doctrine Comes Home* (1996).

65. The national politics that associates victimization by law enforcement with special pleading by minorities makes the voices of white victims difficult to hear. Simultaneously, the relative absence of white voices protesting police violence ensures that concern over this threat continues to seem misplaced. See Katheryn Russell, "'What Did I Do to be So Black and Blue?' Police Violence and the Black Community," in Nelson, *Police Brutality,* 135, 140.

66. José Saldívar, *Border Matters: Remapping American Cultural Studies,* 126 (1997), discussing Kid Frost, *East Side Story,* Virgin Records, 92097-4.

67. Ibid., 126, 128. Saldívar describes such songs as "uncritical hymns of Chicano protonationalism." Ibid., 126. That may be, but I understand them first and foremost to be aggressive expressions of a nonwhite racial identity.

68. Robin Kelley offers the following analysis: "The criminalization, surveillance, incarceration, and immiseration of black youth in the

postindustrial city have been the central themes in gansta rap, and at the same time, sadly, constitute the primary experience from which their identities are constructed . . . The construction of the 'ghetto' as a living nightmare and 'ganstas' as products of that nightmare have given rise to what I call a new 'Ghettocentric' (as opposed to 'Afrocentric') identity in which the specific class, race, and gendered experiences in late capitalist centers coalesce to create a new identity—'Nigga.'" Robin Kelley, *Race Rebels: Culture, Politics, and the Black Working Class*, 208–209 (1996). I agree with Kelley's identification of the importance of structural changes in the economy, as well as his point that class and gender elements of identity are also formed in this milieu. Nevertheless, I emphasize the special role played by legal violence in the cultural context in which young minorities develop their self-conceptions and the resulting importance of race, here captured dramatically by the stylized appellation "Nigga."

ACKNOWLEDGMENTS

I first began this project more than a decade ago while I was still in law school, and since then an astounding number of people and institutions have contributed to making this book a reality—so many that I simply cannot name all those who have helped. Nevertheless, a few people deserve special mention.

First and foremost, my wife, Deborah Drickersen Córtez, shared much of the joy and all too much of the suffering associated with turning a rainstorm of material and ideas into a book. In addition, my parents, Terrence Haney and María López de Haney, my brother, Garth Haney, my daughter, Chelsea Lancaster, and my granddaughter, Lennea Carolina López, all contributed immeasurably to this project, often intellectually but always through their love and forbearance. Good friends who deserve thanks include Rey Rodríguez, whose succinct injunction to my various doubts and delays was invariably "Write the book!" as well as Anna An, Vivian Godoy, Alan Lepp, Bill Levinthal, Soo Ji Min, James Nagle, and Leah Segawa.

I also received wonderful assistance from Priscilla Battis, who battled draft after draft of the manuscript, contributed key insights, and did indispensable research, all while touring the country in her convertible Mercedes. Special thanks also to Rachel Moran, a terrific mentor and colleague. Other collaborators to whom I am very grateful include Tomás Almaguer, Rick Banks, Susan Wallace Boehmer, Lily Castillo-Speed, Dedi Felman, Rosa Linda Fregoso,

Laura Gómez, Angela Harris, Linda Krieger, Kathleen McDermott, Miguel Méndez, Robert Post, Dan Rodríguez, Reva Siegel, Jeff Selbin, Charles Weisselberg, Eric Yamamoto, and several anonymous reviewers.

I also greatly benefited from the efforts of research assistants and former students, including Jessica Delgado, Ron Dor, Araceli Martínez-Olguín, José Palafox, Victor Rodríguez, James Sing, and Gregory Wong. In addition, I would like to thank the participants in the Chicano cases who took the time to talk with me, notably *East L.A. Thirteen* defendants Carlos Montes and Carlos Muñoz, Judge Arthur Alarcon, and attorney Hugh Manes. Raúl Ruiz, a photographer for *La Raza,* generously provided a number of photos for this book.

Finally, I would like to acknowledge a range of institutions. The Oscar Zeta Acosta Papers in the California Ethnic and Multicultural Archives at the University of California, Santa Barbara, provided helpful background material and also kindly agreed to serve as the repository for the court transcripts, legal briefs, and police records I culled from the vaults of the Los Angeles Superior Court as well as from the California State Archives. The Rockefeller Foundation supported work on this project twice, first helping to fund a year at Stanford University's Humanities Center and then putting me up at their villa in Bellagio, Italy. Both the University of Wisconsin, Madison, and the University of California, Berkeley, acceded to teaching-free semesters during which I worked, more or less diligently, on this book. Harvard Law School gave me a grant to fund some of the initial research during my final year as a student there. Law journals at Yale, the University of Pennsylvania, and the University of California published earlier versions of some of the material covered here.

Mil gracias to everyone who helped me with this book. They do not all agree with what I say here, but their input made the final version far better. It goes without saying that any remaining errors are socially constructed.

INDEX

American Civil Liberties Union, 30,
32, 138, 143, 144–145, 154
American GI Forum, 76, 77, 80, 163,
207
Anti-Greaser Act, 66
Arguelles, John, 173
Asian Americans, ix, 212, 248. *See
also* Racial categories
Assimilation: and Chicano movement,
1, 2, 216; and Mexican Americans,
1, 71, 72, 76–79, 163, 164; and
Pachucos, 81; and discrimination,
86; frustration with, 157; and
Valdez, 171
Avila, Robert, 190
Ayres, Edward Duran, 74–75, 136,
138
Aztecs, 172, 216
Aztlán, 196, 215–216, 217,
303nn36,39

Becker, Gary, 107
Bell, Derrick, 260n88
Biltmore Six, 4, 7–8, 35, 36–40, 102,
105, 192
Black Panthers, 162, 188–189
Black Power movement, 18, 161–167,
188–189, 206, 210–211, 224,
292n68. *See also* African Americans; Political activism
Bracero program, 273n144
Brown Berets: and East L.A. Thirteen,
4, 25, 26, 27, 186–189; and youth,
18–19; development of, 18–19,
178–204; and walkouts, 20, 21, 22,
184–186; and school board occupation, 34; and police spies, 34, 35,
149–150, 190; and Biltmore Six,
36; and police, 148, 151, 200; and
López Tijerina, 159; and racial
identity, 178, 179, 184, 188, 190–
191, 199, 200; and police misconduct, 178, 181–182, 185, 186, 188,
189, 190–192, 196–198, 202; and
political philosophy, 183–184, 187–
189, 196–197, 198–200, 298n111;
and gender, 185, 191–192, 198,
200–202; and common sense, 200;
and masculinity, 201–202, 224; dissolution of, 202–204; and
carnalismo, 223
Brown, H. Rap., 162, 180
Brown Power. *See* Chicano Power
Brown race, vii, 1–2, 7, 9, 10, 166–
167, 177, 210–214. *See also* Racial
categories
Brown v. Board of Education, 41

California Rural Legal Assistance,
101, 102, 240
Call, Joseph, 95, 97, 103, 123
Campa, Arthur, 81
Carmichael, Stokely, 132, 162, 180
Carnalismo, 223. *See also* Gender;
Men/masculinity
Castañeda, Carlos, 78
Castro, Sal, 19–20, 21–22, 25–26, 27,
33, 257nn22,28
Castro, Vickie, 179, 180
Catolicos por La Raza, 39, 230
Cebada, Cristo, 190
Ceballos, Jesus, 190
Ceballos, Joe, 35
Census, viii, 43, 44, 51, 52, 54, 82,
253n2, 265n149. *See also* White
persons of Spanish surname
Chargin, Gerald, 84–86, 109, 121,
197, 273n149
Chávez, Cesár, 25, 31, 158, 159, 160,
162, 179, 180
Chicano: and self-conception, 1–2,
152–153; defined, 3; and race, 3, 8,
9, 221; and Gonzales, 160; inven-
tion of, 205–229; as mestizo peo-
ple, 218. *See also* Chicano move-
ment; Racial categories
Chicano Legal Defense Fund, 30
Chicano Liberation Front, 192, 234
Chicano Moratorium Committee,
150, 193, 197, 202

320

Mexican *(continued)*
  white identity/whiteness, 1, 5, 43,
    44, 45, 46, 53, 54, 65, 76–82, 87,
    206–208, 273n140; and race, 1–2,
    3, 41, 42, 43, 52, 58–67, 138, 219;
    defined, 2–3, 254n1; as group, 5,
    41, 42–52, 54, 55, 91, 176; and
    East Los Angeles, 15–16; popula-
    tion of, 15–16, 67, 68, 86, 309n44;
    radicalization of, 18, 23; and grand
    jury, 32, 37, 41, 91, 100–101, 241;
    as distinct class, 41–42; and sur-
    name, 43, 44, 45, 51–52, 55, 82;
    and segregation, 51, 67, 68, 69–70,
    268n63; racial construction of, 56,
    58–67, 157; and miscegenation, 59;
    and barrio, 68; and "una Raza,"
    68; and immigration, 68, 69, 70,
    72; repatriation of, 70–71; deporta-
    tion of, 70–71; and Indians, 75; and
    European identity, 78, 80, 221,
    227; and judges, 97–98; and police,
    102, 138, 146–147; and discrimina-
    tion, 102–103; and crime, 139–141,
    143, 144; and Chávez, 158; and
    whitening, 207, 300n6; as mestizo
    people, 218, 219, 228; and
    mestizaje, 222; and transnational
    consciousness, 238. *See also* Racial
    characteristics (Mexicans)
Mexican Americans: and assimilation,
    1, 71, 72, 76–79, 163, 164; defined,
    3; and white identity, 3, 164, 205–
    206, 208, 238; and police, 152,
    153; and age, 163–164; and Brown
    Berets, 199; and African Americans,
    301nn17,19. *See also* Racial catego-
    ries
Mexican American Movement, 71,
    78–79, 80
Mexican American Youth Organiza-
    tion, 209
Mexico, 2, 70–71, 78, 80, 81
Middle class, 17, 80, 81, 238,
    308n35

Miscegenation, 58–60, 61. *See also*
    Racial characteristics (Mexicans)
Montes, Carlos, 26, 36, 38, 39, 159,
    162, 185, 186, 191, 192, 295n66
Moore, Joan, 42, 43, 44–45
Morales, Armando, 139, 151–154
Muñoz, Carlos, 26, 289n16, 303n41
Muñoz, Rosalio, 296n72, 297n96

NAACP, 138, 161, 275n13
National Congress of Spanish
    Speaking Peoples. *See Congreso, El*
Nationalism, 215, 216–218, 225,
    303n39, 304n45, 308n35
Nationality: and race, ix, 81,
    272n134
National Lawyer's Guild, 30
Native Americans, 67, 211–212, 217,
    221, 222, 268n63. *See also* Racial
    categories
Nava, Julian, 22, 179
Nebron, Irwin, 39
New Institutionalism, 279n5
Nuñez, Ralph, 39

Operation Wetback, 83
"Other white" strategy, 76–87

Parker, Kathleen, 51–52, 91
Parker, William, 134, 135, 136–139,
    141, 147, 148
Paz, Octavio, 272n136
Piranya, La, 161–162, 180, 181, 185
Plan Espiritual de Aztlán, El, 215,
    222, 223, 225
Police: and common sense, 8, 141,
    189, 284n14; and racism, 8, 136,
    137–139; and Chicano movement,
    9, 34, 148, 149–150, 152, 153; and
    racial identity, 9, 247–248; and bru-
    tality, 18, 34, 134, 154, 178, 181–
    182, 188; and Brown Berets, 18,
    148, 151, 178, 179, 181–182, 185,
    186, 187–188, 188, 189, 190–192,
    196–198, 199, 202; and YCCA, 18,

Berets, 200; and Acosta, 242; and Supreme Court, 242–245; and district attorney, 287n1; and nationalism, 304n45. *See also* Racial discrimination; Race; Segregation

Racism theory: common sense, 7, 109–133, 141, 239, 241, 244–245, 284n14; associational, 107; statistical, 107; rational, 107–108, 110, 111; aversive, 131; and cognitive distortion, 131; unconscious, 131; institutional, 132–133, 283n57

Ramírez, Ralph, 26, 36, 38, 39, 162, 185, 186

Rational choice theory, 107–108, 110, 111

Raza, La (term), 68, 170–172

Raza cósmica, La. See Racial categories

Razo, Joe, 25, 169, 173, 174

Reagan, Ronald, 3, 22, 35, 247

Rebozo, El, 226

Reddin, Tom, 22, 148

Rehnquist, William, 276n28

Rendón, Armando, 210, 216–217

Reyes, Grace, 185, 190

Reyes, Hilda, 185, 190, 191

Rhone, Bayard, 47–49, 53, 96

Richmond v. Croson, 243, 244

Risco, Eliezer, 25, 168, 181, 182

Rodríguez, Danny, 194

Rodríguez, Roberto, 286n44

Rojas, Juan, 39

Roosevelt high school, 20, 25, 192, 257n23

Roybal, Edward R., 76

Salazar, Rubén, 163–164, 194–195, 197, 230–231, 232, 234, 250, 254n9

Sánchez, Arlene, 185

Sánchez, David: background of, 25; and walkouts, 25, 27, 186; and Brown Berets, 25, 181, 182, 184, 186; and YCCA, 179; "The Birth of

a New Symbol," 183–184; and police, 190, 192; and gender, 202; and dissolution of Brown Berets, 203; and whiteness, 207; and Indians, 212–213; and race, 229; and legacy of Brown Berets, 299n128

Sánchez, Patricio, 26

Schools. *See* Education/schools

Segregation: and East Los Angeles, 5; and grand jury, 7; and Parker, 51; and Mexicans, 67, 68, 69–70, 268n63; and *Hernandez v. Texas,* 77; and Texas, 78–79; and skin color, 81; structural, 121–122; and education, 273n140. *See also* Jim Crow; Racial discrimination; Racism

Sexism. *See* Gender

Sexuality, 224, 227. *See also* Gender

Sirhan, Sirhan, 93, 275n21

Sleepy Lagoon, 73–74, 136

Social construction of race. *See* Race

Social movement theory, 161, 289n22

Southern Christian Leadership Conference, 161

Spain, 56, 78, 218, 221

Students, 16–17, 18–19, 20–24, 72, 160. *See also* Education/schools

Sumaya, Fernando, 35, 36, 38, 201, 263n129

Supreme Court: and racism, 242–245. *See also specific cases*

Teatro Campesino, El, 171

Thompson, Hunter S., 29, 234–235

Torres, Richard, 173

Treaty of Guadalupe Hidalgo, 62, 158

UMAS. *See* United Mexican American Students

United Mexican American Students, 4, 18, 20, 21, 23, 25, 26, 34, 35, 180, 184

United States, expansion of, 60–62